Once-Removed ...

Ronald Henry Schmidt

Sasha Press
San Francisco, CA
www.sashapress.com

Published 2011

Published by Sasha Press
San Francisco
www.sashapress.com

©Ronald Henry Schmidt 2011

All Rights Reserved. No part of this publication may be reproduced, stored in a retrieval system, or transmitted in any form or by any means, electronic, mechanical, recording, or otherwise, without the prior written permission of the publisher, to whom all copyright inquiries should be addressed.

ISBN-13: 978-0-9788862-7-1

Library of Congress Control Number: 2011935598

Printed in the United States of America

DEDICATION

To my sons Michael (Drake) and Timothy (Tracy) who have loved me in spite of everything with a devotion I have yet to deserve ...

To Maureen (Colleen) who ushered me into radiance and the meaning of magic woe ...

To Bruce Pattee (Degnan) who talked me down from glasses of gin at my lips; taught me, in loving me, my worth as a gay man; so, to whom ... although he will not take credit ... I owe my life ...

To Giovanni Lanni who taught me what the love of one's life means ...

To Tonee Mello, ten years and one month my junior in chronological age, but ever ten years and one month my senior in the art and cause of being ... my beloved mentor ...

To the memory of Harvey Milk, whose call to come out, I answered in these pages ...

SPECIAL THANKS

To Joe Corum who taught me, in my first year of teaching, that there is no such thing as a dumb kid ...

To John Ellis ... my student, my friend, my confidant ...

To Renee, Dan Liner and the other courageous, deeply articulate youth who spoke from their hearts in school district after school district in The Invisible Minority in Our Schools: Lesbian, Gay, Bisexual and Transgender Youth workshops, raising consciousness about their imposed classroom and campus closets ... and breaking out of them.

To Alana Flores, alumna of Morgan Hill Unified School District, who led the enormously successful lawsuit on behalf of five other students and herself against the district's failure to protect them from harassment for their real or perceived sexual orientation.

To my friend Bruce Keegan for his continuing encouragement and amazing technical support. Unquestionably, he is the midwife for Once-Removed ...

To Rick Lawton, my publisher at Sasha Press, for his patient, caring guidance.

To Sally Swope, the genie within Sasha Press ...

To Bernard Arias for our Monday critiquing sessions at Café Flore.

To Richard Baker-Lehne for his thoughtful perceptions.

To Markus Dobler for his sensitive ear, exquisite insight and gentle nudges.

To Gary Bushweiler who put the sticks and stones of coming out as a gay teacher in perspective ... when the names hurt me.

To Parents, Family and Friends of Lesbians and Gays -PFLAG who are determined that no other parent's child will have to endure what their children did.

To the memory of Rob Birle ... inspiring young teacher and co-founder of BANGLE, the Bay Area Network of Gay and Lesbian Educators, and his husband Andy Bowlds.

To Anne Rosenzweig who saw what others saw ... and did something about it.

To Faye, John and sweet Janine ... first to know ... first to accept ...

To my grand sobrino, Isaias, who, at age fifteen, crossed the desert to forge a future and redefined courage for me ...

To Alberto Morales for his patience, kindness and amazing resourcefulness.

To Luke Hickman ... philosopher, renaissance man and fellow septuagenarian voyageur ...

To my cousin Denny Nino, imbued with the spirit of César Chávez in early UFW marches, for his ever-encouraging Sí, se puede vision of the world ...

To George Woyames whose soul is all-encompassing ...

To Barbara Champion, the Mrs. Madrigal of Eagle Street, for chats with Chester in front of the fire ...

To Tsun Yuan for the twenty-seven year ride On a Cairo Bus ...

AUTHOR'S NOTE

To allow myself distance to work through the intimacy, I have used pseudonyms in numerous instances.

Cover photo by author ... Sunset over Santa Clara Valley – 1962

Cover design by Bruce Keegan.

Once-Removed ...

Contents

PROLOGUE 10
CHAPTER 1 THE PROMISE 15
CHAPTER 2 ONCE–REMOVED 18
CHAPTER 3 CHIPPIES 20
CHAPTER 4 THE SMIRK 31
CHAPTER 5 THE FLOURISHING 35
CHAPTER 6 THE PALM APARTMENTS 47
CHAPTER 7 THE ERRING ONE 61
CHAPTER 8 THE BIRD'S EYE MAPLE 71
CHAPTER 9 THE Y 78
CHAPTER 10 THE BUILDING 81
CHAPTER 11 GRAY MATTER 91
CHAPTER 12 PARKS AND RECREATION 97
CHAPTER 13 THE RELIC 102
CHAPTER 14 AUGUST HAS NO HOLIDAYS 112
CHAPTER 15 THE GUISE OF INNOCENCE 122
CHAPTER 16 DAY OF WRATH 140
CHAPTER 17 FIRST PERSON, SINGULAR ... ONCE-REMOVED ... 144
CHAPTER 18 PHANTOM BRIDE 154
CHAPTER 19 OBSCENITIES I: ROLE MODEL 164
CHAPTER 20 THE DISINHERITED 172
CHAPTER 21 THE BASTARD (or HELL IS FOR CHILDREN) 180
CHAPTER 22 SECOND ANDY 196
CHAPTER 23 SEED 204
CHAPTER 24 CANTICLE 210
CHAPTER 25 OBSCENITIES II: THE PERFECT IMPERATIVE 216
CHAPTER 26 MOLOKAI PILGRIMAGE 225
CHAPTER 27 MAUI AUDIT 238
CHAPTER 28 MAUI MAHALO 243
CHAPTER 29 EXILE IN THE GOLDEN CLOSET 250
CHAPTER 30 FAMILY TIES 256
CHAPTER 31 OBSCENITIES III: BY-THE-BOOK RISK 259

CHAPTER 32 CLASS ACT...IVIST 279
CHAPTER 33 OBSCENITIES IV: WHERE WERE YOU? 287
CHAPTER 34 LETTERS TO LOVED ONES 294
EPILOGUE.. 302
RESOURCES FOR LGBT YOUTH...315

PROLOGUE

My forty-one-year-old son's face contorted as he sat across the table from me at Naan-n-Curry on Irving Street in San Francisco. "Dad," he said, "until I was twelve or thirteen, you were drunk every night ... and then you came out ... and you said, 'I'm not the person you thought I was ... ' and I didn't know who the hell you were!"

I set my forkful of Daal down on the plate, taken off guard as much by the expression on his face as by his words .... Indeed, his features could have been those of his twelve- or thirteen-year-old self ... and this the candid outpouring I'd needed to hear since he was that age. If it seemed hurtful, I deserved it to be ... and he had needed to say it for far, far too long ... It was the possible publication of these thirty-four chapters that finally gave voice to that long-repressed hurt ... and as I looked at him across the unfinished platter of Palak Paneer, I ached for the years of uncertainty and pain I'd inflicted on him and his brother. Coming out is a process that never ends for a gay, lesbian, bisexual or transgendered person ... and that is certainly true for their children as well. Each time my sons have gone into a new relationship, they have had to do their own coming out ... I imposed that on them by my own gut-wrenching revelation ... and each of us understands there is no alternative ... not if one is to live with any sense of honesty ... any degree of integrity.

They were fourteen and seventeen when I told them that the man they knew as my good friend was, in fact, my lover. My brother had urged me not to tell them then. They were too young ... adolescents dealing with their own sexuality. He cautioned me against telling our mother because she was too old and our sister as well because "... she couldn't handle it." Such fear, of course, precludes loving ... denies those receiving the news the option of loving enough to encompass who we really are. In fact, what I regretted was that I had not told them all from the very beginning ... when it became clear after the divorce that the psychotherapy I'd subjected myself to for two years had not, in fact, succeeded in making me straight. Schizophrenia had robbed my sons of their mother, and my own irrational fear had robbed them of me. Every day that I delayed was a day lost ... Indeed, they had known only who I pretended to be, sold as I was initially on the success of those two years of what has come to be known as reparative therapy in the case of homosexuals. Further, had I died without coming out to them, they would never have known ... or worse yet, discovered going through my belongings after my death that I had lived a lie to them every day of their lives ... My goal always had been to enable them to be themselves ... and the very best themselves they could be. Coming out after twenty-four years of drinking was not a choice ... as I got sober, it was a necessity ...

Angry at me as only a seventeen-year-old can be at his father, my older son's mouth had contorted around the word FAGGOT and hurled it at me, before he really understood what it meant ... or that I was ... It was the only time I ever struck one of my sons ... and that blow came more from my own utter frustration with my silence than my son's reach to hurt me ... I will never forget the look on his face after that blow ... nor ever forgive myself.

"Give up guilt" ... a later therapist once told me. Easier said than done. Guilt was infused in me with the waters of baptism into Holy Mother Church ... and Holy Mother Church nearly killed me. I was the perfect receptacle ... refusing to question because to question was to doubt, and to doubt was to sin. Pius XII was the pope of my childhood, and the nuns said he was rumored to have visions of the Blessed Mother ... We should believe what he and his bishops taught ... They were learned men, close to God. Who were we to doubt if these holy men believed? We must keep ourselves in sanctifying grace ... that grace essential to be saved. And then, of course, there was actual grace, the grace needed to overcome temptation ... We all received it ... Accepting or rejecting it was our choice.

But, at the University of Santa Clara, I learned that the Jesuits and the Dominicans had argued for centuries over yet a third level of grace aptly titled "efficacious" ... True, God gave everyone actual grace, but actual grace in and of itself was insufficient to resist temptation ... that bonus was the prerogative of efficacious grace, and God gave efficacious grace only to the select. It was the old argument about predestination differently wrapped ... The Jesuits distanced themselves from the Dominican arguments with rationalizations that essentially amounted to the same thing. In effect, not only from the moment of conception ... but from all eternity ... in the mind of God, we are in sealed compartments heading either to heaven or hell ... and it is God's choice.

Good Catholic boy that I was, my head ached over such matters, and I remember the exact cathartic moment provoked by that grotesque nuance of grace. I was walking from class to the off-campus apartment I shared with my roommate, Reed, a recent friend whose unself-conscious masculinity mesmerized me ... Reed was the first man I would ever fall in love with ... my conscience locked in a vise of the Church's making ... Despite all my efforts to live a life of grace, despite the agonized confessions ... weekly ... sometimes even daily, I could not quit what I felt for Reed ... and suddenly, the entire travesty of mind control about actual, sanctifying and efficacious grace converged in my overwrought conscience, and I said to myself, "If God could create me this way and then damn me to hell for it, then fuck Him! I want no part of such a God ..." Suddenly, the years of repressed doubt burst the dam of pent-up fear like a logjam of salt pillars plummeting through my rigid excuse for faith. I stopped dead in my tracks, and my whole being shouted, "I do not believe ... !" Clearly, I had a much more humane and loving sense of what it is to be human than such a God ...

In my need to be me, I have caused those I love to suffer ... and that is a weight heavy on my heart. Causing them pain was never my intent ... and even as I write that I seem to be excusing... letting myself off the hook, so to speak ... saying, "I didn't mean it, but ... here it is ... deal with it ..." What purpose will be served ... Who will be served ... by publication of these thirty-four chapters? Serving some need in myself? Perhaps... I hope it will speak to loved ones of my heart's intent ... of my soul's need ... that they will understand ... that they will forgive if I hurt them ... I hope there will be others whose journey began like mine and who will find courage to be themselves sooner than I did ...

"The world in itself is not reasonable, that is all that can be said. But what is absurd is the confrontation of this irrational and the wild longing for clarity whose call echoes in the human heart."

Albert Camus
The Myth of Sisyphus

CHAPTER 1

THE PROMISE

My father's side of the family had roots in Lutheranism. But he was not one of them; he was one of us ... sort of. He had converted for my mother, even tried to become Irish, but my mother's mother was always there to remind him he wasn't ... Irish, that is ... or really Catholic for that matter. A naturalized Catholic had to be tolerated, but a German who became a naturalized American in the mid-thirties could only be suspect. So, while my father was a citizen of this country, he remained an alien in his own home. He was alone a lot.

His mother was that way too ... alone a lot. We were allowed to call her Grossmama because that distinguished her from our Irish grandma, as tante distinguished one aunt from the other. But we hardly ever said our last name in those days because born-here Americans tended to stretch a finger along the upper lip, raise a right arm and shout, "Heil!" That happened to my father once while he was driving streetcars in San José. My father set the brake, got off the streetcar and decked the jerk. Kids on our block used to sing a song: "Whistle while you work; Hitler is a jerk ..." Hitler was no jerk, but the guy who took on my father was.

Anyway, I started to say how Grossmama was alone a lot. She spoke funny like the rest of that side of the family but her wrinkles smiled, and her eyes held onto us behind thinly wired lenses as she talked. She never seemed angry at my father for converting or the rest of us for taking him away from them. But Tante Gretta and the others did, and they thought Grossmama should too.

That side of the family always talked as if they had ten rows of prune trees between them, and when they broke into their harsh, mysterious tongue and laughed sideglancingly, we knew they were talking about us, as though we were the foreigners.

Tante Gretta married a German-American orchardist out in the Berryessa District. All of their children were giants, which made my mother furious because we were all short, and Tante Gretta was always ready to remind her of it ... that we three were not giants, that is ... short, in fact.

Anyway, Grossmama lived in a one-room cottage behind Tante Gretta's ranch house full of giants, and she stayed pretty much to herself. That was easiest. Tante Gretta had a knick-knack-and-doily fetish. She could spot a speck of dust while it was still en route to a tier table, and her davenport was a place to exhibit afghans instead of sprawling bone-weary limbs. She was easily discommoded.

When Grossmama's age and health intersected, each going in different directions, she was sent to a rest home in the east foothills near Alum Rock Park. It was a lovely old two-story stucco with a view of Santa Clara Valley that was remarkable for its preindustrial clarity. My sister and I went with our father one Sunday to visit.

It was a quiet visit with the separateness of those two, my father and Grossmama, ever so prominent, and I realize now that that separateness has ever been a part of me as well. An end of things was at hand. Grossmama sat like a squat, dumpling-haired troll on the tiled porch steps, her blue lips quivering as she watched my sister arcing stones into the fertile valley. The sun glinted from her glasses, but the wetness I'd suspected was there seeped into the wrinkles below them.

My father sat next to her, his heavy fingers picking against each other's blunt nails. His eyes also studied my sister's slender body. Something of that moment has been becoming clear all these years. My sister was eight. When my father was scarcely more than that, Grossmama had booked passage for him, Tante Gretta and herself, and crossed the mid-winter Atlantic. Behind were graves and wars either undone or in the making. America was the Promised Land of the new century, and she was determined that her only surviving son and daughter should be nourished on its milk and honey. I had not suspected her of courage but, clearly, she had it. I had suspected that in some remote way I loved that isolated little woman, but I could not have defined how.

"I am not happy here, Axel," I heard her say brokenly, and I looked at the dark spots scattering in her lap. A crumpled handkerchief peeked from her sweater's cuff, and she dabbed it up under her glasses. What she asked then seemed to siphon off the flow of my blood for I went cold and dizzy with what I knew must be the answer. But I could only think of the terrible loneliness provoking the plea.

My father's head sank so that his eyes could no longer see my sister, nor the view, nor the promise—only the calloused hands picking one against the other and which were Grossmama's flesh as well as my own. His head shook reluctantly. "It would never work," he said. "You must go back to the ranch when you're better."

When my Irish grandmother recited the Pater Noster on the first bead of each of the five decades of the Rosary, she "Amenned" immediately after "deliver us from evil." That was according to Douay-Rheims. When Tante Gretta said the Lord's Prayer, she inserted "for Thine is the kingdom and the power and the glory forever and ever" before "Amenning." That was as King James would have it.

Things like that used to get in the way of good people and cloud their vision of what is not only common but essential to both versions: "Do unto others as you would have others do unto you," for example. Would that my own vision could always remain as clear as it became that Sunday afternoon when I grasped that the promise that Grossmama had made possible for us had been withheld from her.

CHAPTER 2

ONCE-REMOVED ...

Mass had ended. With the wine and water cruets replenished, the candles flanking the darkly gleaming tabernacle extinguished and coiling their smoky incense into Sacred Heart's hushed sanctuary, I entered the sacristy to remove my altar boy's cassock and starched white surplice. Father Onerazani, his embossed vestments closeted for the next celebrant, smiled his thanks to me with quiet eyes and reentered the sanctuary to make his thanksgiving.

The sharp sun, as I opened the door and coaxed too-long arms into the maroon sleeves of my uniform sweater, quickened the difference between the fluttering, animated world without and the muted, palely contemplative world within. Strange that one could exist beside (or was it within?) the other.

My feet echoed on the hollow cedar steps till I jumped from them to the yielding, newly asphalted driveway and ran toward the twelve-year-old Buick Roadmaster, where my family waited. My father crumpled the front section of the Mercury Herald and grinned over the Korean threat as my mother called from the window, "You looked very nice serving mass today, dear."

My sister Kathleen's blond curls bunched around her left shoulder as she leaned over to unlock Black Beauty's door and then grab the comic section from our older brother, Allen. Sinking against the freshly whisked upholstery, I slammed the back door, and my father pulled away from the curb. Fatigue, enormous and cloaklike, suddenly swept over me, a hollowness that made my head heavy. My heart began a sledge-like thump against my chest and, between the pressured beats in my ears, I could hear voices. Kathleen shrank away from me as Allen leaned across to grab my arm and shout, "Are you okay, Ronald? Are you okay?"

My mother's hands cooled my skin as she knelt on the front seat and raised my face. "Axel, stop the car!" she called. "Hail Mary, full of grace ... What's wrong, dear?" Her hat was smashed against the ceiling.

"Is he going to die?" my sister asked.

Me die? Suddenly the sharp sunlit world flashed again against the muted, pale one, and I knew as never before how desperately I wanted them both.

CHAPTER 3

CHIPPIES

I didn't die; Deirdra did... but I was the one who was sick. Dr. Leone, San José's leading heart specialist, said that to my parents. "He's a very sick boy," he told them, that chrome disk with the peephole flashing from his forehead. "If he were my son, I'd have him admitted to cardiology's first available bed up at U.C. in the City." That's how come Deirdra came to our door.

The doorbell rang during supper, and Kathleen was off her stool before Muggsy could bark. She couldn't handle the way the family was avoiding the issue of my life span. If she looked at me at all across the Italian Delight, her earlier question throbbed in her stare, "Is he going to die? ... Is he going to die? ..." There was, after all, a certain prestige to consider. Not many kids had brothers who did that, not in our neighborhood, at least. Muggsy's nails clawed the linoleum. He closed up headstarts on the hall rug. "Who could that be?" mused my grandmother as she slipped a cheese-coated blade between her lips. Aunt Millicent had dropped a fork setting the table, and I could see Grandma review her roster of female acquaintances for one with the gall to stop in at supper. "Ronald!" Kathleen hollered. "It's Deirdra from Sixth Street. Muggsy, shut up!"

An unconscious protocol stipulated that points of origin extend identification at our house. It was as natural to us as the scriptural texting of Jesus of Nazareth or Mary of Cleophas. Glances intersected. Rising, I brushed my hand against my lips. "Deirdra?" I said.

"Use your napkin, dear," my mother reminded.

"What do you suppose that one wants?" my grandmother asked. Aunt Millicent got up and peered tiptoe through the leaded glass cupboard that opened on the dining room and a view of the door, talking softly to herself.

"Be a little obvious," Allen grumbled, but Aunt Millie muttered on, indentured to her curiosity.

"Should you put Ronald's plate in the oven, May?" my father suggested. "Tell her you're eating, son," he called after me. My father called Allen and me son on occasion days.

My sudden celebrity status had projected me into a kind of aristocracy. Persons designated as that one were not encouraged at our house but could be received in times of trouble or condolence. The usual nature of such occasions required an adult for that function.

"I saw her at the Red and White when I went for the milk," Allen explained as my heels echoed on the cellar air shaft at the entrance to the hall.

I remember the porch light streaming on the pair beyond the screen, Deirdra's bushy hair a nimbus shadowing her facial contour. The color of her visit was red against the January Angelus. St. Mary's tolled the six o'clock summons to prayer behind Deirdra's greeting, "Hi, Ronnie!" No one but Deirdra called me Ronnie. The red weave of the San José High letterman's sweater belonged to the hoop-height Guy Madison attached to her free hand. Its texture swaddled her, which was a good thing because Deirdra wore her black sweaters and green skirts too tight. Discomfort was in, and Deirdra managed to be more in than most. Guy Madison's hair dipped, still damp from turn-out, toward his nasal shaft. He launched spit bubbles from the trough of his tongue as if it were no big deal, and his jaw sported the splendid coarseness of a six o'clock shadow. A slight strabismus made him wonderfully vulnerable, but his cavelike eyes avoided mine. He was too attached to living to flirt with death, and his phallus articulated that fact like a semisoft exclamation against his polished cottons. Even on regular days when he got off the bus at Fifth and William with Deirdra, that's what I noticed first about him, poking against his pants as he walked her down the block. I always needed to go to confession by the time he passed. I wished she hadn't brought him to the door, but I'd have been crushed if she hadn't. I forced my gaze to Deirdra, whose face, especially when she smiled, looked Pekinese.

Smiling was the only way I ever saw her. Deirdra would pause as she loafed past our driveway in saddles and bobby socks to admire my network of roads in the gravel, never hinting that twelve was too old to play cars. She'd shake Guy Madison's hand till he complimented the complexity of my engineering too. "Yeah, it's real nice," he would say, and I'd follow one of his spit bubbles till it popped with its own brilliance. Ten kids could be playing hide-and-seek at our house; Deirdra could spot where I was hiding. She'd crank out a frantic little wave if it was safe to run home or pivot a stay-put till IT hollered, "Olly ... Ollyoxon free." It didn't make any sense Deirdra should die ... and there I was, the sick one.

Deirdra's mom was one of the World War II divorcées that shoved the nation out of gear. Kids in Deirdra's circumstances began popping up all over the neighborhood and not for long. They came and went, rootless and baffled about how to deal with no dad. Deirdra's mom had to work, of course, and Deirdra held Guy Madison's hand all the way up to that Sixth Street apartment every single day. Talk about talks! Deirdra had dirtied the eggs in my family's eyes shortly after she moved to the neighborhood and just before she met Guy Madison. Kathleen came panting into the kitchen one evening as my mother was breading eggplant and demanded, "Mama, what does hideous mean?"

My mother looked at my sister's flushed face. "Well, it means awful ugly, honey. Why?"

"Just what I thought!" Kathleen blurted. "That Deirdra from Sixth Street just walked by and said, 'Tell your brother Allen I think he's hideous!'"

"Deirdra said that?"

Kathleen hitched up her pedal pushers. "Deirdra!" she nodded. "That's the one. She said Allen is hideous."

"Well, that dirty rascal," my mother countered, "strutting past in her old tight skirts and sweaters. Let her walk down her own street."

Perspective, I discovered, is fickle. Deirdra's smile made me feel valued. Her notice warmed me, as it did there on the porch, her left hand crinkling a rolled paper sack. Her eyebrows sketched in each other's direction. "How're you feelin', Ronnie?"

"Oh, fine, thanks," I said.

Her expression claimed she did not believe that, admired my courage, in fact.

"I seen your brother Allen over at Red 'n' White before. He said you was goin' to U.C. up in Frisco tomorrow, huh?"

I nodded, patting Muggsy's whining muzzle as the open doorway sucked January into the warm lungs of the house. A bubble drifted from Guy Madison's tongue, spent itself on the wire mesh. I shivered suddenly.

Deirdra noticed, reached for the doorknob. "We brotcha some funny books so's you won't get bored up there, okay?" She let go the large knuckled grip of her varsity center for the first time in my recollection. Guy Madison looked at his naked hand and immediately launched two more bubbles. Deirdra pulled three comics from the sack and handed them through the breached screen.

I could scarcely talk. "Thhhanks, Deirdra," I said.

"Myself, I figured you'd like these." She spread Classic Comic renditions of Wuthering Heights and The Corsican Brothers. "But Lenny here," her snubbed nose bunched beneath her eyes as she glanced at the six-four roundballer, "he says you should have some v'riety, so he put this one in." Her blanched fingertips raised the corner of a Crime Doesn't Pay selection, the cover ablaze with a good guy/bad guy shoot-out. The latter, bald and obese and snarling comic book expletives, vomited blood and gushed same from a shot-off ear while firing six-shooters with both hands.

Lenny's hand labored its loneliness, veined like accentuated sculpture. It needed a ball or Deirdra's narrow fingers to enclose. I watched it flex around her softness, wishing I hadn't heard his real name.

I nodded, examining the covers like a pair of aces and a joker in my hands. "That's sure nice of you. Thanks a lot."

Kathleen's gambol echoed through the hall sharded by the snapped latch on the swinging door and her own breathless report.

"Don't even mention it," Deirdra said. Her little eyes flecked her crowded features. It was a nice thing to do, and its niceness pleased her too. "You just come home real soon, okay, Ronnie?" Her fingers rippled like antennae from the letterman's rolled cuff. Her other hand shook Lenny's. "See ya," Lenny said without conviction as he tugged Deirdra toward the steps.

"See you, Deirdra," I said, " ... Lenny," I added. But I never did again. Goodbyes ought to be meant.

Judah Street becomes Parnassus on the mount that shoves the medical center against San Francisco's skyline. I was twelve on U.C.'s thirteenth floor when Deirdra died. That still sounds phony: Deirdra died. As if it was easy. As if she didn't mind. Deirdra would have. She'd have hated it, so the fast part of how it happened, at least that was good.

Kids on Ward H were doing it slowly. God, I was lucky. The palpitation that had double whammied me after mass one Sunday petered into a symptom so nebulous it lacked definition. The pounding heart could be controlled by a pale yellow phenobarbital and, in the absence of that, by just pressing the heels of my palms against my eyeballs. Word of honor. Dr. Leone would determine that I had a heart murmur that should be monitored but, aside from excusing me from Bellarmine's freshman P.E. program the following fall and 4-F ing me from a draftable future, should not interfere with normal functioning. In two weeks he would shrug at the results of sophisticated testing. "Maybe you were right," he would say to my parents, his smile less savvy than the one with which he'd dismissed their quaintness at the outset. "Maybe he just grew too fast."

Time would authenticate his prediction about high school P.E., but Oakland's induction center reduce him to false prophet well-paid. Phallus to rump in the jockey short queue, I would classify "A" from anus to eyeball, my murmur in six years gone mute.

Six years isn't a long time unless forty-eight hours seem like them. New admissions to Ward H spent two whole days in isolation sifting their systems of latent virus, guaranteeing, thereby, the vulnerable onward patients against further infection. As well, isolation assessed my own readiness for specialist-prescribed procedures and the ever-present risk of surgery. But the unexpected seclusion reinforced Kathleen's haunting suspicion. "Is he going to die?" worried my silence.

I could have no visitors in isolation. My privacy the first night was disturbed only by the student nurse who initiated my vital signs to U.C.'s charts ... and resembled my cousin who followed her naval officer husband out of their Ste. Claire wedding reception the previous summer on a wither-thou-goest flight to his home in Maryland.

"You remind me of my cousin," I told the student nurse as she practiced her smile. "She's very pretty."

"You've got quite a line," she replied, "for a twelve-year-old." She handed me a thermometer and began unraveling a blood pressure cuff. It was a bit odd, I suppose, the comment; out of character, at least, for me. Forced independence, perhaps, misleads maturity. But what I'd said was true. That the resemblance was limited to looks, however, was reinforced as she glanced up between the stethoscope stems and scolded, "No! No! That's a rectal thermometer!"

Had I been going to die during my stay, it might as well have been then. Were it not for my Aunt Millicent the R.N., I wouldn't even have known what a rectum was at age twelve. It was she who validated excretory and sexual functions with diction beyond toy-toy and toot. But, in my wildest imagining, I would never have thought of inserting a thermometer in my rectum. My cousin's look-alike stood there and scowled the whole time I struggled through that transition.

It was as well I was alone. By the time she left, I couldn't talk anyway. I tried reading The Corsican Brothers, but the idea of those dashing twins having been joined at birth increased the isolation of isolation. I turned out the light and toward the window where the City dropped from Parnassus like spilled jewels beside the sea. The darkness there where the surf should have paled the shore was abrupt and dense as velvet. The fog bank, rolled in from the Pacific, faked the moon along the Great Highway and defined the character of escape.

Feet on hassock, my father would be quartering a Golden Delicious as he watched Death Valley Days on the brand new eighteen-inch Admiral. My mother and Aunt Millie would be vying for the bag of bridge mix while Allen and Kathleen sprawled, hand to cheek, on the floor, and Muggsy edged Grandma out of the Morris chair, snug between its back and hers. Kathleen kept Crime Doesn't Pay to trade with Sidney around the corner. No matter how much Deirdra liked Lenny, I couldn't forgive him his name.

I remember two things about the surgery: not being able to swallow after the anesthetic and vomiting, my head jammed against the bedrail, afterwards. The two-inch incision upper left of my clavicle was the injection site for the dye they traced unobstructed through my cardiovascular system. They wheeled me into recovery, an enigma.

I came to on Ward H. The kid next to me had some disease no one would talk about. He was from Chicago, and his mother looked like Teddy Roosevelt. U.C. absorbed all his expenses for the privilege of studying him. Zack and I wrote to each other off and on after. He was the one who stopped.

Opposite me, in the other window bed, a pasty-skinned diabetic cussed all day and all night even when he wasn't learning to self-inject insulin. God, how he hated those needles. My father, who drove semis across Pacheco Pass, shook his head as he listened to this ten-year-old cuss. Sometimes he'd just cry, "It hurts, goddamnit it, it hurts!" His hair had that pillow slant that makes it sore to comb.

The fourth bed contained a rumple that snored beside an I.V. I woke one night to shadows against his pulled curtain. The day shift aide scrubbed the bed frame, treated the mattress and made it up with fresh linen. Funny how you can get used to a snore. If experience expanded my sense of the world, my Sacred Heart classmates benefited as well. With the post on January 24, I discovered I had become part of the eighth-grade curriculum:

"Dear Ronald,

Sorry I didn't write sooner but I was very busy with my schoolwork ..."

Fifteen renditions of the 200-entry art contest included the facts that Frankie Balasteri had won the dollar first prize and that Sacred Heart would debate St. Joseph's in three weeks. All fifteen hoped I'd be back by then. All fifteen were praying for me. Not even the cotton-voiced Hispanic boy who sometimes ate lunch with me, penned a personal message. Most mentioned they missed my silence, and I thought again of the kitty-corner snore. Thirty-six years later I still wish Sister Mary St. Giles had not made me an assignment.

Allen drove my mother up with the news about Deirdra the day after the Sacred Heart letters. Lenny had sideswiped a telephone pole in his '47 Ford with Deirdra leaning from its window. She was sixteen. Allen listened, his forefinger and thumb tugging his lower lip. So was he sixteen. Sixteen means you live forever. You don't smack wood and die. Leaning out the window tempted fate, but that's what sixteen-year-olds were for. It was the dying that was dumb. Whoever was in charge had to be napping, ought to be accountable. Which should you be more of, sorry or embarrassed, for Deirdra's divorced mother whose daughter's brains, cradled in the polished cotton crotch of an angle-jawed kid, bled into the gutter? None of it does any good—not even anger at star-double Lenny who learned what he lacked with the remnants of Deirdra's smile in his beautifully tendoned hands and him moaning, "Jesus ... Jesus ... Jesus," as if that mantra could make a miracle.

Allen said, "It's like a bad dream, you know?" But thirty-six years later, no one's awakened. Not even Lenny. It was real all right. Lenny's middle-aged now, and his tongue, I suppose, has forgotten the shape of the bubble trough. Three-and-a-half decades of getting by will have weighed the Guy Madison even out of his features and shoveled Deirdra deeper than six feet of Oak Hill ever could. If he thinks of her now, I suspect the pain is vague and embarrassment distant. Time is that kind of friend.

My forehead and nose felt the chill of the glass as I maneuvered a wave at my mother and Allen beside the Buick on Third and Parnassus. They were little wind-up dolls like we must seem to God. I watched as Allen steered the Black Beauty down Judah past St. Anne's before turning left on 19th Avenue. How important, that ritual of the visit, cloaked in the chasuble of grief. They took with them part of my silence and I ... I had retained parts of them - my mother's quaver, Allen's tugged lip, like relics of that splintered pole.

The starkness of life engaged me in a stare down. I was surrounded by life that was nonrenewable. Death came not just to the old, nor even just to the sick. Grossmama, my German grandmother, had died in her seventies feeling used up and wanting to. My Irish grandmother rocked on the Fifth Street porch, callousing her fingers on Irish horn beads, eyes closed so she wouldn't be surprised. But Deirdra was young, and the kitty-corner rumple was just a child. I was sorry for Deirdra, sorry for the rumple. My eyelashes brushed the windowpane. I couldn't be sorry it hadn't been me.

God had become suspect at U.C., though I wouldn't admit it at home. You were supposed to want to be with God, after all. You sort of had to divide your loyalties between family and Him. And you couldn't ever relax. The devil tapped his fingers on your toenails waiting to trip you up during a systole gone askew and carry off the contract on your eternity. There was something abusive about God's end of the loving, particularly if, as we are told, no one is perfect and certainly not all the time. Being human involved a Russian roulette of the soul.

A Jesuit retreat master at El Retiro used to pillage the pride of rock-hard Bellarmine students with his tale of the single mortal sin: A popular, handsome young man, on the eve of his entrance to the seminary, was persuaded by his friends to commit one mortal sin before abandoning the world. How else, they argued, could he appreciate what future penitents would bring to his confessional, after all? The youth consented. Next morning his naked body was discovered by his mother in the thrash of sheets, no evidence of foul play. His heart had simply stopped as he slept off the exertion of sin, before repentance. The parish priest vested at once to offer mass for the repose of the young man's soul. It was, he thought, a mere formality. None but the youth's friends knew of the single sin. Upon entering the sanctuary the priest was thrown back by a vision hideous beyond recognition. It was the voice that gave it away. "Don't bother offering mass for my soul," said the tormented spirit. "Last night I committed a single mortal sin. My soul is already in hell."

God had my fealty, but it was a commitment of torment that laid waste my teens, worsened by the mythology of perversion surrounding the phallus carved like an idol behind my fly. Its demands went without respite until reason replaced faith, negotiating an abrased truce between spirit and flesh. My adolescence stares at my present like the gargoyle whose molten tongue licked my genitals, trapping me between desire and guilt even for retroactive pleasure in wet-bellied nocturnal emissions. I could not detect the quality of mercy in the love of God but left that fear unfocused on the outside chance that when my heart stopped, it might be during a moment's contrition.

I wondered what point there was in praying for Deirdra as the sun flattened past the breakers at Ocean Beach that day. Deirdra's name had rustled like dry leaves across every threshold in the neighborhood. My father made the rumors official. "She's nothing but a little chippy," he declared, and I wondered if even liking Deirdra was a sin, because I did. Deirdra had been nice to me. Would God frown on a requiescat for my friend? Loving God was a lot like being in isolation. Karl Marx was wrong about religion; it's the ball and chain of the masses, the dungeon of the human spirit.

Innocence cannot be retained. The value of losing it differs from person to person, particularly in intensity. Deirdra advertised her loss in an exhibition that sauced up the Mercury Herald's obituaries. I was shedding mine, not agonizingly fast but fast and agonizingly, and there is a difference. And I was shedding it alone. Others could do it in concert. Kathleen was like our brother in that. Both had friends for the covert, to snicker and exchange innuendo. I took God too seriously. Endangering my own soul was deadly enough stuff. Hazarding someone else's was collusion beyond dare.

The night my father called Kathleen a chippy she was herself sixteen. Two years older, I'd begun accessing manhood, having registered to vote and for the draft. I'd begun to accrue certain of the abstract habiliments of adult status. Putting my father in his place was not one on which I'd planned. He was a good man whose heart did his thinking and whose conscience labored with amends for too spontaneous a tongue. Trusting his daughter to the fevered hands of fellows to whom restraint had been cautioned but of whom excess was expected was rough on him. It was rough on me too. Concerned as I was about Kathleen, the tapered muscle that elbowed horns in cars at the dark of the curb primed my own need, stirred my own lust.

Guys in jalopies my father felt easier about. They had values if they had to work for what they wanted and sock away funds for the future. Her date the night of the chippy slur drove a graduation gift from his parents, fire engine red. When he delivered her forty-five minutes late to the door, my father's siege volleyed across the redwood floor like a carpeted cannonade. Inevitably, the element of surprise in the wake of his resolve to remain calm left even those of us who knew what to expect ragged. Kathleen's date could not have touched a single step in his descent of the porch. His revved engine and shrieking tires attested to both the quality of his parents' taste and his coordination. Passion competed with alarm in my sister's face as she searched her bra for his warm, moist gum.

Kathleen was in shock. No one would ever take her out again. My father goddamned his way through one frenzied absolute after another until, his stubby finger wagging in Kathleen's face, he hollered, "You don't give a goddamn about your goddamn reputation, you little chippy!"

Deirdra reeled from the corner of consciousness like old slivers in a present beauty. I lunged between them, ready to shove. "Don't you call her that!" I shouted. "Don't you ever call her that again! She's not a chippy, and nobody better ever say she is!" Allen had confronted our father. Never till then had I. Argued, yes, but confronted never. He was startled. My mother wedged between us. "Go to bed," she pleaded. "Jesus, Mary and Joseph, this is something awful! Everyone go to bed."

My analyst in another eight years would respond to such events recounted with, "You're in love with your sister; didn't you know that? Incest was out of the question for you, so you transferred your love to men rather than be disloyal with other women." It was a theory popular in the sixties. Psychiatry had a decade to process before declaring homosexuality sound and natural to ten per cent of the population. It stunned me then. As the lesser of two evils, it almost made being queer respectable, in fact, downright chivalrous in an unconscious kind of way.

I came through that father/son confrontation with a rapid pulse but no palpitation. The auricles and ventricles were fine; it was the dimension of loving that remained awry. For twenty more years I would make the motions that fitted the norm, isolated in my sexuality. So my father never really knew me. It would be in Kathleen's woman's arms that he would one day weep that he did not want to die, the mass in his chest spreading even as he spoke, come like Mephisto to collect on a lifetime of Camels indulged to the nub. It's a strange mix, family love. I have wondered through the years whether Deirdra's divorced mother ever dared risk it again.

CHAPTER 4

THE SMIRK

The sting of fondant icing lingered against the roof of my mouth, the staleness of twelve extinguished candles probing my nostrils. Eyes closed, I sat at table's head, straining not to cheat at my mother's rayon-rustled approach. Sweat sealed the paper napkin balled in my fist, the residues of lamb, gravy and chocolate ice cream adhering one to the other. The secretiveness of this final gift bothered me, and now an awareness of silence in my mother's wake washed ahead of her, cautioning with the smart of salt. Still, I was unprepared.

I felt her warmth lean near as she pressed her lips to my forehead. "Happy Birthday, Ronald dear," my mother said, and the tempered refrain was echoed by family and imitation revelers about the spent table. Something in her hands scratched lightly across my cheek, trailing an odor mildly pungent, vaguely familiar, and this time caution seized me. Still, I was unprepared.

My eyes snapped open. My breath halted. Lavender beads of potted heather cornered my view of half-smiling faces. I watched through feathered branches as the hunted must fix the hunter when escape is gone. Haywired, my thermostat stoked my cheeks, teared my eyes.

"A plant?" my brother, Allen, asked, incredulous. My ears began to whir.

"Why not? He likes plants, don't you, Ronald?" my father countered.

The whirring cranked into full whine as I tabulated half-smiles aimed at me from around the ribbon-littered table. The explosion of lavender branches was too scant to shelter me.

"Don't you, Ronald?"

I had not answered my father.

"He's a boy!" my brother asserted, his eyes flickering less certainly from me to his friend Barry Margin. Barry had been brought in from up the street for Allen's sake. Barry went anywhere for a free meal. His heavy lidded eyes watched me. There was no uncertainty in them.

I longed for a gallon of fish emulsion to saturate the heather's bound roots. What good, after all, was a bush to the hunted when the hunter still could see him? But my allotted wish had been squandered on the nipples of flame that had seared my cake. I was fresh out.

"That's all right," my father persisted. "He likes to garden. Isn't that right, Ronald?"

I wished he would leave it alone. Regret skewered my mother's soft features. The decision to buy the heather had, I suspected, taken hours of inner arguing to reach.

"Isn't that right, Ronald?" my father pursued.

Nodding stiffly, I shoved the word "Sure" from its grip on my tongue and punctuated the effort with, "Thanks."

"There!" my father scoffed at Allen. "Who knows? Ronald may become another Luther ... What was that old fart's name?"

"Burbank! Luther Burbank," Aunt Millicent piped, "and that 'old fart' wound up well-off, you can be sure, working with all those flowers." She fawned a smile that measured my success thirty years hence.

Barry Margin laughed. So did Allen, but anger shot across his cheeks and his head shook, disbelieving. My sister, Kathleen, screwed her neck into a collar of curls, blond and shimmering.

Next to her under the brass-chained, triple-globed chandelier, Kevin Graham, the preacher's boy, smiled, guileless, pristine innocence ovaling his eyes. He was saved, Kevin was. So were his mother and father and his father's congregation. His father said so. Gosh and heck were cuss equivalents and Kevin shrank when we said them. Piecing together the puzzle of the Good Shepherd he'd given me, Kevin chattered through his adenoids as everyone else at my table fell silent. The blessed are oblivious.

Naked as Adam when God summoned him from behind Eden's apple, I sat aching to wrench the length from those pretty branches. The whirring stopped, but my ears were stuffed, my forehead tight. Adam's shame was not my shame. Suspicion coagulated the bleeding silence but for Kevin's bubbling about the Bible college that would fit him for his father's shoes. The verge of knowledge is a precipitous place, the margin for wonder peaked and narrow. I clung to it still. Their staring stood on my fingers, Barry Margin abrading with his toes. Letting go would confirm for me that Adam's shame was not my shame, that while he had looked on Eve, I looked on him ... knew in my heart I could not get past him.

My father was right, of course. I did like to garden.

My fascination with bronze chrysanthemums striving out of well-mulched soil and the odor of newly turned earth crumbling under my lengthening fingers was part, integrally, of my own striving out of childhood. It was part of my father's own striving, I am convinced, too—the need of his gentleness to assert itself and fulfill him as a man. For a long time he held back, that brusque-bodied, sturdy and stubby German. His early penchant for raked gravel filled Saturdays with the ring of iron teeth, weaving the yard into corduroy patterns. Cutting was another thing. When the wisteria sent out runners and got involved with the oleander, everything got whacked to stumps as if he resisted their need of him, in him. The grease grain calloused in his hands seemed too foreign to the earth ever to be compatible but, in time—as he gradually let them probe roots and enter the secrets of growing things—the look of his hands remained exactly the same, but their touch changed. The grease and the earth made love in his hands and enchanted the yard with fountains and rockery and blooming.

But it was too late for us, or somehow, still too soon. My father and I never really found the way to each other. When he lay fallen with a tumor in his chest, the need for talk strained our visits together. Small talk was the legacy of our relationship, and at that I have never been good.

Barry Margins abound in life, however, and so small talk thrives ... small talk and half-smiles ... or smirks. Smirkers don't ignore you; they let you know they know the score. Barry Margin never missed his chance ... like that Saturday morning after my birthday. I was sitting on the front lawn in the fan shadows of the neighbor's palm when he came by. All around me the grass was quilted with sun. Barry carried his free meals with him. He moved like a dinosaur down the cracked sidewalk. He looked like one too, a brontosaurus, with its massive head moving from side to side, eclipsing the sun as he looked at me ... and smirked.

"What's wrong? I asked.

"If you don't know, I ain't gonna tell ya," he grunted.

He heaved on up the steps to ring for Allen, but the imprint of Barry Margin's foot stayed right in the middle of my chest.

The pleasure I had known at tending seeds, flowers and shrubs was not there when I took the heather into the shadowed yard to plant that afternoon. Nor was the sorrow I'd known when other plants did not thrive under my hand, as this did not ... not even when it died. It had betrayed me ... or so I thought. I had, I guess, betrayed myself.

CHAPTER 5

THE FLOURISHING

Palm Street wasn't called Palm Street for nothing. A great big one grew out of the cement-banked lawn in front of Sacred Heart. It was a neat thing about San José. You could see the palms poking up like curious giraffes for blocks before you got to them, and when you did, you got a crook in your neck from trying to find the tops. And then, of course, they were not giraffes at all but bunches of knotted kites shining in the wind.

They were like people, palms were ... so different. The one in front of the church, for example, had a trunk thick as elephant legs—all four tied together and clipped like mammoth toenails where the old fronds had been. The top of it ... well, it was like a Fourth of July firework, caught mid-burst over Spartan Stadium, that got bigger and bigger without anybody noticing. Orange seeds sprayed from the core like the last gasp of sparks before the firework dies—only these didn't die. That was another neat thing about them.

I used to have nightmares about dying, and I was not at all convinced I was not about to ... die, that is, as Fr. Onerazani's '47 Roadmaster lurched away from the Willow Street rectory, then lurched again onto Palm. Like my father, Fr. Onerazani appreciated a good car but, unlike my father, he didn't know how to operate it. His polished toe worked no better on a clutch than his bare fingers on a cheek. Kathleen always ran for her room when his erratic ring came at our door, and Allen fumed that he was too old to be pinched. He was. He was sixteen. Main thing was it hurt, though ... the pinching. Fr. Onerazani didn't know that and, I'm convinced, he didn't mean it. In fact, he always followed the pinch with a pair of sharp pats that meant you were special. You had to know that about him too, though—that he was special. He got talked about a lot.

Chanting softly, the Roadmaster tempered Fr. Onerazani's prattle as we drove, but nothing could quite counter his laugh. "Cackle" was what adults called it. Fr. Onerazani himself they referred to as "that poor man." I meant to be respectful but, conditioned as I was, my attention surrendered easily to the foreign character of Sacred Heart Parish in which I had not lived since I was two. That year my grandfather died, and my parents, brother and I moved into the family home down the street from San José State College to be with my grandmother and aunt. Kathleen was born a couple of months later, and we never left. Those two facts are not necessarily connected except to show that change didn't play much part in our growing up. Staying in one place did—like driving all the way back to Sacred Heart for thirteen years just because we'd lived up the block from the school when my brother started first grade. We could have walked two blocks to St. Mary's.

Parishes were distinctly ethnic in the 40s, so for me, foreign does not exaggerate the character of Sacred Heart. We'd had a landlord on Palm Street, for example, who moped around his yard every morning plucking snails from their silvery trails and dropping them into a hollow bucket. When the echo stopped, Mr. Farinah disappeared into his kitchen, bucketed snails and all. That, you must admit, was foreign.

I learned later from the Sisters of Notre Dame de Namur that it was all due to the weather ... the large Italian population, that is. San José had a Mediterranean climate, and Santa Clara Valley was one of the world's most fertile. The snails were due to a French vineyardist, Antoine Delmas, same as the street that runs into Willow. Like Delmas, the snails were immigrants, his personal import to ensure bland munching while sipping vintages. Between sips, the little buggers got loose.

Snail collecting wasn't the only thing that distinguished Sacred Heart Parish though. Here and there as we drove, spiny-lobed cacti leaned on chicken-wire fences, their knobby pears glowing in the sun's descent. Tiled roofs, radiant with that descent, dissipated its warmth. Olive trees, veiled with dusk, revolted against sidewalk prisons with a steady, gnarled strength. Bird dirt, nozzled off each morning, collected on the cracked concrete again by evening, an exhibit of contiguous abstracts. Porch mats spread like bristled scalps at the foot of every screen door. Scraping my soles on them matched the scratch of nails on slate. I tried to cancel both out.

Nodding inattentively to his lens-inverted glance, I realized that I had done just that to Fr. Onerazani—canceled that poor man out—and

I felt guiltily ill at ease. I did not like being plunged into the eye of new events, and there I was setting out on the Feast of St. Joseph to bless altars in his honor in homes whose native tongue was reputed to be Romantic, yet was spoken at such a clip that I could identify not even a semblance of the Latin from which it derived ... and of which I knew only altar boy responses anyway.

"Why does he want me to go?" I'd urged as late as supper, still in the hope of being let off.

My Irish grandmother, blowing across the tea pooled on her saucer, looked up. "You can bet the wops themselves will all be celebrating, that's why." Tea dribbled from the saucer's edge.

"Grandma ... !"

"Hush, now, Grandma's only fooling, Ronald," my mother said. "Aren't you, Grandma?" Tea spotted my grandmother's gingham lap. She could not answer.

My father, who wasn't even Irish, grinned also. "Fr. Onerazani knows you want to be a priest. He thinks you'll enjoy the altar blessings, that's all." While that was true, he winked at my mother. I was not convinced.

Two days earlier we had celebrated St. Patrick's Day. We'd even driven to the City on the weekend for the parade. In fact, Archbishop Mitty dispensed the Lenten fast every March 17. It was an occasion all right. But what St. Joseph had to do with the Italians, I never could figure out. The nuns said that angels had carried the Nazareth home of the Holy Family to Italy; maybe that was the connection. I mean, who else could boast a home built by the man who taught the world's most famous carpenter everything He knew about the trade?

The prattle had stopped, I suddenly realized, and I didn't know what had been asked. It struck me as well that for several minutes there hadn't even been a cackle, so that whatever was afoot was serious stuff. That poor man watched me from his Roman collar turret, his eyes sunk in lenses. My scalp prickled with the rebuke echoing in my own Gethsemane, "Could'st thou not watch with me one hour?" and my temples went damp. I struggled for some gist of Fr. Onerazani's question and saw that he was pointing. Leaning forward, I followed the direction of his index finger aimed like Flash Gordon's rocket ship through the windshield. But there was nothing foreign in the iridescent, pulsing sky. My eyes returned to the thick, rigid consecrated index finger, and suddenly

I knew that it was not a rocket ship at all. My father's wink shuttered in my mind. My back sought the pleated solace of the Roadmaster's cushion. Fr. Onerazani's voice cracked unevenly. Tenting my fingers in my lap, I watched, wordless, as the sacerdotal circle of left index finger and thumb descended over the right index finger, his right thumb hooked on the steering wheel, driving.

"Do you understand, my boy?"

"Yes, Father," snagged in my throat. A bit of bile washed past my tonsils on the back of my tongue. I swallowed the reflex to throw up.

"Do you have any questions?"

The back of my hair mussed against the cushion. "No, Father." I ached to be elsewhere. So, from his expression, did he, this man who had taught me to go in to the altar of God and assist at the holiest of rites. In the ensuing silence we did not look at each other, and it was obvious that this latter teaching had been a weightier affair for him as well as me. The clear flight of Sanctus bells through Sacred Heart's nave was infinitely preferable. Besides, that which I had begun to suspect about myself he had not so much as touched upon. How then could I ask?

In the basement, a week before, as my mother fed sheets through the wringer, I had asked, "Are you and Dad supposed to ... tell me about things?" She and I did not look at each other either. I thought she had not heard me over the wrenching of the washer. But then she said, "What kind of things?"

Clorox stung my eyes. I shrugged. "How babies are born ... things like that." Cobwebs, snagged on redwood beams, drifted above my mother's prematurely gray hair. In the refracted light from the ground-level window, I watched the imprint of worry that had already marked her loveliness—the prophecy of age at work in her features. She had calmed me out of a nightmare once by promising me I would never die. Now she studied the thorn-stemmed Talisman rose hedged beside the driveway. "How babies are born" was easy, actually; it was "things like that" that had us stumped.

"Most boys hear about that from other boys at school ... but ... I guess you don't listen to talk like that, do you?"

My cheeks burned. "Huh-uh..."

The washer clicked. A thick black hose shuddered, then spewed turgid suds into the rinse basin.

"How did Allen find out?"

The flush of the Talisman set in her skin. She bit her lip. "Oh, ... partly from other boys, I guess ... and ..."

"And what?"

"And your father took him to see a movie."

"A movie?" The Monitor's headlines blazed in my memory, the ink still fresh. "That Mom and Dad one?"

My mother nodded fugitively.

"But that was condemned by the Legion of Decency!"

Her tone was compromised. "Yes, now, I know it was, but not everyone takes things as serious as you do."

The gray waste boiled in the basin; the drain sucked the whirlpool that would stink finally on the Alviso wind and buoy the seagulls cavorting for Vahl's starched-linen diners.

It was a mortal sin to see Mom and Dad. I stopped short of asking that. "Would you ask Dad to talk to me about it?"

"About the movie?"

"No, ... about things ... You know!"

"Well, can't you ask him?"

My head shook emphatically, but I shrugged. "I'd feel funny. Will you do it?"

My mother reached across the wicker basket of sheets webbed like the salt-water taffy she loved to buy on the Boardwalk at Santa Cruz. She brushed my loosened wave off my forehead. There was no coarseness in her touch. "Such a nice boy," she mused, then added, "I'll ask him." She tugged the collar of my uniform shirt and squinted. "Why don't you take that off so I can have it ready for the morning?"

The Roadmaster white-walled the curb behind a driveway-segmented chain of other machines. Tepid air, nonetheless revitalizing, gushed in around us as Fr. Onerazani and I heaved open the doors. Spattered olives squashed underfoot as I stooped beneath the ashen drape of branches. Only our shoes, as we fell in with each other's pace, wordlessly brisk, registered sound. My parents had set us both up.

Our destination in the middle of the block was clear. Sun-burnished men, Sunday-suited, dark brows beaded with the unseasonable March, chatted on a sulphur-colored porch. Left hands trailing smoke, right tumblered with wine, they moved, caught in a primal sensing of one another, before a bay-window eye curtained with recessive images. I watched the steps as I mounted behind the priest into that unsubtle setting of male ritual. Porch sealer layered old scars like sins on a confessed soul. I wished I could bathe and feel the way I used to.

Absent narcissi scented the raked yard, their stems oozing clear blood in the corduroy soil. It was not, I knew, the fairness of my skin but the shadow on my soul that caused the rapid flux of tongues resonantly awash on the dusk. I saw it in the single glance I allowed to sweep their faces; saw it in the light in those eyes shining with relish in forbidden fruit, and I knew that they knew that I had been to the Tree of Knowledge too ... but was not one of them ... that the taste of forbidden fruit was different against my tongue ... and God, I did not want it to be. While their voices smiled over unsatisfied appetites, the morsel of my tasting had lodged in my throat, and I knew only its pain. I wanted to throw it up and swallow the core at the same time. With the priest's approach, innocence foamed upon the dialogue, but nothing could dim the eyes guarding those cherished reefs around which they guided his voyage past them.

My head jammed under Fr. Onerazani's shoulder blade. He had paused midstair to shake hands and to prattle. Sensuous lips, shadowed male, smirked over lines of teeth holding their truths at bay. My careful wave splintered under the working shoulder blade. That poor man's cackle stirred my distress. Anger was a sin whose mortal bounds I exceeded without sufficient reflection. Black gaberdine stung my jaw as Fr. Onerazani turned to my rescue. Tempered laughter washed beneath the cresting cackle. Pain throbbed at my set jaw. I had my mother's weakness for flushing. I wanted to cry.

"What if they're all cheek pinchers?" my brother had baited, his mouth full of meatloaf at supper.

My watery appeal searched the priest's eyes. The tautness of my skin, minus two fingers of cheek, shook my distress like signaling linen from that sulphured porch. I bit the tremor from my lip as the sharp slaps fell, an equal pair, upon the smarting pinch. "My-y-y goodness! I'm sorry, Ronald!" His sincerity shoved reflection to the brink of sufficiency. "Ronald!" he announced to the knowing eyes. "This is Ronald! Shake hands, my boy!" He pulled my wrist clear of its cuff. My hand pumped skin the texture of damp chamois. My eyelids concealed my shame from eyes that brandished theirs. The air, dense with Cribari burgundy, soured my nostrils.

Big brotherly advice eked residually into my consciousness as the porch light switched on. The pallor of sulphur deepened. "Take a deep breath before you go into their houses. They fart garlic." The screen door budged open. Italians swarmed within.

"Scrape your feet, my boy, scrape your feet." I cringed then stepped on the bristled scalp. Loquat leaves leaned darkly inquisitive across the balustrade to whisk my shoulder and whisper, "You're the boy who steals loquats!" And that was true. I liked those pear-fleshed pits. No one picked the tree from which I ate, at least not the Virginia Street side that hung over the fence behind the Jackal Club. There was a man at the Jackal Club who took the 3:10 sun and used to hug my sister if my mother was late and we'd walked that far. One day my mother drove up during the hugging and bounced Black Beauty against the curb. The man grinned and hurried into the club. After that he stopped taking the sun at 3:10. Anyway, it was true I always looked around before I picked the loquats, so I guess I stole them all right.

Sacred Heart Grammar School was still on Palm and Virginia then and had three-quarters of a block just to itself. Seventh and eighth graders were taught by the principal in the same room on the first floor. She kept the spanking machine there, the principal did. None of us ever saw it, but we heard it. Sr. Purissima could turn it on from any room in the building. She had a secret switch on every teacher's desk. All she had to do was stand in front of a desk with her hands behind her habit. None of us needed to see it.

The inside stairs to the lower grades had brass edges for coordinating first and second graders' feet. The outside stairs tremored like the Alps under Hannibal's herds when Sr. Purissima marched the third, fourth, fifth and sixth graders in from recess, reviewing their silent formation and clicking her wooden signal toward those guilty of infraction.

Pepper trees leaned like drifting galleons in the wind on the girls' playground. Swing sets with teeter-totters and monkey bars separated the girls' side from the baseball diamond and football field. The only grass that grew shouldn't have. When you fell, you knew it. Sr. Purissima used to egg me on to play ball, but I knew I would strike out or drop a pass, and I always did. Captains never chose me; one of them got stuck with me. Most recesses I spent on the down side of a teeter-totter wishing the bell would ring.

Cyclone fences ensured our safety, containing us and the infidels in contiguous blocks along Virginia Street. We didn't think of ourselves as caged, but we did them, the non-Catholics at Woodrow Wilson Junior High. Their backstop, fences and even the sidewalk blazed with the F word. I asked my mother what the F word meant when she picked us up on the emblazoned cement squares once. The chalky F had imprinted my right half-sole. "Oh," she said, "that's a terrible, dirty word, and don't you ever say it!"

"I wasn't going to say it," I said, "I just wanted to know what it means."

"Just never you mind. It's a terrible, dirty word, and don't you ever say it!"

That sort of confirmed what the nuns felt about Wilson kids and the needle's eye not being just for rich people.

The thing was, though, my father used terrible, dirty words all the time—well, most of it, at least—especially when he got angry. But I only heard him say the F word once. That was when the shop steward at the pump company had been picking on him for a long time. He took pride in his work, my father did. In the twenty years with that company that ended his work life, he was late only once, and that because his Baby Ben had ticked its last at 3:37 A.M. To hear him rant, anyone would think it was Big Ben that had failed and the heart of England gone off kilter. He was that conscientious. The shop steward could be a son-of-a-bitch!

How did I get off on that? Loquats, that's right. Next to the screen door with the mat scraping under my soles.

It was even warmer inside the sulphur-colored house, and despite my resolve to the contrary, I gulped a breath of air before entering. My brother smirked in what grownups would call my mind's eye. The room glowed with lamps but seemed muted. Darkness went with Italians. They wore black, and their skin was shadowed bronze. The young ones had black hair, but the older ones didn't go white like my grandmothers; they went iron instead. Muted, always muted.

The smell, when I had to breathe, was heavy but not with garlic. I remembered the bleeding stems in the yard. The March 19 garden had been moved inside. It was more than narcissus though. Odor coated the air like frosting on the glazed rolls and buns plattered at the feet of the plaster saint, visible between the Richter-registered movements of those come to do homage. The archbishop had been heavy-handed with dispensations that week.

The scent of tallow and burning wick curried my attention. I searched above those dark forms with vigorous teeth and roped pearls for the improvised altar. Thermal patterns pulsed about the candle-barred saint. Clouds of homegrown stock banked him securely within the hovering tapers. It was the stock that smelled—like too-sweet icing, not garlic. St. Joseph clutched his sculpted lily in a static ascension from a spray of hothouse gladioli. A McTwins floral card vibrated below the surging blooms—trumpet blasts of white victory.

Frankly, St. Joseph looked as out of place as I felt ... and vaguely familiar.

A hand, warmly possessive, slipped about my shoulder and hugged. I looked into the shadowed eyes of an iron-haired woman whose smile glowed and whose voice buffed English with Latin curvatures. Pressing a tumbler of red wine into Fr. Onerazani's hand, she asked to be reminded of my name. "I see you serving 8:30 mass with my Anthony," she said. "You are always so serious."

Anthony? Anthony had eyes like a lizard. They slid to the back of his head and copied my answers in class. I decided she had gotten the wrong baby in the hospital.

Nylon whispered upon itself as she leaned to ask, "Are you permitted a little wine?" Fr. Onerazani cackled, but she did not notice. Would Father, when he had refreshed himself, bless the breads so we could all eat? Sobered, he drank covetously and returned the glass to her waiting palm. The reversible folds of a white-and-purple stole followed his hand from an inner pocket, flamed satin as he draped it about his neck and bowed to the saint. Hushing pursed the mouths of the pious like shell's echo, ebbing sound. I moved to his side.

The screen door wheezed, inhaling the porched resonance. Fr. Onerazani pressed a silver vial of holy water into my hands and let fall the gold-leafed pages of the Rituale Romanum to the ribboned rite of St. Joseph. "In the name of the Father ..." The Sign of the Cross hung fused on scents of fire, flower and flesh. Fr. Onerazani cleared his throat and read:

"The just man shall flourish like the palm tree; he shall grow like a cedar of Lebanon planted in the house of our Lord, in the courts of the house of our God ..."

I thought of the giraffe-necked palms with their kites shining in the wind; I thought of the elephant-trunked palm with clipped toenails and firework top, and somehow neither image seemed to fit in the house of our Lord, in the courts of the house of our God. I looked then at Fr. Onerazani but could not see his eyes striving behind their flashing lenses. His attention was focused on the surrogate father of Christ. His voice had lost its nasality, descending like the Roadmaster into full throttle. Silence drew in about him. Candles fluttered in ascendant tongues—Babel fashion.

"O Lord, may the merits of the spouse of your most holy Mother assist us, so that what we cannot obtain through our own efforts we may have through his intercession."

Italian women shone under their muted skin; the men fidgeted without stirring. Fr. Onerazani's instructive index finger tapped the black binding cadently, jarring words from the text. It was rigid again.

His head lowered, and I saw his eyes open upon the page. "Joseph the just was a man of great silence. Scripture records no word spoken by him." I had not known that, and it struck me that perhaps he had used terrible, dirty words like my father ... I would have to confess that.

Closing his eyes, Fr. Onerazani looked back at the saint. "Beloved of God and men, whose memory is in benediction, He made him like the saints in glory, ... He sanctified him in his faith, and meekness, and chose him out of all flesh, ..."

Heads angled ever so slightly toward that poor man as he continued to pray. His voice, unconsciously intense, was of a tenor unknown to his congregation. Some private vacancy or inner occupancy stirred within him.

"O Lord, you made him excel by your choicest blessings; you placed on his head a crown of precious stones. He asked life of you and you gave him length of days forever ... His posterity shall be mighty upon the earth ... The just man shall blossom as the lily, and shall flourish forever before the Lord. Alleluia."

Flame did not flutter nor fabric rustle. It was not the words so much as the drama of the priest that bound us. Fr. Onerazani leaned forward and whispered the angel's counsel from Matthew's Gospel, "Do not be afraid, Joseph, Son of David, to take to thee Mary thy wife, ..." He paused, eyes flashing beneath the glass, "for that which is begotten in her is of the Holy Spirit."

The saint with the lily relaxed—or so it seemed—comforted, as it were, by one who understood the weight of precious stones bartered against conjugal caress.

"Amen." That poor man closed his Rituale Romanum and kissed the cover's gilt cross. Taking the silver vial I held, he blessed the breads in a cross that unraveled shimmering beads upon the glaze. He kissed the stole as he removed and refolded it, accepted more wine and resumed his cackle-punctuated prattle.

I remained in the vestibule of the blessing, under the palm in the house of our Lord ... alone ... watching.

That St. Joseph had been made to excel by the choicest blessings of the Lord was a theological subtlety that as yet escaped my notice on that March 19. My concern with free will in those wasteland days of adolescence focused on whether my consent to the onslaught of carnal thoughts had been full or not. I did not know that God's blessings could tip the balance and so could not have measured the fairness of that.

As I watched Fr. Onerazani moving among the other guests with his replenished glass, I saw that people made reasons to escape him, and I knew then that his cackle and his prattle were masks he was forced to wear. Like a revelation, I understood why St. Joseph had looked familiar ... in his isolation. Even in the prayers just concluded he had figured only as an afterthought: the son of ..., the spouse of ..., the beloved of ... and never as a person in his own right, that poor man.

It seemed clearer now to me that salvation lay in complete dedication to God and that, for me, even the priesthood would not be protection enough. Those same sensuously shadowed males, drawn in from the porch, sobered of their grins by prayer and talk of everlasting flourishing, coaxed back their venal smiles with renewed drafts of tumblered wine. As their eyes sampled the women leaning over trays of blessed breads, I sensed with deepening disquiet that it was not the object of their desire that ran like mercury in my chest but rather their own searching expressions, the set of their dark-lashed eyes, the character of male flesh feathered with unruly coils and leashed across the bone of brow and cheek and jaw. Desire was different for me, and I could not vent that difference with a smile. I had to cut temptation from me like the frond stubs on the trunk of Sacred Heart's palm.

March was the month devoted to the study of vocations, and the isolation of the mystics reached out to me with its promise of anonymous peace ... a Cistercian cloister, even a Carthusian cell with steady contemplation the copula between God and me. My eyes closed tight and cold upon the vision, and I pledged to God my celibacy.

My father was already in bed when I arrived home. In fact, only my mother and Aunt Millicent rocked by the radio, fastened to the narrow glow of I Love a Mystery.

"How did it go, dear?" my mother asked, breaking their spell.

I turned to hook the screen and bolt the door. "Oh, fine," I said. "I even learned the facts of life."

I knew they would be grinning when I looked. They were. I smiled too ... not with amusement but rather to mask what I'd learned of loneliness in the courts of the house of our God.

CHAPTER 6

THE PALM APARTMENTS

The Palm Apartments anchored our block to the corner of Fifth and Reed like a two-story fortress with parapets and mustard-colored ramparts of smooth-lumped stucco. When my grandfather died and we moved in with Grandma and Aunt Millicent in the middle of the block, the apartments were owned by the Schulers, a snow-peaked couple who lived in a detached duplex next to the row of rear garages and fronting on Fifth Street. A rib of dark tile ran around the duplex just below its paned windows. Mr. Schuler taught violin, and Mrs. was just cultured. Together they nurtured a rustic garden at the base of the battlements—spindly palms and ground cover with Let's Pretend yellow blossoms covering rocks. Lightly fuzzed maples grew out of the narrow curbside rectangles owned by the City of San José.

The Schulers sold the property to what my grandmother called an Okie success story, a skinflint man named Jordan with bad teeth, soiled skin and clothes that followed his body round. His two boys tagged at his heels, two hims all over again. Tenants complained that he never fixed anything, and that was true. He moved like he was always busy but got into the Mercury Herald for making tenements out of decent places. When things got bad enough, he just sold and moved on. Lots of people didn't like him. Mr. Jordan wouldn't live in the Palm Apartments himself—too much obvious disrepair and too many tenants to notice. The row of rear garages began to lean like sheds, and shingles were loose; the dirt cracked, smelled hard and pushed up weeds in clumps, the kind that stuck in your socks and your dog's ears. I always called them "why lotes," those stickers, till one day Aunt Millicent articulated the d's and t's for me. Foxtails was another name for them, but they irritated just as badly. Every time Muggsy made a run for it, he came home with his tail-stub between his legs and one of those things worked into his ear, whimpering.

Muggsy was a neat dog. I had a sore throat the night my father brought him home. He was driving a truck for Wieland's Brewery then, and he'd stopped for supper over in Crow's Landing at one of those scrubby cafés tucked off the side of the road behind lined-up semis. He always claimed that if you wanted good food, you should look for a truck stop. Set gears and idling motors were the best recommendation in the world. He never took us to them though. My mother was afraid of grease, and truckers' clothes like truckers' hands never quite came clean. Without seeing them I supposed the towns my father talked about along his truck route were greasy too.

Muggsy fit in the palm of his left hand when my father brought him into the house for the first time. He was going to be a black-and-white fox terrier, but that night, in front of the gas stove with blue flames lacing up the asbestos grate, my feet soaking in mustard and water and my throat pinned in flannel wrap, he was all puppy ... a pink-tongued softness with moist eyes and freshly bobbed tail. The waitress at Crow's Landing had been holding him and crying because the boss threatened to drown what was left of the litter by sunup ... in the sink she used to wash stainless steel pots. She wanted Muggsy for herself, but my father said he wouldn't take a female, so she gave him up to save another one.

I can vouch for the fact that a new puppy gets rid of sore throats. I got to hold him before Allen or Kathleen because I'd been sick, and I remember the way he whimpered when my unskilled fingers tried to fit under him and lift him out of my father's calloused, solid palm. I guess Muggsy didn't mind grease.

He grew up with us, Muggsy did, and like any kid, he had a favorite habit that put our teeth to grind. He loved to run off. I don't know; maybe it was that long truck ride in my father's glove compartment that jarred the roaming instinct into his blood. Whatever it was, we held our joy at his returns, scolding and spanking him for his having gone in the first place.

Palm Apartments people couldn't have pets except for sneaked-in cats now and then. Mostly, tenants didn't stay there long anyway. My grandmother used to call them transients and us landed, and even they seemed to sense the difference. If they had kids, they went to school at Lowell on Sixth and Reed like the other non-Catholic kids in the neighborhood, but we played with them when we got home and changed our uniforms. Aunt Millicent used to say that the Palm Apartments was like a book of short stories waiting to be written, but the characters kept getting up and moving away ... sometimes in the night, like the Arabs in that poem she liked to quote, they would silently steal away.

To show you just how different they were, Kathleen as Bo Peep and I as a mandarin went trick-or-treating with our friend Sidney from around the corner one October 31. Sidney never got to eat his treats; his mother saved them till the next Halloween. His father couldn't work anymore. He had spent a lifetime treating his lungs to cigarettes, and they had finally given out on him. When the three of us walked up the tiled stairs between the ramparts and stood on the high porch, it was just dusk out, but those still, wide corridors within the swinging glass entry smelled like a stale cave and single-globed themselves out of total darkness. People didn't own TVs yet; only someone they knew did, and Walter Winchell crackled behind brass-numbered doors with cracked enamel or slid out on light slivers underneath.

Dovina Hench was going with us, so we climbed into a second-floor haze of liver and onion and knocked at her door first. Dovina's mother stopped yelling at her boyfriend so she could yell at Dovina, "Dovina! See who's at the damned door." She waitressed in a tavern on South First just off Reed. My mother said she was well suited for the job because she was hard-faced. When she got a permanent, it screwed the red curls all the way into her skull. She sketched on her brows over tight little eyes that clashed with the white spots showing through freckle. Her voice rasped and rolled out of her mouth in balls of swallowed smoke.

In the overstuffed chair, as the door opened, slumped Leon, Moxie Hench's boyfriend. Moxie wasn't Dovina's mother's real name. It was what her first husband started calling her when he found out she had so much of it. Leon's shirt never buttoned over his navel and, as he listened to Moxie Hench four-lettering his ego, his cheek hung from the edges of his left hand. With his right hand he fingered the condensation on an amber beer bottle with foam in the neck. Nobody could figure out how Moxie and Leon got together. My father said Leon must have a lot of what none of the rest of us could see, and the grownups, even my brother, Allen, laughed. Dovina's little half-brother, Leo, sat on the linoleum in squashed diapers banging a greasy spatula against his father's khaki shin. Dovina's face was tight red from crying, but she steamed off her tears in front of us. There was no softness in Dovina Hench and no loose parts.

She was grownup anger stuffed in a kid's body.

"I can't go!" she said to our decorated faces. "My mom's got to work an' Leon don't know how to change Leo. Leo's got the shits again."

Through the slits in her mask, my sister's eyes moved like sun-quickened leaves over the scene and returned to fondle Dovina's face. "I'll save you all the Snickers I get, kid," she said. Snickers were Dovina's very favorite.

A crease moved between Dovina's eyes. She snuffed and closed the door on us.

Kathleen's blond curls bounced as she spun away from the door and beat the dark air with her shepherdess' staff. "Bugger! ... Bugger! ... Bugger!" she hissed.

"Who?" I said. Sidney shrugged. He was Long John Silver, but his peg leg looked phony and was coming undone.

"That little red-haired brat with the smelly pants."

"Well, he can't help it," I reasoned.

"Yes, he can!" Kathleen snapped. Her mask was white, but her soul was bitter. "He does it on purpose. Every time Dovina wants to do anything, he shits!"

"Kathleen!" I gasped. Sidney turned his head to laugh in his cupped hand.

Kathleen strutted up to another door and turned on me now. "I don't care. It's true. And God's not going to put me in hell for saying that word once. Dovina says it all the time and ..."

Leo with the smelly diapers loomed into our minds as a fate possibly worse than hell, and Kathleen paled to the lips. She turned to knock on the door, and Sidney's head bounced with amusement. The right side of his charcoal mustache had come off on his cupped hand.

The numerals twenty-two jiggled on the door under Kathleen's sharp knuckles, and almost instantly the door swung open. A woman with bandannaed hair and darkly furred upper lip registered surprise. "I thought I heard voices," she said huskily. Mid-thirties shot the wiry coil escaping down her forehead through with white runners. "Godsake! I completely forgot about Halloween!" Genuinely flustered, she wrung her damp, naked fingers in her Hawaiian-print apron. "Sorry, kids, I'm afraid I don't have a thing in the house for you."

We stared at her, clearly disappointed. Her eyes misting, she stuck her nose in the V of index finger and thumb. "Tell you what," she mumbled. "Come back in an hour, and I'll have fresh baked oatmeal cookies. Okay?" Her eyes smiled kindly.

My sister picked up the hem of her dress—daintily and unnecessarily for it already revealed ten inches of pantaloon—and said, "Thank you very much. That would be very nice," and turned toward the stairs. Sidney and I followed. Kathleen had no intention of coming back, I knew. She was being too polite. It was her "serves-them-right" tone reserved for people who weren't prepared for eventualities. Besides, she hated oatmeal cookies.

But that's what I mean by the Palm Apartments people being so different. How do you forget about Halloween? The year before when we trick-or-treated the rancho style apartments in the three hundred block, there was a woman who lived alone too, but she hadn't forgotten. She invited us in, and she looked like Linda Darnell in a long red evening gown with her hair fixed on top of her head. Hi-fi records spun smoothly on a console turntable, the needle softly weaving Mantovani into the muted lamplight. She led us to a tray of frosted goblin cookies with a flickering jack-o'-lantern in the center and admired our costumes while we ate our fill. That was the only time we ever saw her. During the summer when we walked down to Margin's grocery on Fifth and San Salvador to get Double Bubble, the James Van Lines was loading her hi-fi, lamps and all. She wasn't around to say goodbye to, but then she probably wouldn't have recognized us without our masks anyway.

The first twins we ever knew lived in the Palm Apartments too. Their mother always acted ashamed to be there and kept saying how there just wasn't any place to rent right then and how, anyway, they were saving to buy a home in Willow Glen. Willow Glen was the district where all the Italians who could afford it lived. The Cetitti twins were Italian too and identical ... except for a cheek mole and one letter in their names. Gina had the mole, and her head shook when she got angry. When Tina got angry she just cried. They lived in the apartment with a small sitting porch under Dovina and Moxie Hench. But Hench's apartment had a box window that sat out above it and gave them a view of the Cetittis coming and going. They couldn't see Moxie, but they heard her laugh out the narrow side window and saw smoke floating on an updraft. She liked to make up limericks out of Cetitti and belch beer gas when she finished. We could hear her laugh all the way down at our house. The twins' mother pretended she didn't hear.

The evening the Cetitti twins called Kathleen and me krauts they got paid back good. My mother, when we told her, said, "Well, of all things. Those little wops called you that? That just proves they're wops." We had heard wop often enough in our family but didn't know the Cetittis were ones. "Go right back out there and call them wops ... and dagos. Call them dagos, too. That'll fix them."

We did, and was she ever right! Gina's mole shook to her chin and Tina burst into tears when we came charging out the screen door and down the steps yelling, "Wop! Wop! Dago! Wop!" The twins no sooner got up the porch stairs to their apartment than their mother slammed out the screen door and hollered down the block, "Ronald! Kath-a-leen! You come here!"

Right away a puff of smoke drifted from Moxie Hench's window, so Mrs. Cetitti slammed her fists on the banister and ran down the stairs like an old-fashioned movie clip. My legs went weak, but Kathleen made a beeline for our porch. "Ma!" she hollered through the screen door. "The twins' mother! She's coming after us!" And she was ... marching ... her arms like shouldered weapons on either side of her aproned body, and stepping on sidewalk cracks.

"Ronald! Kath-a-leen! Did you call my kids wops and dagos?" she demanded, standing her ground in our driveway.

We didn't answer, knowing that our mother had moved into place inside the screen and was waiting to fire. Aunt Millicent and Grandma were shadows behind the living room curtains.

"Well, did you?"

"Yes, they did," my mother said coolly. "I told them to."

"*You* told them to?"

"I sure did. They called my children krauts. If you don't want your children called names, you shouldn't allow them to call others names. My children are not even full German. They're Irish on my side."

"My husband and I were just eating supper ..."

"You have a husband, do you?"

" ... and when I heard, I threw my fork down in my spaghetti and said, 'Nobody's going to call my kids wops or dagos!'"

"My children just did."

"Not and get away with it ..."

Silence. My mother's smile lit up the screen.

The twins' mother grinned whitely. "We'll be moving out of this neighborhood in a month or two and so glad to be out of it."

"Yes," my mother countered, "and we'll be glad to have it back."

World War II had been over for five years. Korea was ready to break, and neighborhood skirmishes were the order of the times. People seemed in the habit of battling. The Palm Apartments was a scale model of the world in a way ... troubled and insecure ... especially, for some reason, the Cetitti apartment. Their screen door banged loosely in the wind when they left for Willow Glen. My mother said Mrs. Cetitti had left it open on purpose.

A young couple moved in next. The husband sold shoes at Leed's on First Street and walked with some sort of defect my grandmother called splayfoot. His wife walked past with him once in a while, always too frightened to talk, mincing steps as if to avoid stepping on the cracks. One day he came home very early, his lunch still brown-bagged in his hand, striding as fast as splayfoot allows and straining to see ahead to his apartment. Not long after, a kind of ambulance pulled up, and his wife was taken away between two attendants. The next family had a sitter who poured scalding soup on their two little girls. Nowadays people say things like that didn't happen then ... but they did. I think it was the war.

And I guess it was the war that was responsible for so few fathers being around ... like the girl who used to sit on the mustard-colored lumpy battlements encasing the tiled porch, quietly, always aloof, looking as if she needed a shining knight and that her need alone would create one. Word got out that her name was Fairy, but we doubted that. Her mother stayed in their second-floor apartment, and I don't think any of us ever saw her. We just heard she had one. Fairy rode her bicycle over to Red and White when they needed groceries. Her long hair hung on the wind as her bobby-soxed legs pumped. She rode like she was mounted on a white stallion. We would think she wasn't paying us any attention at all, when all of a sudden she would turn her head toward me and call, "Hi, Duke!" only she said, "Hah, Dewk!" in southern talk.

Embarrassed, I would call back, "Who you calling that to?"

And she would answer, "Yew ... Hah, Dewk!"

Kathleen and Sidney and Dovina laughed, high-pitched, and imitated, "Dewk! Dewk! Dewk!" like some weird bird call. Muggsy just smiled and wagged his stub. Flustered, I would call after her pedaling form, "That's not my name!"

But she would just say, "Yes, it is, Dewk! Bah, Dewk!"

"What's your name?" I hollered as she slowed for the corner once.

"Fairy!" Her voice came softly.

Sidney held his sides and Kathleen and Dovina each other as my cheeks burned. With both hands cradling my voice I shouted, "My name is Ronald!" but she was gone around the one-armed attorney's house, content in the way she would have things. None of us really believed her name was Fairy any more than we believed mine was Duke, and although I found her interest in me privately fascinating, I resented the association because we had begun to suspect what fairy was going to mean when we grew up.

We never played with Fairy. The closest she ever came to any of us was one afternoon on her way to Red and White. She rode into the gutter next to where I stood on the lawn, slowing herself with a bobby-soxed hop along the curb and handed me a carefully folded piece of grocery bag. "Hah, Dewk!" she said, and her eyes held mine briefly before she rode off into the Alviso wind.

I opened the brown sacking to find a note penned in Palmer method: "Duke, I like you ... Fairy."

Kathleen, Sidney and Dovina came running to see what was in the note. At first I tried to fold it up and stuff it in my pocket, but they got it away and read it, so I laughed and yelled out loud what it said, "Dewk, Ah lahk yew!" and hooted.

Fairy pedaled around the one-armed attorney's house, out of sight and out of our lives. Like the Arabs in the poem Aunt Millie liked to recite, Fairy and her invisible mother were gone next day. I guess she heard me hooting that way, too ... about her note, I mean.

Roberta Dore's mother had no husband either, just Roberta and a little boy who ran around the house without diapers pissing on things. They rented the duplex longer than anybody we ever knew in the Palm Apartments. Roberta and her little brother were like water colors without skin tones. Their mother yelled more than Dovina's mother, Moxie, and she didn't work.

At first there was a couple who moved into the other half of the duplex, and she had only one leg. The other one was wood. Leslie was young, about eighteen, and friendly, but her husband didn't talk much or smile even. He had a short, stocky brother who wore a hat and used to park behind the duplex beside the garages. He didn't talk either except with Leslie and his brother, low, like he expected someone else would listen.

Nobody had much money those days, but Palm Apartments people seemed to have less. A heavy-set man who smoked all the time, wore a shiny suit and drove a 1950 Chevrolet sedan started coming and going to Leslie's all the time. Roberta Dore's mother told my mother that everybody called him P.I., and she giggled and shrugged her shoulders. Her gums went all naked when she smiled. She was an Arkie.

Later, as my mother, grandmother and aunt eased back and forth in the oak porch rockers, sipping tea and snacking on buttered toast and neighbors, my mother said about Roberta Dore's mother, "That silly woman. It wouldn't surprise me if she went to work for P.I. too." The hr-r-rack ... nok of the rockers unevenly punctuated their conversation.

"Well, if hipple-dick can do the job with one leg, I guess Roberta's mother can do it with two," Aunt Millie said. Quiet laughter washed over the banister onto Muggsy and me lying on the shadowed grass.

Staring into the burning sky, I massaged the black-and-white head panting beside my leg and asked, "What job? I didn't know Leslie worked. What job?"

The rocking stopped. So did the conversation. "Oh, you'll know soon enough, Ronald," came the reply. More quiet laughter.

The older I got, the more I heard that answer. The afternoon the ambulance rushed Sidney's father to the hospital, Kathleen, Dovina and Roberta were all playing in Roberta's house and wouldn't let me in. The night before, Kathleen confided that the three of them had climbed under Roberta's mother's desk and taken all their clothes off.

"That's a sin!" I told Kathleen. "Did they make you do that?"

"Huh-uh, I wanted to."

"You've got to go to confession and promise never to do that again. You won't do it again, will you?" Kathleen popped her gum and shrugged. "I don't know."

She was like that. Sometimes I couldn't understand her. "I'm coming into Roberta's with you tomorrow."

Kathleen blew another bubble.

But the next day they locked me out, and I could tell from the way they laughed inside what they were doing. When I banged on the door, Roberta's mother shoved open a side panel of paned window and leaned out. Her bare-bottomed son hung around her neck, and she yelled, "What the hell are you doing banging on the door like that, Ronald?"

"They won't let me in ... They locked the door," I complained.

"Oh, for God's sake. You're too big to be playing with girls. Go find some boys to play with."

"Sidney's father's sick, so Sidney can't play, and there aren't any other boys around here anymore."

Roberta's mother's gums gnashed at me. "Then go home and play with yourself, and quit bothering the girls!" She slammed the side panel shut, then shoved it back open because of the heat. Kathleen, Dovina and Roberta were laughing inside.

Angry, I sat on the stairs in the breezeway between the apartments and the duplex, locked my arms across my knees and dug with my chin to hold the tears burning in back of my eyes. Behind the dark bulge of screen directly ahead of me, I suddenly realized I could see Leslie sitting on a chrome chair at a formica table, the nylon sheathed wooden limb angled awkwardly in front of her. She towelled the back of her neck under the fall of moist black hair, and when she stood against the light to get a beer, you could tell she didn't wear anything under her rayon dress. A weighted wind blew floral-print drapes in curved shadows across the sun rectangled on the formica top.

"Do you work, Leslie?" I asked.

She sat back down with the cold beer, stuck the foamy neck in her mouth and swallowed thirstily.

"My mother says you do," I coaxed. Leslie was pretty enough but she had too many teeth. She lowered her eyes and spoke carefully.

"If you have two-fifty, I'll show you what I do. It's a lot better to show you than it is to tell you. And I would only charge you two-fifty since it's your first time ... It is your first time, isn't it?"

I didn't know what she meant, but I nodded my head against my knee-braced arms and said, "Oh, that's all right. I just didn't know you worked." Leslie's teeth shone like the grill of a new Buick, but she wasn't laughing at me. Somehow I knew Leslie wouldn't ever do that.

In fact, the only laughter I heard came from under Roberta's mother's desk, and I lowered my eyes against my arms. When Robby Dravou used to live in Mrs. McNabb's rear rental two doors toward the college, he and I played that way once, and that's why I knew it was a sin. We used to like to pretend ourselves into the time of the Corsican Brothers and the Three Musketeers we'd read about in my Classic Comics and dress ourselves in towel cloaks. Usually we wound up dragging out old blankets that became flowing gowns and we, vulnerable beauties suffering the most harrowing of dangers. While I found myself easily absorbed in such pretense, I dared not share the dimension of my imagining with anyone but Robby.

Robby's brother Billy was the same age as Allen, but they didn't hang around much. Billy painted watercolors of Red Ryder and Little Beaver that no one believed he did. They were beautiful. Billy didn't wear any underpants, and the crotch of his jeans had worn through. We found that out when he leaned over to hike Allen a football one evening. It didn't bother him any; he just fingered himself back in.

One afternoon in that August, though, Robby said to me as we laid aside our seventeenth-century garb, "I'm all sweaty. I'm going to ask if we can take a lukewarm bath." He looked at me and then added, "All right?"

I shrugged supposing his mother would say no, but she didn't. She made sure the tub was scrubbed and started the water for us. The tub was the antique kind that stood on eagle's feet and allowed for stretched-out soaking, but it seemed short for us, and our knees touched often. Robby giggled a lot like the girls in Roberta Dore's house, and we visually examined each other's bodies. Robby began a game of trying to touch my penis, his hand snaking through the water, and I felt panic rise in my chest. The shrinking I experienced when first I took off my clothes and stepped into the tepid pool had changed, and I feared I would stiffen down there instead. Watching that hand come closer and closer, I backed against the water spout and, when his fingers were still inches from me, I felt their grasp and myself go hard. Robby laughed delightedly and pointed first to my organ and then to his own, rigid against his belly. I grabbed the towel from the stool beside the tub and got out. He had not touched me there, but I wanted him to; my throat was dry with it. So I knew it was a sin - what was going on under Roberta's mother's desk.

Sloughing footsteps interrupted my reminisce, and I realized there was a present stiffness between my legs as well. I looked up to see P.I. hefting into the breezeway toward Leslie's apartment. His suit coat flapped around his middle, and you could tell he was all sweaty because of the wrinkles under his belt. Smoke climbed from the slit in his face, staining his upper lip, screening his narrowed eyes. He must have seen me, but he pretended not to. Ash fell from his cigarette as he clubbed the screen door.

"It's open, P.I.," Leslie called.

P.I. stepped back so he could clear the screen door. His voice was fat. "Linin"em up on the young side, arencha, Les?" The screen door absorbed him, and the formica-topped rectangles blacked out.

Sidney's father died that night, and Sidney and his mother were finally able to move to a home of their own off the Alameda. My mother left me over to play one day, but it wasn't the same anymore. We never did go back again.

Charles didn't live in the Palm Apartments or even on our block. He just rode into our neighborhood one day with a string of toughs in tow and decided to stake his claim. He hated my guts. Once when I was arguing with Dovina, Roberta and Kathleen, he skidded up on his bicycle, let it slide from under him and came to a running stop. "Leave 'em alone!" he snarled and his fists were ready, clenched for contact. His dark eyebrows met across his nose, and his eyes were brittle with anger. His chin curled vindictively. His features were clean and hard, his skin smooth and taut over patrician cheek bones. He could have been the prince in pauper's jeans, and I stung under his unreasoned glare.

"None of your business!" I stammered.

"I'm makin' it my business, you son of a bitch! Now get out of here! You're not wanted in this neighborhood!"

Moxie Hench chuckled above.

I knew I should do something, especially because of what he had called me, and my father, when he heard, was disappointed in me. He said that it was an insult to my mother and that I should never allow that. I had done a few "Oh, yeahs?" and "Says yous!" but gotten ultimately on my own bicycle and ridden from the challenge.

"It takes more courage to walk away from a fight than it does to fight," the nuns always told us, and so did my parents. But that was one of those things you were expected to believe but not do ... at least if you were as terror stricken as I was.

My mother said I had done the right thing, and she called Charles "some sort of Jesse James." What I didn't know then was that Jesse James was generally revered for giving to the taken from the coffers of the takers.

Moxie Hench's chuckle followed me for days.

Muggsy never cared about any of those things. Right or wrong, hero or coward, he loved me ... accepted me, even my abuse when I could heap it on no other. He lay with me on the lawn, his muzzle snug in my armpit when the toughs circled behind Charles like bicycling vultures, hooting epithets that stung all the way to my testicles. Muggsy's breath came in warm snorts against my flesh. Sometimes, if their circling came too near, I could feel his growl vibrate against my rib cage and his ears flutter like bat wings against my tee shirt. When Charles rode up on the lawn and clipped me on the toe with his bike tire, that was it. Muggsy's forepaws dug into my chest and his teeth glowered with pursuit. He was fast even though he was no longer young. The vultures winged off in different directions but Muggsy's teeth stitched themselves in Charles' jean cuff. White-faced and badly balanced, Charles kicked with his heel, and Muggsy yelped through his growls, hanging on tenaciously.

"Let go of my dog, you son of a ..." That word stuck in my throat. Standing on my toes I hollered, "BITCH!" Muggsy's jaw let go of the cuff, and Charles, deciding I was no longer worth the effort, rode out of the neighborhood.

I loved Muggsy fiercely, ... guiltily. Generally, I manufactured burdens out of life for my family ... like threatening to tell on Kathleen for taking her clothes off with Dovina and Roberta if she didn't go to confession. Kathleen's face turned beet red, and her blond curls vibrated. When she could speak, her freckles bunched about her nose. "See if I ever tell you anything again!"

"See if I care! That was a mortal sin, and you have to confess it."

Kathleen knotted fists of her fingers and literally growled at me, "I hope you get hit by a car and God puts you in hell!"

I don't know what shocked me more ... that she had wished such a fate upon me or that, like Charles, I had caused her eyes to turn brittle with hate.

Things like that I took out on Muggsy. Invariably, it was those times I decided Muggsy needed to be trained, and I would vent my wrath on his laidback ears for his stupidity ... or stubbornness ... or ... Anyway, right through it all, he waited for some sign that I was over it, then wagged his stub till, full of remorse, I hugged and petted him.

We had him fourteen years but never broke him of his need to roam. In the end, distance took Muggsy from us as it had once brought him to us. Nearly blind, almost deaf, he limped down the gravel driveway one day, past the bougainvillea, and we never saw him again. He passed from our lives in much the same way the Palm Apartments people had.

CHAPTER 7

THE ERRING ONE

Allen was in a body cast. He had graduated from Bellarmine and I from Sacred Heart in that same June of 1950. The accident took four lives, those of the three soldiers who crossed six feet over the center line of Highway 17 just below the Santa Cruz summit, and one of the two friends with whom my brother had gone to the Boardwalk's Friday night dance at Coconut Grove. The dashboard crushed his friend's chest and shoved him into the back seat. The left shoes of all three soldiers had come off their feet, tied, in the impact. Allen's other friend, the driver, remained unconscious for six weeks, shouting obscenities the whole time. In the hospital, in those dark early hours after the call had wakened us, as my father drove the bloodied S-curve shimmering with windshield fragments and my mother's voice riveted Kathleen and me to the Rosary, all fifteen mysteries, Allen's heart stopped.

It was the swing-shift nurse who told us about it. The doctor had pressed his stethoscope to Allen's bruised chest and shaken his head. The swing-shift nurse thought of my mother, she said, whom she didn't even know, and began to pray ... and Allen's chest expanded with breath.

She was a sincere woman with a wasted look, the kind that is burned fleshless with the energy of visions. In time, she admitted having them, visions that is, from the Holy Ghost no less, and she was committed. So we were never sure of the straight story. The doctor, steeped in science, seemed reluctant to talk about that emergency-ridden morning.

Anyway, that was how my mother and I started sleeping together. When Allen was finally ambulanced home from the dance at Coconut Grove, he needed a hospital bed and someone constantly at hand to see to his needs. Since I was a thrashing sleeper and my father a light one who dug wells and installed pumps for a living, my mother moved into Allen's space in his and my bed. Kathleen, of course, shared Aunt Millicent's room since Grandma died.

If my thrashing kept my mother awake, she never complained. She would have lain sleepless endless nights to minister to any one of us children in need. Her gratitude ran deep for our being and the marginal safety of her scarred and broken eldest child. Mend he would. She would see to it.

Allen had only to shift his iodine-swabbed toes at the mouth of the cast or moan frustration through his wired, tooth-decimated jaw for her to throw back the covers and pad to his side, the flashlight moving like stagnant pond ripples across the high-ceilinged room. With my cheek sunk in the pillow, I watched one-eyed, the lid burning with interruption, the glow palely reminiscent of the glare the kitchen light had shed that 3:30 A.M. as my father shivered at the phone, his thick hand bracing his tufted head, repeating, "God! ... Oh, my God! ... Oh, my God!" the rest of us frozen in fearful and nameless obeisance about that black oracle on the wall.

I listened to the steady pinging of urine against stainless steel, the rustle of sheet against plaster and the stretching of floorboards under tired feet as the concentric Eveready rings ebbed once more to my side.

Sighing, yawning, my mother sat on the bed's edge, ricocheting echoes through the springs as her weight settled into the lukewarmth of her earlier lying. I clung to my edge of mattress, fingers locked in the coils beneath, knowing that if sleep claimed me, I would gravitate toward her night-gowned body. What to do with the stiffening between my legs was bad enough when Allen shared my bed but with my mother ... Lust as yet was a singular and private enterprise for me and, indeed, it was not desire but confusion that wrapped my knuckles in those chilly coils. In fact, reluctance to touch her compacted my limbs, left me aching for rest upon rising and drove me darkly whispering into velvet-draped confessionals. Sleeping with Allen should have been okay, but it wasn't. His absence made that clear. It was Allen I wanted to touch.

The snapped-out light ushered in my mother's soft snore and out my reverie. Allen cleared his throat and, for a moment, I was unsure whether the sound echoed in the questionable safety of that sleep-saturated room or against the slamming lockers and shower spray of the dressing room at Santa Cruz's salt-water plunge where two, three years earlier he had ridiculed my shyness. Like the other males, he and my father attending to stripping as if it weren't happening, watching the trunks they shook out to step into, toweling as if another man's eyes on their own flesh were the furthest parameters of their interest. But it wasn't so for me. The privacy of the body had gone shamelessly public ... Shameless is not accurate either. Visual avoidance of each other's privates gone public loaned that fact emphasis as did the self-conscious chatter of projected voices. Naked men in a locker room talk louder.

I could avoid none of it but needed to. My eyes scoured male contour, a smorgasbord in all stages of undress. Tan lines sharpened the explosions of pubic hair and the dalliance of unencumbered lengths—straining my own hairless little organ against the fly I refused to unzip.

"Ronald, ..." Allen said sharply as he tied the drawstrings under his flat belly, "Why aren't you changing? We're ready to go in."

My father turned. "What's wrong, son?"

"I don't want to," I said.

"Don't want to what?" Allen pressed.

"Go swimming," I said.

"What are you talking about? You couldn't wait ..."

"Ps-s-st," my father interrupted. He leaned down, one strong hand easy on my shoulder, the other tugging my clutched towel. "We're all men in here, son. No one's going to notice."

"Aw-w-w, little Ronnie is shy."

"Dammits, Allen, stop it ... Ronald, we all look the same."

But we didn't all look the same; I wasn't blind. My father had a shank of skin neither Allen nor I had; everyone sized out differently, and some strutted irresistible physiques. Besides, were I to set aside my towel and take off my pants, I had very hard certainty that everyone would notice. I had no guarantee at all, either, that what had happened that spring in my imprimatured history lesson would not happen to me in front of everyone—with no shorts or corduroy pants to soak up the white stuff.

That afternoon Sr. Mary St. Giles had assigned the class to read how the Franciscan missionaries had brought God to the New World heathens beginning on page 43 of our history text. I'd found myself hoping there would still be heathens to convert when I became a priest as I read to the bottom of the page, reached up and turned to read on. As page 44 fell flat on its predecessors, however, I was stunned. Sketched above the continuing text was a line drawing of those heathens, stark naked, as they moved about their village. Men, women and children with not a stitch on. I had to shift suddenly on my seat. Quickly I thumbed back to the copyright page. Sure enough, under the nihil obstat of the censor deputatus, Archbishop Mitty had stamped his imprimatur. The archbishop, Sr. Mary St. Giles had explained, was the prince-in-residence of matters moral. His imprimatur meant that he approved of the book, so we could be sure that everything we read was true. It was a safe book to read.

But what was happening between my legs was not safe. I moved to relieve the pressure and found the motion pleasurable. My face felt hot and my temples throbbed as I studied the tiny line drawings with globed breasts or tubes between the legs. I couldn't tear my eyes away, and I couldn't quit flexing my thighs against my own stiffened tube. I didn't know what was wrong with me, and I was terrified that Sister might ask me a question, requiring that I stand up. I squeezed and released, squeezed and released, squeezed and released until suddenly my groin convulsed and I struggled not to cry out. Surge after surge jetted from my swollen tube as I bent over the text, thighs nearly cramping. But for the pleasure, I thought that God must be killing me for relishing the naked heathens.

"Ronald! Stop squirming," Sr. Mary St. Giles said sharply, "you're distracting the people around you."

That had been God's opportunity. I was sure my heart stopped for good on that rebuke, sure the good nun was going to make me stand for further reprimand, sure that whatever was leaking from my body would drain on until I dropped over stone dead ... but I didn't.

I looked beyond my father and Allen. It didn't matter that there were no globed breasts, the tubes caused my stiffness; the primed muscle with the sun's signature weighted my eyes with its own reflection. My father and Allen were determined.

"You stand in front of me then," I pleaded, "and turn around."

Allen folded his arms against hairs sprouting between his nipples. "Shit!" he muttered.

"Here, now! You're not so big that I can't ... "

"Sorry," Allen said and about-faced elbow-to-elbow with my father.

Squatting at the pool's edge, I set aside the towel and eased into the shallow end. My mother and Kathleen tried to draw me into splash games, but I hadn't the heart. I pressed my back to the yellow-tiled circulating fountain and let the warm salt water plunge over my head, face and chest. From time to time I leaned forward to glimpse a tight-calved diver prance on the high dive, his tubular bulge jostled in cloth, before the graceful arc that seemed to suspend his stretched descent into the water. The ache in my need to watch transcended the pleasure of a well-executed dive, and I knew I could say that to no one ... as I could explain no real reason for needing my own bed now.

As Allen convalesced, a composite of his high school classmates and teachers visited his bedside—laughing, regaling the room with retrospective renderings of life among the Jesuits. Harsh and foreign to the hovering glide of nuns I'd known in grammar school, those tales infected the final days of my summer with foreboding, clinging like gargoyles to ceiling moldings and haunting the time I dared not sleep.

I began, finally, to visit these fears on my mother. "I don't know how to describe them," I would say, "I just have these feelings and ... I'm scared of going to Bellarmine."

She would put her arms around my own cast-layered emotions and say, "It's all part of growing up, Ronald, that's all. The feelings will go away. You'll get over them. Don't worry."

But the feelings didn't go away, not until far into my freshman year, at least. By then we'd developed a pattern, I of needing comfort, she of giving it, and that pattern took the frequent form of diversion. We did things together, more so than ever, in the manner of outings that offered escape.

My mother appreciated many of the interests emerging in me. I was drawn to Playhouse 90, Mantovani—even to opera—while my father, settled into his upholstered rocker, his elevated legs peeled of their rubber stocking skins piled in a soft stink at the base of the hassock, thrived on the fights—boxing, even Tuesday-night wrestling—the phonier the better. He loved them.

Aunt Millicent, who was convinced that every trait is gened to us, was at a loss to explain my interest in theater and classical music.

I rode the bus to Bellarmine, caught the number ten line at Fifth and William in front of the one-armed attorney's house. He was the only professional on our street. His wife wore pince-nez and morning caps, and even on hot days he wore a tie and suit coat with the right sleeve retired.

Most of the 8:00 A.M. crowd unloaded downtown in front of J.C. Penney's, Roos Brothers and the Bank of America, so I could claim a seat from First and Santa Clara all the way out the Alameda.

I remember one particular Tuesday in November, my polished cotton lap steadied with Latin grammar, general science, English lit, algebra, history and religion, the windows of the bus dribbled steam and frosted store fronts as we pulled into the zone for Hester Elementary. Mufflered children, rain-coated, stepped into the hissing stairwell as if they were toe-testing water. Across the street the Hester Theater had just changed hands, and Towne Theatre was newly ensconced above the foyer. Art films had come to San José.

The glass squeaked as I fingered a viewing space. La Traviata strode across the marquee like a proud, bold signature. My pulse quickened. The bus geared away from the curb spewing diesel fumes after the slickered children. Using my palm as a squeegee, I rubbed wider and pressed against the cold, flat window. I knew that name and, struggling, called melody from memory ... an album of operatic preludes, the distinctive characters of which lay merged in indistinct splendor. I could discern none of La Traviata's parts from the whole of that album, but I knew that I had to see that film.

The machinists' local called an emergency strike-vote meeting that night and my father had promised to pick up a fellow worker whose license had been revoked for repeated DWIs. "Ends Tonight" postscripted the Towne's listing in the Mercury Herald's movie guide, so my mother and I took the bus. The day's bluster pelted the early dark, unabated, revealing street lights in anxious liaisons with rain against the windows. Captive on the interior of the glass, my mother's and my own reflected faces watched, intent upon that rain. I was, in effect, taking a night off from my studies, although I'd sat down and translated Caesar out of Gaul and begun memorizing Shylock's rebuke of Antonio on both sides of supper. The latter lines edited my concentration still:

"Signior Antonio, many a time and oft
In the Rialto you have rated me
About my moneys and my usances.
Still have I borne it with a patient shrug,
For suff'rance is the badge of all our tribe ..."*

Sufferance my mother promoted to the rank of Cardinal Virtue in those last months since the accident. Focused on her reflected features, I studied the victories age had won in the battles waged for her beauty and wished I could save her from that war. Nervous tics tugged at her eyes and mouth. The white that would beset her hair in later years intruded a commanding presence even then. Addiction to sweets in general and Schurra's chocolate in particular expanded the boundaries of her body, that gentle country that had naturalized my passage into the race.

The thin light in the bus cavity cast the few passengers oddly for viewing. Rigid seats, mostly vacant, rehearsed their potential for occupancy. An old man, whose neck piled out of his overcoat collar, fidgeted under the No Smoking sign, the cigar stink residing in his damp wool staling the air. Two women, opaqued in plastic and bandannaed, bounced with bus palsy, staring mutely through rimless lenses. A subtle sense of embarrassment at being caught altogether in this place kept the quiet distance of mutual disregard.

Dimming further, the lights surrendered to the doors' need, spitting hydraulically into the hiss of rain and depositing my mother and me on the curb at Hester Elementary.

Because of its expanse, the historic Alameda was now equipped with occasional undercrossings. Early settlers traveling from the Pueblo de San José to Padre Serra's Mission Santa Clara had not had speed to contend with.

"Can we use the undercrossing?" I urged, head angled into the damp wind.

"Oh, I don't know, Ronald," my mother hedged. "Those old tunnels are so long and hidden, and there's not a soul around if you need someone."

She had meant nothing by it, but it stung nonetheless. Unconsciously, she had served up a platter of my assuaged fears. After all, she was the comforter, I the comforted. What reason had she to feel protected?

"Come on," I said boldly, "let's do," and tugged her from the Alameda's surface, the lights of the Towne beckoning on the other side. The descent of our footsteps raced ahead, across and back to meet us. The concrete corridor narrowed the glow of two naked globes too widely spaced, the walls scarred with hastily coupled names and words we ignored. The dampness smelled like the cigar smoker's overcoat and urine.

Midchannel the clatter of running leather tensed my mother's gloved fingers on my arm and we paused. It was impossible to tell the direction of approach and, suddenly, voices, sharp and callow, spilled into the Towne side stairwell, shattered into laughter and retreated on leather-soled echoes. The gloved pressure at my arm eased, and my cocooned testicles averted further shrinkage. Neither of us spoke. Like the words on the wall, we ignored the incident and hurried to be on time for the film.

Through the curtain rising against the screen, I discovered the translation of my first opera, that celluloid La Traviata. It meant The Erring One. From the first chord of the prelude, Verdi's genius struck deep within me, separated out from those melodies merged in retention, and held me rapt throughout the ill-fated story of Violetta and her youthful lover Alfredo. It was, it turned out, the story of Camille, a scandalous tale by Dumas that had brought recriminations from all quarters and been placed squarely on the Index of Forbidden Books. I did not know that at the time, but my suspicion, as the opulent, immodest love scenes unfolded and my mother clandestinely unwrapped Walnettos, swelled to the brink of conviction that we should not stay, that the movie was doubtlessly condemned by the Legion of Decency.

But I belonged to that music for as long as it lasted. Without willing it, I had become committed to that tempestuously matched pair, to that hollow-eyed, vulnerable beauty Violetta, ravaged with illness and remorse; drawn even more disturbingly to Alfredo, that lithe and easy victim of deception. She, whom suffering had purged into a marginal madonna, lay among pillows and comforters while he, like a rutting squirrel, pranced bare-chested on the mattress at her side, his entire presence a throbbing erection. Hers, paradoxically, was the voice of a seraph coaxing the divine spark in my breast but his, ... his set fires under my skin and stiffening between my legs. Scruples waited in the wings for absorption to pass.

In the foyer later we drank coffee. The California, Mission, State and Padre theaters downtown never served free refreshments. Clusters of professorial sorts sipped from paper cups and enthused behind horn-rimmed glasses about the eloquence of "Addio del passato" and the unique character of the lovers' duet, "Parigi o cara." I felt strangely as I did when I woke in the night with my fingers aching in the coils of the bedspring ... but this time wanting to let go.

My mother and I edged out of that crowd toward the exit, a napkin insulating my gloveless fingers against the coffee's sting. The marquee grazed the November night, fluorescent, as we walked to the corner and stood, curiously disquieted. In a matter of hours, I would be on the bus traveling the opposite route to first-period Latin, unrefreshed from slumbering at my mother's side, and the "feelings" merged their descent with my tardy scruples.

"It was awfully good, didn't you think?" I asked, imitating a comment I'd heard inside. The bus sign rattled with wind, trembling damply.

Poking her tongue against some wedged Walnetto, my mother nodded. "Yes, ... " she said, "it was."

The cold took hold of me and shook. "I loved the music, didn't you?"

Actually, the intensity of Violetta's deathbed vocalizing had strained our faith in the reality of opera. My mother nodded into her coffee cup, steam mixing with breath to fade an escape. "It does sort of drag on though. I thought for a while that poor soul would never pass on."

My novice's loyalty dismantled my laugh, but I had no mask for my smile. My mother's face lit up. "You thought so too, ... I can tell." Humor had not eased her features since the accident. It freshened her loveliness, and I knew that she loved me very much. I felt the wings of my feelings lighten, begin to rise, then swoop again.

"They weren't married ... Alfredo and Violetta." Tremors seized my softly furred jaw. My scruples gnawed.

"No," my mother confirmed, "they sure weren't."

"But they slept together ... They shouldn't have done that ..."

My mother studied me, briefly. Handing me her empty cup, she broke her visual grip. Down the expansive Alameda, the reader board above the bus' windshield rotated to 10th and Keyes as the bus angled away from its stop in the line of traffic. I dropped the cups, hers inserted in mine, into the corner disposal, and we edged toward the curb.

"Do you think it was okay for us to see that movie?" I asked.

"Well, we didn't know what it was going to be about before we went in, Ronald."

The driver, as the bus approached, bounced like a loose pupil in a giant eye.

"I know," I said, "but I guess we should have left when we found out."

Illuminated frames from a film clip, the bus windows reeled in above us, images, spaced irregularly, disinterested. The braking down-throttle exhausted itself in a great sigh.

The fetters of indecision reclaimed my mother's features with cruel transiency as I watched. My courting of detail, my bondage to that buzzard of inches and els with its talons in my skull, chewing on my conscience, pierced the harmony of everyone in the family.

"Is it a sin—our sleeping in the same bed, I mean?"

The bus door slammed open. My mother looked at me as if she were seeing me for the first time ... seeing someone she'd rather not see.

"I *am* your mother, for goodness' sake. Surely ..."

"Step up, lady. I'm behind schedule," the driver called.

"We hadn't enough beds ..." she whispered.

"I know," I stammered, but she didn't hear me. She stepped across the gutter trickle into the stairwell, her blue leather knuckles gripping the loading bar. "I know, Mama ..." I continued, grabbing the cold steel to hoist myself onto the bus behind her. She who had joyed in my naked emigration from her flesh, glimpsed me naked again, an émigré from an innocence she still possessed, and she turned from the vision, wounded.

The Towne Theatre shows only porn flicks now, and the corner of Fifth and William, in front of the one-armed attorney's house, is grazing turf for prostitutes. Of course, the attorney is long gone. Everything, it seems, changes.

*The Merchant of Venice by William Shakespeare
Act I, Scene III, Lines 107-111

CHAPTER 8

THE BIRD'S EYE MAPLE

Aunt Millicent was a tiny woman—a maiden lady who defined herself as a fragile creature whom life had sponsored through the College of Hard Knocks. We grew up calling her Peewee and never thought that odd until long after we should have. While in nurse's training at the old Columbia Hospital, Aunt Millicent came down with colitis and nearly died. She blamed her fragility on that episode, her fragility and the nervous disposition that plagued the rest of her life.

Not one to do things in half-measures, Aunt Millie earned herself the distinction of Registered Nurse and a full-blown neurosis about germs. Her profession and her emotional makeup grappled together into her nineties with no truce in sight even then. When Allen, Kathleen or I needed to use the main bathroom, the wash basin invariably reeked with a pool of Hexol disinfecting the porcelain or some innocent article she'd had in use. A cry of "PEE...WEE" rang through those curved-corniced rooms as we danced cross-thighed, waiting for the ritual draining. We dared not wash in that purifying puddle lest we reverse the effects of the soak. To pull the plug was to throw down the gauntlet, and only my father's frustration forced that. He did it on our behalf. He never used that bathroom himself except to shower, preferring the back-porch toilet for the privacy its undesirability ensured. He did his morning wash and after-toilet hands in the kitchen sink—which kept Aunt Millicent in a churn, but she had, after all, conquered the convenience of the main bathroom between their two bedrooms and so kept a disgruntled silence about his kitchen cleansing.

Impatient with fate, in which she trusted implicitly, Aunt Millicent once rendered her palm to a patient who offered to read its lines. Frowning, the woman pulled the scrubbed flesh to the tip of her nose, squinting, solemn. Aunt Millicent caught her breath, and a flush sprang across her cheek. "What is it?" she asked. "Do you see something wrong?"

The reader cupped my aunt's palm in her own, her eyes gone gray with revelation. Her illness caused her to clear her throat often. "My dear, ... an auto ... will strike you down. You ... will die in midlife."

Poor Aunt Millicent fretted about that for the next thirty years, paranoid about setting foot from a curb, straining to see up and down the street for approaching vehicles and muttering to herself, "... an auto ... will strike you down ..." She did not even know what midlife was in her schedule of years.

Going to a fortune teller was a sin, of course. Aunt Millicent knew that. "'Vengeance is mine,' saith the Lord."

The muttering, we had grown up with also, and, while we noticed it, we paid it little heed unless an outsider came among us and refocused our attention. Muttering is not an accurate word choice. Aunt Millicent was a full-blown soliloquist. She could reconstruct both sides of entire, lengthy dialogues and recreate the energy emoting from whatever conflict lay memorized in the breach of her angry soul. Angry soul suited Aunt Millicent well, I'm afraid. Early on she decided that God had dealt her out, and she never forgave Him. Eldest of three offspring born to my Irish immigrant grandparents, Aunt Millie and her father were each other's heaviest cross. Love between them was a duty arduously contended and grudgingly executed. It didn't work except inversely as guilt.

It was the anger in her soul that torched those spontaneous reruns and startled Miss McCaffrey who used to drop in of an afternoon, unannounced, to savor a cup of my grandmother's milky tea and buttered toast sprinkled with sugar. Grandma concentrated on keeping the conversation relaxed and Miss McCaffrey's curious eyes engaged as Aunt Millie poked the air with her surgically deformed index finger and intoned, "I said to him, I said, 'Now what business is it of yours if I'm still single?'"

How did one pretend not to hear? Yet Grandma held onto Miss McCaffrey's attention as if nothing in the least untoward were going on ... and, indeed, nothing was, for our house. It was an unconscious eavesdropping, and we came by it with effortless innocence. Some things, I suppose, had to register and leave their mark. The mono-dialogue ran on at length, aloud. It was in the air we breathed, in the silence we only approximated. Somewhere in that big house Aunt Millicent's resonance kept the air charged like a lone telegrapher tapping continuous reminders of survival to anyone who would listen. But we had tuned them out.

My grandfather, who had been dead since I was two, remained a presence in that house. Aunt Millicent could not let go of him or of her argument with him. That was the model for her relationships with other men as well. The telephone remained listed in his name for as long as the family had the house. Insurance agents still called him forty years after he'd moved to Calvary.

That love which my grandfather disallowed, Aunt Millicent redoubled in my grandmother's direction so that too great a closeness bound them together. That he was a difficult man she emphasized unconsciously whenever she spoke of him through the years, her words fatigued, her eyes dredged of feeling. She had, I think, been devoted at least to the concept of loving him and hurt, always, that it failed to work—hurt, immeasurably, that his features never softened in her presence.

He was a cripple, my grandfather was … lost a leg to a railroad car and a false report of another train on the same track. Artificial limbs were heavy and unrefined then, and the stump of his severed leg put the promise of pain into his working, daily. Southern Pacific assigned him to a signal shack at the North Fourth Street crossing, and he grew morning glories that trumpeted the sun, up the side, between trains. That fact, like a less persistent telegrapher's tap, invites a probe inside the callous of my grandfather's sternness.

It was expected in those days that children should marry in the order of birth, eldest first and youngest last. Otherwise it made some sort of statement about the eldest and drew the focus of attention to her age and diminishing prospects. Had my mother and Uncle Vincent waited, theirs would have been sterile sacrifices to unreasoned tradition, and they become bound to each other, remnants of mindless obedience, infirm with regret.

When my mother and father announced their intention to marry, a good face graced the whole affair, but rancor burst like blemishes through cracks in the makeup. Aunt Millicent veiled herself in humiliation. The impact was no easier when Uncle Vincent married. His spouse would not even convert. A taciturn Norwegian, she suffered family dinners, collecting innuendo, and awaiting worse, the half-tailed smirk chiseled on her features her only defense against the Irish rancor. She had, after all, put one over on the matriarchs. In the end, she enjoyed bitterness as much as Aunt Millicent, but she stored it up. Our holidays were doozies.

It was not, you understand, that Aunt Millicent never had any beaux.

She did. But none of them was ever the beau ideal ... with the possible exception of the doctor. She didn't know him well. He interned at the old O'Connor Hospital and caused a flurry among the nurses with his dashing Douglas Fairbanks looks. He had paid attention to Aunt Millie. When he smiled at her across the wards as she charted TPRs, his eyes flashed. Indeed, photos from that period portray my aunt as a dark haired beauty. Intelligent, well-read, capable of wit and charm, she'd have been a catch for a young intern, but Zukor's got in the way.

Between cases one August 15, Aunt Millicent took her name off call at the Registry and drove downtown with my grandmother to shop for a new dress for a staff picnic. They'd planned a day of it, attending mass first in observance of the Feast of the Assumption and lunching afterwards at O'Brien's. With the '28 Dodge parked on San Fernando beside silver-domed St. Joseph's, they conveniently completed their holyday obligation and worked off lunch with an arm-in-arm stroll down First toward Hale's, poking about in the abundant dress shops en route. Awnings had been lowered from most store fronts to protect both merchandise and shoppers from the throbbing heat. Mannequins, stylishly poised and cool in glass cases, leaned toward Aunt Millicent to chide her for her hot, sticky condition. Her hair, in full-scale mutiny from its pins, she had scheduled for a shampoo and set next morning. She had eaten off most of her lipstick at the San José Creamery, and the caramel syrup from her sundae had dripped a fecal-colored stain on her blouse. It was her time of month, and nothing went by design despite her efforts at renovation. She had not planned on seeing anyone she knew, certainly not the young intern, yet there he was, on the far side of the gaping jaws of a sidewalk freight elevator, striding comfortably suited, despite the temperature, toward them.

"It's the perversity of life," my grandmother consoled later, rocking on the front porch. The sun, setting between the houses, tossed the Rose of Portugal, trellised at their side, in fragrant and fragile shadows upon them, inviting the dusk. A gentle wind blew in from the Bay at Alviso, fingering the wisps on Aunt Millie's lowered head.

"There you were but a day's distance from having your hair done and on your way to buy a new dress when he shows up. It couldn't have been tomorrow on your way out of the hairdresser's ... It had to be today." Her frail fist shook in the filigreed breeze. "It's the perversity of life, I tell you!"

Aunt Millie's eyes glazed with her folly. Seeing the intern, she had clutched her purse to her blouse and pulled my grandmother to look at the fall line of knits on Zukor's snub-nosed mannequins. In the glass as he passed, she saw the doctor's clouded face turn from her, and he never smiled at her again. In time, of course, his internship completed, he moved on, but Aunt Millicent could never let go of him.

She kept her name off call for a month after that incident and, I think, never fully trusted her judgment again. She chattered almost incessantly to herself. Her fragility and her nervousness began to intrude between her and other people more eccentrically and, as if to thwart the hand of fate, she went out one day and bought a chest of drawers and a dresser made of bird's eye maple, with a matching pair of caned-bottom chairs. Whether it was a costly gesture of one-upsmanship on hope chests or a concession, investing in spinsterhood, is hard to say. The blond wood with its myriad eyes shone like golden peacocks vigiled silently in that high-ceilinged bedroom, expectancy veneering its surface. Aunt Millie's size emphasized the unused space in its flawless glass. Her muttering would sometimes stop like the interrupted hum of the refrigerator, and she would examine the unused reflection, puzzled, her look one of wonder and searching.

I remember one afternoon that she had come in from the beauty parlor. She was in her early fifties then. She settled her handbag and gloves on the glass top she'd had cut to protect the dresser's surface and leaned toward the mirror. The boudoir lamp softened the dark cream of her Celtic complexion as she turned her features this way and that, studying the beautician's skill. Coming out of the bathroom, I paused at her side, privy, as it were, to some mystical Eleusinian experience.

"Your hair looks really nice, Aunt Millie," I said.

She smiled, still studying her reflection, and announced, "I was a pretty woman."

Aunt Millie could not let go of my grandmother either. In that winter of her decline, Death announced his intentions with pneumonia, and Grandma wanted to receive him in her own home. Aunt Millie was frightened. Medicine was dedicated to keeping patients alive, not helping them die. Death meant that the patient had been lost. Aunt Millie could not brook the notion that that should happen to her own mother in her care ... especially considering her nervous disorder. She compiled a blame list of possibilities for herself that virtually immobilized her as a nurse and cited the equivalency that doctors do not operate on their own. So Grandma was ambulanced out to O'Connor's one morning as the French lady who rented from Mrs. McNabb passed, garbed in black, on her way to daily mass at St. Mary's. She paused and blessed herself as she watched the final emigration of that Irish matriarch.

And she died, Grandma did, one morning with none of us there, probably on purpose. Sr. Rita, whom Aunt Millie always referred to as "that good woman," called to say that we should come but not to hurry, so we suspected Grandma was already gone.

That good woman was waiting for us on one of the wide bricked verandas shaded and scented with magnolias, the wings of her white bonnet quivering with warm wind, her face sober and serene in its message. My father took my mother in his arms and squeezed till the sobbing ceased. Aunt Millie sank onto a porch divan, pressed her forehead against the nun's hand clasped in her own and wept with an abandon I had never known in anyone—peculiarly, eccentrically. My grandfather's harshness toward her stood among us wringing her like a personified, "I told you so!" Allen, Kathleen and I studied the format of sorrow ... Peewee's most of all.

Grandma's death put Aunt Millicent even more in mind of her own soul after that, and she struggled with God and loneliness. A stoop grew out of her back. Jansenism had made its mark among the Irish, and Aunt Millie was convinced when she sang, "O Lord, I am not worthy ..." to receive the body, blood, soul and divinity of her Savior in the ritual of Holy Communion. Always meticulous about examining her conscience before confession, she dug now into the unused corners of intent, accused her innocence and maximized her venial sins into mortal ones. Doubt became her master, and God withdrew in jealous pique, stranding her in the most solitary of isolations. Under the threat of hell, Aunt Millicent bought a Smith-Corona Clipper and set about typing her confession lest she forget anything in the telling and nullify absolution after the fact. For two years, day after day, Aunt Millicent plunked on that typewriter, coaxing sins from its keys and impatience from the rest of us. Conflict raged in that house.

The mouth of the pit seemed a relaxed yawn beneath that scruple-ridden soul. I persuaded my mother to visit my current confessor at St. Joseph's, fearing that at any moment Aunt Millie could die without benefit of the sacrament she so painfully labored to complete.

"You tell her that I want to see her tomorrow afternoon," Fr. Aragho said, thumping an index finger against the other palm. "It's time we put an end to this business!"

Aunt Millicent's muttering rolled through that house like thunder the whole evening. The main bathroom went under siege with incessant washings of personal items, especially soiled panties, and ritualistic bathing of her own person in preparation for the event. Being human was hard on Aunt Millie.

Her annoyance with my interference relaxed when my mother pleaded my concern that she might die without the sacraments and be separated from us for all eternity. Indeed, still fresh in my memory is the question of a sixth-grade classmate whose divorced mother had remarried. During a catechism lesson on the justice and mercy of God, the girl had asked, "Sister, how could I be happy in heaven if God put my mother in hell?"

"Ah, but you see, Tomasina," the nun smiled sadly, "you have your answer in your own question. God does not put anyone in hell. They choose to go there by not following His will."

The girl's lower lip lost control. "But how do we know God's will?"

"That's the beauty of being Catholic, child," the nun said radiantly. "Mother Church tells us God's will. All we have to do is follow it."

Whatever Fr. Aragho said to Aunt Millicent carried the weight of Mother Church's authority. She retired her little Smith-Corona Clipper—but not her scruples—and it stayed in her closet till I needed it to vent these goings-on within my own soul. Aunt Millicent remains a tragic tenderness housed within my being.

CHAPTER 9

THE Y

Catholics were not allowed to belong to the Y.M.C.A. when I was twelve. It was a religiously based organization, and we admitted no truth but our own. It was only when I discovered that men swam nude at the San José Y that I risked the fires of hell and entered that multi-storied building on the corner of Third and Santa Clara, an easy bike's ride from home. Risked is the wrong word, actually. Desire had unseated conscience, and ignorance begged off from every pore in my body. I was a breathing receptacle for things sexual, and everything sensual had become sexual. I say it was an easy bike's ride, but my legs, as I touched concrete and lowered the kickstand, trembled from pumping and resentment that distance of any kind stood between me and my need. I did not risk because I could not. My body had taken my soul out of my hands.

Damp-headed boys with triangles stamped on their tee-shirts snapped gum as they exited the building, limp towels caught in vigorous hands, an easy arrogance in their unseeing eyes as they passed me. The asphalt-tiled lobby, punctuated with chairs Spartan in character, collected echoes—animated, robust, staunchly male. Breath came raw from my throat and swallowing hurt. If the gray-fringed clerk at the desk read the flush in my cheeks as he glanced up from the form he penned, he gave no indication. "Is it okay if I just go in and watch the swimming for a while?" I asked. My whole chest, I knew, was splotched red with anxiety, and I was grateful his seeing stopped at my collar. "I like to watch swimming," I added.

He continued to write, his eyes framed and distant with lenses. My eyes began to burn, and my heart jammed my ears with thrusting. I was afraid I would not hear his answer, and then he jerked his pen toward the half-dozen wooden stairs surmounted with swinging doors. Unawares, I swallowed. My pocketed right hand held rigid my excitement while the left sought to anchor my trembling. I gave him neither chance to rethink nor retract. I turned quickly, but not lightly, my soles sanding the steps as I climbed. Priestly warnings about the perils of sin reached for me—the spectral face of a youth who had dropped dead in the midst of his only impure act and was damned for eternity. But the sour-sweat scent of locker-room reek sifted through those doors, and blind chase seized the remnants of my will.

The clamor of masculine camaraderie, hollowed against steamy tiles, bounded through as I nudged open the door. Sunlight cut the water from high transoms, glittering in anxious patches on the clear-chlorined, slender bodies within—tawny-skinned, tight-ribbed, beige-buttocked—arms and legs athrash. Had these been women, my watching would have been wrong, but less wrong than this. My lust was for males, and my eyes searched their forms with quick gluttony. Breath snagged in my quickened chest. The threat of instantaneous climax benched me at once in the elevated spectator section where I sat alone in the grip of desire and despair. My eyes scoured the nakedness, lest God suspend my breath before I could devour enough. I did not know what to do with my want, and it twisted inside of me, an unheard scream.

I envied the swimmers their bare-bottomed cavort, begrudged them their laughter and their fun, hated their apparent immunity to conscience. The binding of my clothes intensified the binding of my guilt, and any motion at all, I knew, would explode the orgasm so tenuously verged and pulsing.

Spraying the textured cement with running streaks, the seal-slick head of a tall youth launched free of the pool, his glimmering body twisting to a bare-flanked squat at the edge. Non-stop he gained his footing and shook as he trotted directly toward me. The view was unobstructed, his male endowment swing-bouncing from its shadowed cove of dripping coils. Quickly I crossed my legs, and the explosion ripped through me. Desperately I struggled to betray nothing of my condition as the youth leaned on the iron railing and grinned whitely.

"You're Allen Schmidt's kid brother Ronald, right?"

I nodded, certain that if he knew that, then he must know what was happening and why I was there.

"Don't remember me, do you?" Droplets traced paths down his chest, dripping from one of his taut nipples. The inner surge had begun to ebb.

"I'm Sonny Edsyle ... Used to live across the street from you. Me and Allen used to hang around some."

"Oh, hi!" I managed.
"'Member me now?" he snuffed.
"Yeah, sure," I said, and I did, much to my chagrin.
"So what're you doing?"
"Just watching the swimming," I shrugged.
"Why don't you come on in?"
"I don't have any trunks."

Sonny's head pitched back in the transom light, and his laugh ricocheted off the tiles.

"I mean ... I don't have any money," I stammered.

"Hokay," he grinned and slapped my arm good naturedly. "Tell Allen hello, hey?"

I started to nod, and in one supple move he arched into the air and back into the pool. The pressure of his hand remained wet and warm against my arm. I'd never been touched by anyone naked before, and it was an intimacy that sustained my arousal despite the release just experienced. I ached with aftermath and prelude all at once. Guilt would vie with desire and win only when desire was drained and resistance unarmed.

I returned to the Y in subsequent years. Sonny never ran into Allen, and I never ran into Sonny again, so no one in the family knew. One other person knew, though. He was a salesman for a printing-supply company that serviced the shop I part-timed for during college, in the old Victory Building at 45 North First. By that time I'd found my way to the Y's sun deck, but shorts had become mandatory because secretaries in the Bank of America Building were binocularizing the unclad males on top of the Y, and their bosses were complaining. Anyway, he was on that roof one day, fully clothed, watching the street and me alternately. Neither of us pretended to recognize the other. He drove a new pea-green Mercedes. I'd seen a sailor in the car with him once and, God, I didn't want to be like him ... but I wanted him to notice me and the unsubtle straining at my shorts.

It was all so very furtive, and guilt never left me. I remembered those incidents years later when finally my need led me to a bathhouse and I found youths scarcely older than Sonny had been, as at ease with their gayness as he had been with straight sexuality. I ached for the wasted years and the feelings I'd left unshared in dark gropings and anonymous fear.

CHAPTER 10

THE BUILDING

We're still pulling up stink trees. Like snails, they can't be gotten rid of. Yanking them up by the roots only wakens dormant seed, dropped into cracks, years old, and Lord, it makes your hands smell! The biggest ones I ever saw grew right next door at the back of Hawkie's lot on the right and the Blackspots' lot on the left ... as if they were part of the conspiracy. They hurt your neck looking up into them and dusted your hair with yellow pollen. Every spring they layered our yard so thick you couldn't tell we had gravel unless you walked on it. It's a wonder the sound wasn't muffled. They patterned the base of the sky with their wild grace and, in a wind, must have made God sit up the way our English walnut did us, rubbing against the building.

Betty Smith taught me to love those trees, but I was grown then. Page after page of A Tree Grows in Brooklyn held me as realization, like the tenacious seedling itself, crumbled my preconceptions and returned me to the graceless battleground of my grandparents' feud-flanked backyard. Francie Nolan's glorious Tree of Heaven, I discovered, was none other than the stink tree exacerbating neighborly strife.

I can scarcely remember the Blackspots, that's how long ago they moved from the block, but they're indexed in family legend under "Humdingers." Dark-complected Portuguese, they worshipped God like us but at Five Wounds Portuguese Parish and not, I guess, in their hearts next door. Their daughter was best friends with Hawkie's Belinda, for whom family legend developed no category, and between them they wove misery into my family's daily fabric.

I have no personal recollection of Belinda, mercifully, but then none of my memories antedate the building. The family home, centered on South Fifth Street, was a single-story valley house whose redwood beams weathered ought-six and lesser disasters without so much as a stretch mark. Not so its inhabitants. We're a family that grayed early over old rancors.

My grandmother, for example, looked over at the Blackspot father once as he squinted into the sun and said to the Blackspot mother, "Your man there looks like that Jap emperor." That was shortly before the Blackspots moved to Gilroy without even saying goodbye.

It wasn't a neighborly remark, of course, but then neither the Blackspots, nor certainly Hawkie's brood, had made neighborliness even an effort. Hawkie's boy hadn't the smarts for malice; it was Belinda who put him up to his worst. He looked like the blond Katzenjammer Kid, which is why we called him Fritzie. Hawkie, the pair's widowed mother, chirped nasally beneath a beaked dominance, endorsing Belinda's fun. It was how she got by.

They hung from their back porches, Hawkie's two and the Blackspots' daughter, hollering across our yard, usually about us. My grandfather had to stump around the yard on his wooden leg with them catcalling over his head, and that was no picnic. When he caught Fritzie imitating his limp, all hell broke loose. My grandfather had a temper. Even Belinda lost her sneer under that tongue-thrashing.

Anyway, that's why the building went up. Two stories of tongue-and-groove shell from the back of our house to my grandmother's chicken yard were too much even for Belinda to holler across.

"What's that?" Mrs. Gottmuller asked when her family bought out the Blackspots. Shielding her eyes on her laundry porch, she studied the screen-windowed structure rising out of our English walnut. The Gottmullers were Wagnerian people—massive except for Mister, who owned a pharmacy but couldn't treat hair loss. The women were huge and moved with a deliberateness that looked like grandeur. They didn't come out the front door; they proceeded. They were the block mastodons. When their son Cuthbert took a leak in their toilet across the driveway from our kitchen, you'd swear an elephant was pissing in a bucket.

"Oh, it's just a sleeping porch," my mother told her, and that was true. My father slept there on August nights in a metal-frame bed, the tar paper warping between exposed beams like ledges of dust.

Allen, Kathleen and I tried it a couple of times, sleeping out there, but I came in. The walnut used the building as an emery board and, even with Muggsy on our feet, I could never get to sleep.

A steamer trunk of odds-and-ends dishes butted against the beams under the second-story stairwell. My German grandparents hung there, under glass, more together than fate in thirty years had let them be. Grossmama watched like her own warm hug, but Grosspapa referenced only a footnoted past, the Atlantic distance forever between us.

"He was a stern man," summed up that mustachioed patriarch frozen in ferrotype. It was the kindest remark my father, Tante Gretta or Grossmama ever mustered about him, and that after a "Let's see..." pause. I pick back through memory, incredulous, but it's always the same. "He was a stern man." The unspoken positive, even though it forced my father from gymnasium into workplace, was that Grosspapa died young. But for that, the Schmidt seed might never have made the crossing.

A third photo, hung from a contiguous beam, documented a gathering of Finns at Lake Tahoe in a moment congenial enough to pose. My recently widowed grandmother had the arm of eldest, unwed Aunt Millicent—one of whose beaux hovered in the backdrop of that prophetic grasp. My newly married parents smiled for posterity beside a sober Uncle Vincent and his reserved Nordic Protestant. Issues, like wedges, dictated, even then, the horizontal slant of that family shot. Small wonder it had been consigned to the building.

It was a cocoon of sorts, now that I think of it ... the building, I mean. I did a bit of processing there myself, especially upstairs. I followed my phallus to the second-floor privacy, secreting muscle slicks that powered the thrust of semen straight from my soul. Fingers awed by the wonder and guilt of erection, I measured the clandestine leap of my seed, examined the distance of spurts as the breath of the English walnut stirred afresh the hair on my descending testicles before I could even pull my pants up and I had to go at it again.

The second story was remote. I remember the smell of corroded wire as I flicked the meshed screen, exploding residue into the broad, lucent leaves at that level. The English walnut, apricot and Grandpa's little almond were the only cultured trees on the three lots. Hawkie, the Blackspots and even the Gottmullers contented themselves with stink trees. Pressing against the screen left little grids on my forehead and nose, but I could see into Gottmullers' back bedroom, where by night, Doc, their roomer, kept his own counsel. By day he ground powders and mixed elixirs for pharmacist Gottmuller... until the morning he scooted under his burgundy Chevy and connected its tailpipe with his windpipe ... and gave the neighborhood pause ... all but Gottmuller, that is. He was a chemist, after all, a pragmatist with a business to run. When he noticed the coupe idling at the curb, he shut off the ignition and did as circumstances dictated. Doc had a replacement without missing a shift.

We could have caught Gottmuller poisoning Grandpa's almond, I'll bet, if we'd staked a watch in the building. His wall of variegated ivy was warping our fence, after all, and my father asked him to trim it back. He listened, the stink tree pollinating his fringed head, lenses pocketed on either side of his nose, just listened until my father added that it sure would be nice to get rid of all those stink tree blossoms covering our yard and his head. Gottmuller's eyes flickered. "I wouldn't cut that tree down for anybody," he grinned. Next time he looked over the fence, it was to cluck with shame that Grandpa's almond was dead. Stink trees were already sprouting at its base.

On tiptoe I could see all the yards to the Palm Apartments, even across Reed Street to the Vaughn house, where Armand was fucking Tom McCartney in the loft over the garage and, God, I didn't even know it... not till I was forty-two coming out to my brother across coffee on my circular dining table in the Sierras. When he recovered enough to gasp, "Why are you telling me this?" Allen explained, "My only experience with homosexuality was watching Armand and Tom fuck each other in Armand's outback loft on a Saturday sleepover. They wanted me to join in, but I wouldn't ... I couldn't believe my eyes," he added and lowered his eyes from mine.

I can still remember the sun on the honeysuckle climbing the siding of that loft and the way the steam sifted from grass robbed of nightshade between my polished oxfords and the chewed base of the sagging door. It was the same morning; I know it was. The warmth was dense on my back as crazy guffaws thunked about me, randomly aimed, in answer to my call. "Allen? Mama says to come home and get ready for mass... right now."

The loft doors never budged, but I could hear the hysterics good and plain. Armand and Tom were going at it right then, I'll bet, with Allen on an elbow declining a three-way, sort of stunned, pretending to be amused.

I tend to think Allen actively protected me from that. They could have invited me up, after all, and talked me into the experiment. Chances are I'd have freaked. Not only was I four years younger, I was the family saint. "Let your conscience be your guide" was not an admonition Allen needed heed; he had me for that.

On the other hand, I was drawn to a difference I knew to keep quiet even then. Had they asked me up, it might have been Allen who freaked. There was, after all, the time I tagged after him and Tom McCartney on bikes down to Coyote Creek behind the Home of Benevolence. I dropped off a log following the leader across the meager stream, and they made me strip down, spreading my clothes to dry on branches. Lolling against the parched bank, they snickered, egging me through a hula with bramble for a grass skirt and I did it, totally out of character, excited by the naughtiness of the exhibition, a taste of what lay thirty years ahead of me in the corridors of gay bathhouses. Voices other than ours raided my burlesque. Allen and Tom scrambled for my tee shirt and jeans, and I, frantic not to be left (though Allen never would), struggled into their warm dampness. We pedaled like hell for home.

Mr. Gottmuller, I think, suspected my difference, watching me from the ivied crest of the fence. My father had rigged an incinerator out of a fifty-gallon drum mounted on little red wagon wheels, and that's how I mostly disposed of muscle slicks and pocket books once I'd abused myself into contrition. I stoked some impressive conflagrations in that old can, probing with a smoke-tipped stick to ensure against tell-tale pages too thickly layered. Despairing at the caveat that the bottom of hell is paved with good intentions and, therefore, what possible hope could there be for me, I tried, by standing close, to sear desire from my system, confronting the rigors to be realized in my hell-bent destiny.

I would look up then from the flames, sensing the chemist's pocketed eyes, nesting in the variegated ivy, under the stink-tree canopy where the wind sifted burned-off oxygen.

"You folks burn a lot of trash," he would observe cannily, and I was never sure whether he knew what I was up to or simply fretted that I might set my next match to his house. Gottmuller measured normalcy against his own family and seemed smug about their rarity. They were republicans, masons and nondenominational theists who claimed as much virtue as people who keep holy the Sabbath. The women, including Cuthbert's wife, who swelled to Wagnerian dimensions upon marrying into that family, belonged to the Daughters of Pythias, and their lodge night was our three-ring circus. Their white-gowned descent from porch to Pontiac rivaled any routine we had in place. Wednesdays we made sure we took the air on our own porch, adults in rockers, kids sprawled on steps, appraising the Pythians. Their own daughter Chloris, without exaggeration, draped four hundred pounds in full-length chiffon. The wind was our puckish ally, venting their backsides as they maneuvered into the sedan, exposing their stacked joints like piled columns. The last door slammed, the Pontiac glided from the curb, three Pythians in a fifties lowrider.

Missus had a carriage the girls lacked ... height and the bearing found on old coppers. She was San José's answer to San Francisco-dressed women. Lodge or no lodge, every day was a day to receive. She was like that. Lace-strung glasses rode the plane of her breasts, where she tucked Kleenex for patting perspiration. She was always properly, if thickly, hosed. Muggsy lifted his leg on hers where she stood chatting with my mortified mother once, and she just laughed. She had a pretty good sense of humor if you got her off politics and religion, which wasn't often. She was a good woman. They were good people, actually. Well, the chemist was questionable, but what fenced us out of each other's grace was not so much ivy-split planks and dead almonds or even stink trees as it was the ego involved in casting a vote and offering a prayer. When I was a child, both issues were one. God the Father, Son, Holy Ghost and F.D.R. inhabited democratic sanctuaries. The meanest thing Mrs. Gottmuller ever did was to slam through the screen door onto her back porch and announce to my mother, who was hanging out wash in the yard, "Well, this country's got no more king!"

I looked up from my gravel roads at my mother's incredulous expression. She understood at once yet couldn't take in the trumpeted declaration. Her fingers clutched a sheet scented with stopped wind. The walnut leaves held their stir.

"What?" she said.

Mrs. Gottmuller's upper arm quivered beneath the pulley where she'd hung her hand on the clothesline. "Roosevelt!" she chortled. "He's dead."

My mother stared at her. Wisps loosened from Mrs. Gottmuller's combs, careless as her victory.

"What an awful thing to do!" my mother said, as if Mrs. Gottmuller had personally pressed a pillow against the face of Falla's war-weary, paraplegic master. Then she burst into tears. Plopping the sheet back in the wicker basket, she walked through the mottled shade toward the house to tell Grandma and Aunt Millie. Neither pausing nor turning, she said brokenly, "Come in now. I don't want you out there where that battle-axe can gloat over you."

The gravel bit my jeaned knees as I scuffled to my feet, grabbing a car for inside. I glanced at the battle-axe still hung from her line and saw in her face the grace to regret but not to say, "Sorry."

Cold war was a principle I understood from experience before the Mercury Herald or my U.S. history text undertook to interpret it. It was the way neighbors loved one another. The cold war between our houses continued till the chemist succumbed to a heart attack and my mother took over a casserole. Neither God nor F.D.R. mattered for the moment. A woman was widowed, and she was right next door, as if she'd been right in our own home. And now, in spite of herself, Mrs. Gottmuller had something in common with Eleanor and with my grandmother and, in time, so would my mother with all of them. Now, too, Mrs. Gottmuller understood about Grandpa's dead almond because Mister's variegated ivy taught her from the fence dusted with stink tree pollen. The denominator of loss was a common, after-the-fact bonding, altogether ironic.

For Hawkie, too. Belinda was dead, killed in a car, and Fritzie was working on it. Out of work, he staggered after the lawn mower or sucked Lucky Lager in the sun on the stoop beside the yellow Scotch broom and began to chat with us as if the building had nothing to do with him. He took up, for a time, with an older woman across the street who stood his drinking to lie in his warmth, until finally he succeeded in failing. And Hawkie was alone. And we became friends, neighborly in need.

Hawkie's nieces drove up in quiet Lincolns and parked under the elephant-trunked palm at the curb. They had connections, those two. One had been friends with Carol Henning in the days when John Steinbeck was only courting her, and they picked up Belinda for outings. In those days Steinbeck's renown lay in wait for him, his greatness nonetheless immanent in the measure of his soles on those next-door steps. I keep searching his novels for foul-mouthed Belinda and marveling that our building never became famous.

Hawkie couldn't stay warm at the end, pulling sweaters up her thin arms, checking the kettle level on top of her gas stove and rocking as close as she could to its BTUs. But for the Mercury Herald, Hawkie didn't read, couldn't afford T.V. and was too deaf even for the radio. Visiting her strained the vocal cords even with her hearing aid at feedback volume. She had nothing but memories, few of them sweet, and more than enough time to review them.

A demolition squad with bulging muscle and no sentiment shoved an iron ball into Hawkie's echoes at the end of a short coma. The nieces repainted their Saratoga places, and apartments went up at our side. It was the beginning of the end of the neighborhood. San José State had metamorphosed from normal school to state college to university, encroaching on its environs like a figment of bad sci-fi. The original Spanish-tiled tower remained the ivied core reminder of what might have been but for the grotesquerie of nondescript economics. One by one, family dwellings fell to the wreckers or absentee landlords who modified porches into communal quarters to reap the harvest of postwar students. When the Pythian daughters helped Cuthbert carry out the Gottmuller casting couch, our house became the victim of buildings, a vintage piece caught in the thighs of progress.

Allen, Kathleen and I freed up funds by coming of age, and our parents cashed in on the landlord trend. The building was plumbed, sheetrocked, painted and tenanted. For the first time in the family's history, strangers came in to reside.

Being a landlord distracted my father from the emphysema that forced his retirement and the cancer that lanced his lungs. Conscientiously, he conditioned my mother to become landlady, but no amount of prepping could have inured her to the devotion with which collegiate youth study Human Body I, II, III and IV.

Allen, Kathleen and I tried to dissuade her, when we came home to visit, from extending proprietorship into tenant morals. Aunt Millicent, though discomfited, could chuckle some at the stealthy procession of co-eds treading gravel down the driveway. But my mother pursed her lips, watching the apartment we still called the building, and fumed, "The worst part of it is, the little buggers think they're putting one over on me."

One strapping redhead, confronted with the fact of his fiancée up there on the second floor, packed himself up in a rage. When the couple's peninsula wedding was recorded in the Mercury Herald that June, my mother glanced up from her reading to emphasize that the bride had worn white.

Inevitably, the building did exert an erosive effect on both ladies' levels of tolerance. John XXIII abetted that condition by happening to the Church, casting in haze all the old constants. For my mother and Aunt Millie, there seemed little any longer to cling to. And, so, the only change in foot traffic among tenants-in-tryst was that the sneaking stopped.

I owe a lot to the building.

By the time my mother began to suspect my resolve to stay single following my divorce, she could listen to my affirmation of gayness, accept that Degnan my friend was Degnan my lover and reserve for us both an unreserved embrace.

As I trimmed the yard prior to her eightieth birthday celebration, my mother pointed toward Grandma's decaying chicken yard. "Oh, look, Ronald," she said, "there's one of those old stink trees getting a start."

I looked at her, hard-pressed to mask a smile. The English walnut was a stump now. In summer, the afternoon sun baked the building, the backyard and the kitchen without mercy, and I remembered the cool canopies of Hawkie's and Gottmullers' pollen shedders.

"Let it grow," I suggested.

My mother shielded her eyes to look at me.

"Let it grow?" she repeated.

I nodded. "We need it," I said. "It would shade the yard again and cool the draft when you leave the doors open in summer."

Her shoulders sloped around her strength. Clearly, this was one adjustment she had never considered. I hugged her.

"They only stink if you try to pull them up," I said, studying the spindly stalk of splayed leaves. "You can't really blame them for that. Besides, they're a famous tree."

"Oh, go on ..."

"Cross my heart. An author named Betty Smith wrote a book called A Tree Grows in Brooklyn."

"I've heard that title."

I nodded. "It's a wonderful story about an Irish family, so you'd like it, but the tree ..." I stabbed the direction of the leafy stalk, "the tree is the same one you see pushing aside those chicken-coop slats,... right there."

"Well, I don't know what your father would say."

I laughed, softly. "He'd want you to be comfortable."

"Are you sure it's the same tree?"

"From the moment I read the description, and I've never forgotten it. Listen: 'There's a tree that grows in Brooklyn. Some people call it the Tree of Heaven. No matter where its seed falls, it makes a tree which struggles to reach the sky. It grows in boarded-up lots and out of neglected rubbish heaps. It grows out of cellar gratings. It is the only tree that grows out of cement. It grows lushly ... survives without sun, water, and seemingly without earth. It would be considered beautiful except that there are too many of it.'"

My mother's lips twitched. "Mrs. Gottmuller used to call it that, the Tree of Heaven. Of course, we never believed it."

"I know."

"You think we should leave it then?"

"I think it's time," I said.

CHAPTER 11

GRAY MATTER

I knew something was wrong, seriously wrong, as I sat under St. Joseph's cherubim dome and watched the man who had kept me from communion receive it himself. True, Fr. Aragho purged Saturday night's sinners in his box beside St. Michael's defeat of Lucifer, but penitence claimed no quarter in my need just then. I wondered, in fact, as I shifted my knees to allow my sister back in the pew, whether it ever would again. Kathleen's crinoline whispered against my slacks and, noting a damp spot on my beige crotch, I lowered my missal in my lap. Residual seepage was the plague of heavy self-abuse. It wasn't that I was without regret, but I'd been victim long enough of my lust to suspect that the real issue was when I would submit, not whether. I was further experienced enough at fourteen to know that neither an environment for remorse, nor contrition sufficient to make absolution stick would grace my ardor till my genitals hurt too much to get hard, and my guts, like putty, were ready to reshape. I sure wasn't there.

St. Joseph's had organ-quality choirs in those days, so the communion was upholstered with a full-bodied Panis Angelicus, my all-time favorite. He followed a trim-hipped blond woman, that man who kept me from communion, hands clasped to his dark tweed in cumbersome devotion. He had impressive hands. I'd noticed them last evening as he handed me the book I'd ultimately shredded and bagged at the bottom of the garbage. Already I regretted that righteous zeal, that fear of detection. Already I needed it again and weighed the options for slipping up to Second Street for another copy ... God! For all of them! I'd need them in short order. He counted on that. You wouldn't think so, watching him walk behind the woman's taffeta wiggle, but he did. His jaw worked slightly, moistening the Bread of Angels on his tongue.

"Have you seen these?" he'd asked, his warm voice aware, his index finger bleached against the display case. He had followed the train of my browsing, noted the intent of my pocketed hand. "They're brand new."

His left hand slid open the back of the counter, performed in the fluorescence. Hair rippled the edge of his French cuff as his wrist extended, the large knuckles and blunt nails articulating the grasp as if it, too, were brand new. "They're selling fast," he coaxed.

Some moments you just know are turning points. I didn't breathe.

Even flaccid, I remained swollen because of him. The blond woman would be surprised, I'd bet, to know that. I leaned into the cover of the couple ahead of me, without need, as it happened. The blond woman stepped into a pew near the carved Pieta at the base of the Crucifixion altar. He followed, reflective, with no thought of me or anyone else whose endangered soul stuffed his wallet with collection-basket bills.

Eyes closed, he leaned into his thanksgiving. A couple of yards beyond, Christ bled lipstick from marble wounds on Mary's cold lap.

The nave swelled with the wondrous affair that gripped the congregation, the tenor turning Latin syllables on the lathe of his resonance: "O res mi...ra...bi...lis..."

"Fabian Originals," he had said, "really a hot item."

His hands covered his whole face. I wondered how he breathed. The blond woman's pearls softened Christ's dead eyes. It is a bleak altar.

I moved as little as possible, shifting the missal to check the damp spot. Even limp, the shaft of my phallus throbbed. I'd purposely broken my fast, feigning forgetfulness, to avoid questions. I mean, I always went to communion. So it was the perfect excuse. You could go to hell in those days for not fasting from the midnight before you received ... unless you had a dispensation.

The coarseness of my missal contrasted sharply with the pocketbook's slickness. The Fabian Original had actually slipped in my fingers as I studied its cover fantasy: three husky guys boarding a boxcar with a girl who couldn't undress fast enough. The woody pages opened to Chapter I. "He couldn't keep his pecker in his pants ..." I came on the spot, my engorged penis wrapped in my pocketed hand, desperate to quell the thrill of climax, wondering how in God's name I could contain the warm, wet mess. My face was afire. Wetness dripped down my leg. Fumbling, I pulled a crumpled dollar and all my change from the pocket not bulged with my fist.

To the left of St. Joseph's shell-hooded pulpit, to the left even of the patrician-featured patron of Ireland, St. Aloysius studied his lily, resolved to have no truck with the impure and unrepentant.

"Pau...per ser...vus et hu...u...mi...lis..."

The book dealer was more generous. Tax totaled me out five cents shy, but he bagged it for me anyway. He glanced pointedly at the knotted fist in my darkening pocket, winked and said, "Give it to me next time."

Versed to completion, the Panis Angelicus yielded to simpler fare. "Oh, Lord I Am Not Worthy" faltered into its aftermath like a veiled virgin taking the measure of the center aisle. The last communicants folded their limbs in reverie, and the celebrant tapped God fragments from the gold paten into the gold chalice for his final draft. I studied my parents in profile, noting the value their fingers lent, bead by bead, to their separate rosaries. Between them on the kneeler, my mother's purse rested still unclasped from her puzzled search for Offertory change.

I'd taken greater risks, but none more shameful. The dowdy owner of the College Market at Eighth and William followed me onto the sidewalk once and watched, hands on hips, as I hurried down William Street, the paperback slapping the flat of my stomach below the undone button. The cover alone had validated the risk. I knew then the color of compulsion: male skin toned by desire, deepened with sun, lightly furred between taut bronze nipples, tapered down the rib cage. I'd had to have it.

Between secreting funds back into my mother's purse and feeding the parish poor, restitution calloused my hands and kept me indigent. "Stores shouldn't be selling that trash anyway," Fr. Aragho counseled in the confessional. "Put the money in the poor box." I couldn't mow lawns fast enough. As my coins rang in the vestibule's vault for the hungry and homeless, my lips went dry, "Lord, ... make me like the rest of men."

Somehow I didn't have that "Ask and you shall receive" business down quite right. I knew I was in trouble.

"Bu...ut speak the wor-r-rds of comfort, my spir-r-rit healed shall be..."

Down shed from the cherubim dome, softening shame, beckoning with the thrall of the great placebo. "He couldn't keep his pecker in his pants ... pecker in his ... An...nd humbly I'l-l-l receive The-e-e, the Bridegro-o-om of my soul-l-l ... peckerpeckerpecker..." The blond woman looked at the book dealer, her smile luminous. Didn't anyone listen to the lyrics? How could they sing it if they did? How did the Church allow it even to be written? The Bridegroom of my soul? Jesus H. Chr... I stopped.

Claude could sing that. How could I have forgotten about Claude? Was he even there? Of course he was. My eyes knew his place by heart, found him with ease—first pew, center aisle, right side—God's left. For years Claude had worked for the Jesuits and haunted the night, till one morning he made the Mercury Herald. After that he just haunted the night ... in his narrow overcoat... and kept his front row, center aisle seat. Some said that was audacity. It was, undeniably, remarkable. He walked everywhere, showed up on unlikely street corners, his white face set in the dark collars of his coat, looking as if he'd never seen you before, and you saw him every Sunday in that same damn pew. "There's that Claude," my mother would remark as we drove. My father would say, "Uh-huh," as we paused for a light to change. I watched Claude from the Buick's rear window, slumped in the seat so he wouldn't see me, dreading the prophecy of his mere existence.

"No-o more by si-i-in to grieve The-e-e ..."

Did I ... Could I cause God to grieve? Mother Church did a signal mix on that; it was like the dispensation thing. The higher one went in Catholic education, the more in umbra slipped subtlety, the more circuitous became exception.

Even as I blamed him, of course, I realized that, ultimately, the book dealer did not own my impurity. What angered me most was that I could not make him really responsible. It even crossed my mind that, had he noticed me at mass, he might be scandalized that a Catholic boy had bought such a book. Granted, he'd put the Fabian Original in my hands, but he was just making a living. I was buying it to masturbate.

That whole issue came into focus with the pharmacist father of a Bellarmine classmate. He sold contraceptives with the Church's blessing, not because he wanted to, mind you, but because he'd go out of business if he didn't. If a customer wanted a rubber, after all, and the Catholic pharmacist couldn't supply it, the customer bent on sinning would just buy it from a competitor. "I don't carry condoms, sir," meant you didn't care about what the customer perceived as his needs or that you passed judgment on that perception... or that you were a stupid businessman— any one of which could cause financial collapse. My classmate's father managed quite successfully, keeping condoms under the counter with the Playboy magazines. He raised the considerable results of his rhythm-and-restraint, funded them, in fact, through Catholic universities. It all had to do with "the greater good" concept. Unscrupulous non-Catholic businessmen made such competitive practices necessary in the first place. Conscientious Catholics shouldn't bear the brunt of someone else's decision to sin. Besides, a condom, like a Playboy or a Fabian Original is just an object, neither moral nor immoral. How a customer used it gave it that kind of value. The seller had no control of that.

What's good for the pharmacist is good for the theater entrepreneur, of course. When the long-standing steward of San José's First Street films opened the city's first open-air theater at Thirteenth and Gish and gradually bled his profits into or out of porn, who could fault him? His issue proliferated across Catholic campuses as well, and those tuition tabs were costly. He merely catered to what his paying public would have gone to a competitor for. It is a far, far better thing to have well-heeled Catholics who can support Mother Church's charities ...

It wasn't so much that white was not always white as that black was not always black ... except in cases like mine ... yes, and Claude's. I probably read every Fabian Original ever published before graduating to Nightstand Readers and, finally, the stuff Amendment One batted a home run for. By all reasonable standards of that era's thinking, I should have been insane by eighteen, my mind laid waste by a phallus that should have dropped off in my abusive hand. Regular fellows eventually plugged their fantasies into weddings with nice girls. For Claude and me, there was only the headline to risk or deception to pass off as commitment to women moved by respect for their bodies.

Gray matters are those that turn a profit. Shading comes from financial feasibility. In my youth Catholics were forbidden membership in the secret fraternal order of Free and Accepted Masons under pain of mortal sin ... unless one sought membership to enhance one's business and did so quietly to avoid scandal among the at-large flock. Now, even the pretense has been dropped. Now, even the Catholic pharmacist may sell me condoms, from an above-the-counter display, for acts his Church confirms as abomination ... because dispensing Claudes and Rons from lifelong abstinence still isn't financially feasible.

Even that Sunday under the cherubim dome, I sensed that the spirit of God did not move in dispensation. But the habit of hard-line belief is hard to break. Given the intensity of my nature, I sometimes fear that, had my own homosexuality not forced my humanity to the surface, I might have been one of Mother Church's deadliest bigots. It is a fear that makes me very grateful.

CHAPTER 12

PARKS AND RECREATION

That thing about Claude hit the Mercury Herald one Saturday morning. Not that it was news to anyone ... about Claude, period, I mean. It's just that no one could ignore it after that. Suspicion become official is rumor promoted to scandal. Confirmation in black and white is intrusive enough to make even bacon and eggs confrontational. The neighborhood buttered its toast with "How dare he's!" Claude had solicited a sophomore in the university gardens. How dare he, indeed.

The item cheated my mother ever after of her rhetorical questions about him. "There's that poor, odd Claude," she would observe to my father, the Roadmaster's headlights thinning the fellow's features. "What do you suppose he's doing way over on this side of town?" Invariably she would add, "... at this time of night?"

That we were also on that side of town at that time of night had no significance because, of course, we were in the Buick. Claude walked everywhere. Well, everywhere except to and from his secretarial job on the Jesuit campus. Then, and only then, he rode the bus, his narrow lineaments juggled in the window like a post office mug shot minus the I.D. number.

"Uh-huh," my father would concur, his toe idling the accelerator. He couldn't do that anymore either. Ignore the question about Claude, that is.

Sunday after Sunday Claude knelt behind his Windsor knot in his front row, center aisle pew, one of the more conservative of St. Joseph's communicants. Clearly, he shocked the faithful by showing up as usual for the 12:15 mass the very day after the item, looking not in the least abashed. It pissed people off.

Out-of-towners, who still took Sunday obligation seriously, were known to detour from 101 to catch the last mass if it looked as if they couldn't make the City on time. It was with them that ushers fleshed out seating alongside Claude. In those days it was more common than not to know your pew mates, and parishioners who knew Claude wouldn't sit with him. In all fairness, he did nothing to abate a disturbing resemblance to Bela Lugosi. Students called him Bela behind his back, in fact, and did that Lugosi tongue roll. Nothing about him invited kindness, especially his own inability to initiate it. Strangers ushered to his pew rose from genuflection to Claude's naked gaze and never repeated the error. He could smile but it seemed contrived, almost private.

Claude epitomized stereotypes. Despite eighteen as the first demarcation of manhood, parents cling to the boys-will-be-boys concept of college-age sons so that the Mercury Herald item established Claude as a pederast—a word the sound of which drives splintered stakes in the hearts of the genteel.

Students seeking recourse through the vice-principal dealt tongue-in-cheek with Claude from their first encounter. How, after all, could those who fawn on power take seriously a male secretary? Unfailingly volatile, Claude could range from relative calm to a campy snit without notice. No one expected claims to be processed with equanimity. Complete opposite of the broad-shouldered, square-jawed director of discipline, Claude brought to that office an extended dimension of the term "prick." But then, what V.P.'s office is meant to be easy? As long as Claude kept his place, it seemed not to matter what anyone thought; the V.P.'s protection remained in place, too.

With the Mercury Herald's documentation of everyone's suspicion, even the V.P. was powerless. Claude had to be let go. There was nothing else to do. It was unthinkable that Claude might offer his lips to crown the jewels of other scions among Santa Clara's Catholic dynasties. Who could measure the trauma of such a proposition on the tender hopes of such well-bred youth?

Claude was not the sort to commit rape. Like everyone else on that all-male campus, he was the sort to need sex. Had the proposition come from the broad-shouldered, square-jawed director of discipline, in fact, it's conceivable that the only result would have been quiet satisfaction. But it came from that poor, odd Claude ... and that could not be brooked.

He comes often to mind, Claude does. That's interesting because I doubt that I ever come to his. I can remember only one instance when he looked closely enough at me to take any notice. We both had our flies open, standing thigh to trough in the stinking latrine at St. James Park.

For years I had run my mother's letters in and out of the post office across the street, memorizing the texture of loitering under the elms, the darkness quickened with cigarettes at the mouth of the bunker-like structure. The deeper puberty impaled me with desire distinct from my brother's, the more compelling became those figures pretexting the face of need, until I went in, breathless, refusing to think, desperate for the secrets of that inner sanctum. I hadn't voided for hours, ensuring a reservoir equal to my own pretext. But, genitals exposed, I couldn't swallow and I couldn't piss. I waited and waited then looked up at the form moved in beside me, and it was Claude, three steps to my right, studying my phallus and then my face, working on recognition. Where had he seen me? Blood blocked my ears. I scanned the dull shapes stalking the doorless stalls and panicked. Convinced I'd contracted V.D., I zipped my pants and fled, pleading with God to spare me existence of that quality.

It is the kind of memory you never lose ... that particular mime-like silence flawed by the whisper of stained plumbing, sanded leather on cold concrete, smoke and urine mixed on a chill staved-in with longing. That I begged a deaf God, I suspected even then.

Still, I tried to help Him out ... maneuvered myself through Francis Thompson's "the labyrinthine ways of my own mind" in the delusion that I could become therapeutically straight, convinced that only therein lay sanity and salvation. Belief moved me from conviction to marriage and two children so that one afternoon at Seattle's Woodland Park Zoo, I dutifully led my sons to the restroom before the forty-mile drive to what was then our home in Tacoma. Their mother was still with us, though ill, sunning herself on the grassy slope where Drake, Tracy and I had tossed the frisbee following lunch.

To this day, public restrooms mortar up a little cloister of terror within me. That day I had only to cross the threshold to know what we'd walked in on, Claude watching from three sets of shoulders.

"This restroom's too crowded," I said, pivoting. "We'll go somewhere else."

Drake dug in his heels against my tug, crying, "But, Dad, I have to pee! I have to pee!" unaware that my deafness was a response to a deafness far less reasonable. I fled not as much from the coition we'd interrupted as from the exquisite desolation that haunts its risk, hating the baldness of need so naked, willing my sons elsewhere that I might rush panting back inside. I thought only to spare them the starkness seeping through the cracks of straight morality. One has to probe for the beauty in toilet sex. Children haven't the skill.

Six years into my commitment with Degnan, Claude's narrow visage watched me again from the printer's ink of the St. Louis Post-Dispatch. It was August 26, 1986. That summer we spent in St. Louis was the same season religious mercenaries forged the climate of November elections. The Supreme Court upheld Georgia's sodomy law in the case of a man arrested for homosexual acts in his own bedroom. Lyndon LaRouche set his dogs on California gays. Fury became the uneasy holocaust of those months headlined with rights denied, even retracted—progress gone to regress in the frenzy to be on the side of right. The August 26 headline synthesized the tragic and the absurd in the high court's biblically backed decision: "Police Arrest 109 Men in Park."

Crackdowns on flagrant sexual conduct between men in Carondelet Park restrooms netted that number from "all over the metropolitan area and from all walks of life" in a single summer. Sgt. John Burke of the St. Louis Vice Squad bragged, "It was a very popular meeting place. There was not a single repeat offender among the 109 arrested."

What an indictment of straight mentality, ... of straight morality.

Officers of the law modeled its transgress, loitering through presumed consent to fondled genitals, rights recited and handcuffs slapped on wrists given to trust. What kind of man trains to entrap ... grabbing that bulge, refining the dialect of his eyes, decoying desire with entreaty? Who teaches an officer of the law to steady his outrage against the fit of another man's fingers? Does Sgt. Burke do that? Is it his grasp that carries the scent and size of his squad's endowments? Or does the squad itself rehearse the methods for putting the make one on the other? Have they hired a homosexual consumed with self-loathing, eager to pay his debt for his difference? Just what kind of man entraps? And, God, how do you find enough of him to snare 109 victims on the same turf in the same summer?

"Not a single repeat offender..." is a curious phrase. Did they all go straight? Never have sex again? Does it mean that Sgt. Burke's squad were merely selective or that the once-entrapped declined the offer of a second feel; or that the arrestees moved their cruise to Tower Grove Park where, the article lamented, a less-successful "campaign" had been waged?

One hundred nine had to have a satisfying sound for heartland homophobes who would ignore the fractional factor of the offending catch. That most of the men "from all walks of life" making "popular" the scene by "frequenting the facility" went home from their blow jobs unimpeded would be overlooked by decent readers who don't know any queers personally but can't get a straight answer to what keeps a husband, father or son irritatingly late at times.

At the rate of one arrest plus per day, what caused the Carondelet risk, those flicking tongues like moths set on the flame? The word had to be out. Crackdowns intend that, depend on their power to deter. Why Carondelet with arrest the imminent end of every reach? And why any park at all with desire in a dead heat with AIDS in that summer?

The primacy of person moves in the risk, the integrity of difference demanding recognition—an unconscious leap toward the legitimacy of relationships straights exclude from their decent standards. The Carondelet one hundred-and-nine are martyrs of democracy run biblically amok, of minorities refused constitutional guarantee.

The Post-Dispatch staff writer, in that 109 Men in the Park piece, mentioned in the ninth of eleven paragraphs that another two hundred men had been arrested in a two-week crackdown on prostitution on St. Louis' South Jefferson Avenue. Two hundred men in fourteen days as opposed to one hundred nine in ninety. This is outrage gone askew, objectivity out the journalistic window. That the story's lead begged revision of its five w's impugns the standards of the Post-Dispatch's founder and creator of the coveted Pulitzer Prize. Reporting facts is an obligation secondary to the slant that sells the papers.

Claude was that kind of victim of his victimless crime. I hope the slant of his notoriety freed him from the small despairs of chance sex and that he stocked his bed with the integrity he brought to his pew. I hope he charmed out of the hedges, home from the flawed scent of ill-lit latrines, a firmly contoured, unthreatened warmth to assuage the disquiet of solitary sheets from his own nebulous definition. I hope the toss of passion against his pillow softened Lugosi out of his features and taught him to smile through the extended awe of repeat lovers. Disgrace can be that kind of blessing.

CHAPTER 13

THE RELIC

Word was that it was remarkably preserved in its glass-and-gold reliquary. The nuns' cheeks pinked within their wimples as they primed us for the phenomenon which would coincide with Sacred Heart's February novena to the Lady of Lourdes. Monsignor Farrell, whose mission it was to conduct the nine-day devotion, had negotiated with the Jesuit Fathers at St. Joseph's to detour the holy relic on its way through San José. After all the pennies we had pinched to feed mission babies, God was blessing us with the very hand that had washed paganism from countless thousands of their ancestors' brows and marked their souls with the indelible character of Catholicity. Clearly, an air of the bizarre caught us up and held us fast. St. Francis Xavier had been dead four hundred years.

On the day the relic was to arrive, the principal brought the monsignor into our seventh-grade class to finalize for us the importance of the event. Side by side Sister Purissima and Monsignor Farrell looked alike—even talked alike—modified New England from the left side of the jaw. They were San Francisco Irish. And they were both tall and distinguished, trim black with white accents and ammonia-rinsed rimless glasses. Monsignor wore a cloak over his cassock and held its edges at his thighs with long, easily bent fingers. He was outlined in crimson piping like some character who'd stepped out of Prince Valiant in the Sunday supplement. When he moved he did so deliberately, and his cloak swayed above his shining heels, the crimson piping frank as neon against the black gaberdine. He knew when to pause, the monsignor did, and he would look down at the oiled floor and pace off his thoughts before beginning to speak again. He wore a stark black crucifix strung about his neck so that the gold corpus hit him mid-chest and the bottom tip tucked inside the cincture snug about his waist. When he began to speak again, his right knuckles went white at the base of the corpus while his left hand clung to the fabric draped from his squared shoulders. Lowering his jaw to raise his voice, he spoke ... and he could be heard anywhere he wanted to be heard ... even if he whispered. His voice caressed the Spanish-Basque saint as though he were an old friend and gave him a bearded presence there in the room with us. When Monsignor's hand thrust suddenly toward our second-floor windows, our attention went with it to the Pacific and the bay that trickled in and out of its Alviso bladder.

"'Go!' St. Francis was told by his friend St. Ignatius, 'and set all on fire!' St. Ignatius meant the Orient, boys and girls, and the fire of which he spoke was the love of God, for he knew how deeply it burned ... *burned* in Francis Xavier."

Both his hands raised above our heads slowly, till our necks strained with the tilt, and he articulated the exotic names: "Goa, India; Travancore; Ceylon; Malacia; ... Japan. He'd brought the word of God to five pagan countries, but was that enough? Not for Francis Xavier. No ..."

There was that pause as Monsignor looked at the floor and, cloak caught in fingers, he paced. ... and paced ... then stopped abruptly and, turning toward us, whispered, "Do you know how he died, boys and girls? Do you know?"

Sister Purissima's eyes blinked at Sister Agatha Julie, our seventh-grade teacher, muted against the blackboard. Monsignor's voice had the timbre of seasoned wood and left no echo. "He died on Sancian Island, four hundred years ago, waiting for permission to enter China ... still *burning* with zeal for Christ's mission."

Salvatore Barbino yawned.

Both of the monsignor's hands disappeared in his cloak, and again he looked down. One shoe drifted sideways then back, as if shifting gears, and his mood seemed to lighten.

"In the mass on December 3, celebrating the Feast of St. Francis Xavier, we read from the one hundred and eighteenth psalm, boys and girls, verses 46 and 47. Now, a psalm, you understand, is a song ..."

Sister Agatha Julie's wimple whisked against her veil as she nodded to reinforce the fact that she'd taught us as much. She hastened a glance at the principal.

"... and the song used for St. Francis goes like this ..." Monsignor cleared his throat, raised his jaw, and the corpus dipped forward on his chest. "'I spoke of your testimonies before kings ...'"

Gino Cattansara's shoulders bounced as the resonant chant filled the room, and his mouth sputtered like a deflating balloon. The principal's veiled hood jerked slightly but efficient as cobra puncture. Sister Agatha Julie shrank into the diagrammed sentences chalked behind her.

"... and I was not ashamed. I meditated on your commandments, which I loved dearly.'"

Without organ accompaniment, the rounded tones searched for places to go. Like everything else about him, Monsignor's voice was magnetic, but in that classroom context, it was as undeniably stark as if he'd walked into our midst naked. Gino's chin quivered on interlocked fingers, still in the grip of Sister Purissima's visual jaws. His distress coursed along his arm against the desk and dribbled anonymously from his elbow to his gray cords. In the vestibule of his left nostril, a bubble swelled, receded, swelled again and popped.

Monsignor's pause let the words find niches, and then he carved them into place. "There is a lesson for all of us in those words, boys and girls. St. Francis spoke the truth about Christ wherever he went—in India, in Travancore, in Ceylon, in Malacia, in Japan. And he went to the leaders, to the kings of those countries, as well as to the people themselves because he knew that if the kings believed, the people would follow... and he was not ashamed to spread the teachings of our Lord just as you and I must not be ashamed. Rather be *proud*! We who have the truth must be proud of the truth and share it with as many souls as we can. That's part of our mission, you know, ... each one of us ... spreading Christ's word." The left side of his jaw smiled, his head raised toward the ceiling and suddenly he was back on Sancian. "But in 1552 God said, 'Enough! Well done, thou good and faithful servant. Come home where I have prepared for you one of heaven's many mansions.'"

There were many mansions on Seventeenth Street across from the park on Coyote Creek. Kathleen and I skated the twelve blocks down to them to sell Christmas seals every year, so I could picture many mansions easily enough. It was the four-hundred-year part that was hard to get in touch with. I mean, in school the nuns talked to us about Jesus, Mary, and Joseph all the time, and they lived two thousand years ago ... but we didn't have parts of them attending our novena to the Lady of Lourdes.

One woody snip from Sister Agatha Julie's signal brought us to our collective feet as the principal and the monsignor bade us south-jawed farewells and exited the room. "Good afterNOON, Monsignor Farrell," we said in precise time with Sister Agatha Julie's exaggerated lips. "Good afterNOON, Sister Purissima." As the door shut, it was not so much Sister's signal as her beatific, wimpled expression that sent us squirming into our seats again. It was a look that meant she was susceptible to sidetracking.

Both of her hands grasped her polished signal in a kind of parade rest as Sister Agatha Julie said, "That visit was a perfect example of Actual Grace, boys and girls. Can anyone tell us why?"

Having misjudged the undercurrent of exuberance among us, Sister sensed that whatever had us keyed was waning with the strain of her question. The realization that a visit from Monsignor was hardly parallel to one from the Holy Ghost edged her features with a more factual cast. There was a glint of tears in the recess of her hood and, ever so briefly, she bit her lip. With her next breath she smiled, however, and said, "Well, then, I will tell you. Monsignor's visit was like Actual Grace because it came when we least expected it and helps us choose the right thing to do. I'm sure, after hearing what Monsignor told us about St. Francis, that all of us will come to the novena tonight to receive the blessing of that holy hand. Of course," Sister paused deliberately, "it was also an example of how some of us can reject grace, ... wasn't it, Gino?"

Gino gave a mucousy sob.

Beverly Ann's hand began to flop in the air like a frantic pigeon. "S'ter! ... S'ter! ..." she pleaded, and her braids fidgeted about her squat neck.

"Yes, Beverly Ann, what is it, dear?"

Beverly Ann gripped the corners of her desk and wiggled back to her feet. Tugging the navy blue pleats caught in her behind she said, "Sister, if that hand is four censhries old, what's it really look like, anyways?" Her shoulders hunched about her ears, forcing her tongue from her mouth, and she resumed her seat, one exposed thigh squeaking against the wood. "I'm going to close my eyes when it blesses me," she summarized.

The rustle of necks against collars gave proof that Beverly Ann's was not an isolated concern. Sister Agatha Julie frowned and sent her signal into action. "CHILDren! CHILDren! ... I'm surprised! Why, God can do anything. Surely, if He made this whole world, He can keep one little hand fresh for four cen-tu-ries."

"Okay, Sister, but how come they hacked it off?" Salvatore Barbino asked.

"Ew-w-w! ... Don't say that!" Beverly Ann cringed.

Immediately, Salvatore grabbed his right elbow in his left hand and bent his right fingers into a claw. Beverly Ann led several girls in a shriek, and Sister Agatha Julie's thumb went white with its rapid-fire pace on the signal. "That's enough!" she shouted, and this time the tears had invaded her voice. Turn to page forty-two in your Catechisms. That's Lesson Eighteen on Sanctifying and Actual Grace ... Certainly an appropriate lesson for this class!"

"But how come they hacked it off?"

"I said, turn to Sanctifying Grace!"

My faith was unused to wavering. It was a sin to doubt. I was a believer in miracles. The crutches and canes flanking the statue of Bernadette Soubirous in Sacred Heart's shrine to the Virgin were as genuinely castoffs of the cured as if San José had been the Pyrenees town of Lourdes itself. I was convinced of it. But I had seen human flesh that was hundreds of years old before, and it was a most unholy sight. Fear, however, took charge of doubt and would not let me call it that name.

My parents had taken Allen, Kathleen and me to the Rosicrucian Museum on Park and Naglee to view what were basically Egyptian artifacts. Catholics couldn't be Rosicrucians because Rosicrux was a religious society that, according to my grandmother, had gotten its real boost during Prohibition. All of its male members, at least, shared some degree of priesthood that allowed them to take wine. The Rosicrucian priesthood was not, of course, celibate, which must explain why there was no corresponding run on the Catholic priesthood of the same period. Catholics could, however, visit the museum for its historical value, for which it had no parallel, certainly, in the South Bay.

Despite my faith, I feared death, even then, and closed my eyes in passing the glass-encased mummies shrouded with eons. I felt, instinctually, that those remains had best been left in sand-driven graves or pyramidal vaults. The sleep of death, after all, was guaranteed undisturbed until Final Judgment. It was serious business we were about, walking among rumored curses and the contents of unsealed crypts.

"You can open your eyes now, wimp!" Allen said as our footfalls echoed in the corridor connecting exhibitions.

"Scaredy cat!" Kathleen taunted. "Those mummies didn't even scare me! They were dumb!"

"Ps-s-st!" my father hissed, turning from my mother's side. "Do you want these people to think you do nothing but fight?"

"We don't," Allen replied.

"Dammits! I said, stop it!" my father glared.

"Well, he makes me sick. Scared of dead mum..."

The cold ceiling recorded the flat of my father's palm against Allen's Hawaiian-print shoulder. Rubbing the stung flesh, Allen regrouped. "That, my friends, is the sound of one hand clapping."

My mother tittered through her fingers. Even my father's displeasure wavered.

"One hand can't clap," I pronounced as we entered another chamber. "Dad just proved it."

"Tch! ... And anyway all mummies are ..."

Kathleen stopped. Her eyes went wide and she gasped, "Oh, God! ... Don't look behind you, Ronald!"

I did, of course, as she knew I would. I spun about to find myself staring straight into the empty sockets of two heads the size of Kathleen's discarded dolls. The skin, shriveled and taut on the facial bones, was mould green, and the mouths were sewn shut with bold criss-cross stitches. Black hair hung in uneven wisps from the crowns of the heads, and skin wedged about those sightless cavities in an endless anguish.

My father's voice read, the remnants of his mother tongue a mild clutter in his speech, "... a religious rite of retribution amongst warring tribes and the mouts sewn shut to prevent uttering a curse against dere enemies."

When we grow older, we learn to shrug as we mutter, "Man's inhumanity to man ..." and we stop there as if a gilded phrase can condone the acts that give it rise. It took longer for me to discover that what Burns actually wrote was a lament:

"Man's inhumanity to man
Makes countless thousands mourn."

And I mourned. All at once and intolerably. Those heads were poetry gone graphic, religion become satanic, and I gagged with the awful despair of those stitched lips and gouged eyes. My stomach summarily heaved into my chest, and I threw up on Allen's high-top Keds.

A woman wearing a name tag and glasses with tortoise-shell rims on a chain fluttered among the displays, calling over her shoulder for a custodian and paper towels. When she saw that my mother could not turn my head from the shrunken pair in the case, she intruded herself between me and them. Sobs ran a loose gamut in my body. Terror seized my mind like talons. Kathleen's morbid attention was divided between me and the heads as if she were sizing me for a similar fit under glass, but pale streaks lay at the corners of even her mouth. Allen, cursing me in the direction of his soiled shoes, scrubbed them with paper towels, then turned and stalked toward the exit and air.

"Let's take him into the planetarium," said the lady with the tortoise-shell rims, and her gentle hands nudged me toward tall brass-handled doors that opened soundlessly on darkness. My heels scraped on the hardwood.

"You'll like this, Ronald, dear. Hush now. This is going to be so pretty," my mother consoled.

The light vanished in an arc as my father's strong hands lifted me under the arms and the doors shut noiselessly behind us. "Look up," my father coaxed close to my ear.

"But ..."

"Shut up and look up, Ronald!" Kathleen snapped. "Crimany sakes!"

"Ps-s-st!"

In the fresh darkness the woman with the tortoise-shell rims had a velvet voice. "Watch now ... Sh-h-h ... Keep looking up and you'll see the stars come out. Have you ever seen the stars in daytime ... What's his name? Ronald? ... Ronald? We can see them whenever we want, right here in this room. Watch now ..."

And she was right. A faint flickering bloomed into a full galaxy above and around us as we watched, cooling my terror like a compress against my skin. The soft husk of her voice directed me through the Milky Way while the placenta of fear hung on the doubt birthed in my mind, muffling its cry. It was a sin to doubt ... but ... where was God when those lips were sewn shut, the eyes gouged out and the heads cut off?

A pendulum, glowing gold, adrift with Greenwich-mean accuracy, bribed us finally from that celestial interlude. We stood in the foyer of the planetarium, measuring the steady, silent traverse. I pressed close to my mother at the circular railing and felt the glow of that golden sphere on my own skin and the beat of my own pulse slow, finally, to the pendulum's pace.

Xavier's hand was not preserved, not, at any rate, well. I looked at it straight on as Monsignor moved to me in the line of kneeling venerators, and I held fast to the communion rail. It was as dark and shriveled as the membrane of dried peppers, ugly in its glass-and-gold reliquary. It was not shock I experienced then, for the mummies and shrunken heads had initiated me to the bizarre but sinking confusion that the taint of savagery had infused the trappings of my own faith, and there seemed no answer to Salvatore Barbino's question: "How come they hacked it off?"

I would learn, of course, that fire and the sword rivaled the waters of baptism in the trinity of techniques for spreading the word of God. Kings used them as inducements for those reluctant to follow. Death and dismemberment are not novelties in the cause of salvation; neither are they always overt.

Years later, at my own wedding, I would enter the sacristy of St. Thomas the Apostle to find Monsignor Farrel preparing to enter the sanctuary as guest clergy. Friend to my fiancée's family, he shook my hand and smiled from the left side of his jaw. Time had diminished none of his distinction and none of his charm—rather it had been enhancing. He, of course, had no recollection whatever of the child he'd edified long ago in that South Bay outpost of the archdiocese but was pleased, as we chatted, to be reminded of his days on the mission band and those San José sojourns. One of those individuals whom age cannot shrink, he bore himself still with the assurance that security breeds. The Church had been good to him and he to her. Pastor of an affluent parish he had single-handedly raised like Lazarus from debt, he stood in that vestibule of varnished cabinets and stained-glass light, a resplendent figure, his surplice a cascade of lace over the monsignorial plumage of crimson taffeta. His hair had gone gray and his lenses thick, but his aura went undiminished.

Emotion fleshed the recollection of Xavier's hand for me as Monsignor's vigorous grip shook my own, but I dared not mention it. Just beyond that sacred hand in my mind moved the memory of two other relics religion had spawned, and the attending omens were too heavy for so joyous a day. Then, too, time had, I anxiously believed, changed me.

Having recognized the fear at the basis of my faith, I had transferred my allegiance, by then, from God to a woman, second among ordered priorities for those of us with indelible marks, professing a truth that was still not my own. The real me I'd exiled to an inner Elba, vanquished, I thought, and overcome.

I had, in fact, traded religious fantasy for a fantasy of science, believing the psychotherapeutic theorem of the sixties that if a homosexual had desire sufficient for change, his chances of going straight through therapy were 50-50. Continuing attractions to men I attributed to statistical data then-current that it is normal for normal persons to experience occasional same-sex attractions. The real me continued to do time in the purgatory of my own spirit.

"I am what I am," I inscribed my bride's silver goblet, "even to the haunt of past echoes ... All that I am loves you."

But all that I am I kept hidden from her, and the haunt of past echoes would not be still. I loved her as fully as I could while denying the self I could not let her know. The real me was a shrunken head with stitched lips, a sightless self, a shriveled member in the reliquary of my soul.

Monsignor's vestments whispered, as he moved, among themselves, reciting the Litany of Western Civilization with tongues that articulated power, wealth and the jurisdiction of matters moral. If truth be known, of course, a sizeable segment of my early devotion in those Sacred Heart novenas went not to God at all, but to the stunning mortal instrument who served as liaison between Him and me—Monsignor Farrell.

Nowhere in the fabric of that litany was there mention of the me sewn securely out of sight ... not even a lisp. Homosexuality suffered the ban of contra naturam. The me within was a nontopic, a judgement foregone.

Forty years dismembered from the core of my self. Four decades of denial and deceit, the threat of hell stitched like bold strides up and down my lips by the ministers of a loving God. And I'd let them.

Don't trust the priest, it's the poet who's whole:

> This above all: to thine own self be true,
> And it must follow, as night the day
> Thou canst not then be false to any man.*

I have stopped hiding, my soul, from my truth. I have shattered the reliquary and set free the embrace of my exile, made whole the self I should always have been and it is warm ... exceeding warm.

*William Shakespeare
Hamlet, Act 1, Scene 3, Line 69

CHAPTER 14

AUGUST HAS NO HOLIDAYS

It's true, of course. August has no holidays. Eighth on the roster of Gregorian calendar months, the name derives from Latin and means sacred, venerable, majestic. So how come it has no holidays? August is to summer what Sunday is to weekends, and maybe that's the problem—the finality of it—the closing down and then the gearing. Commitments. Deadlines. August can't be enjoyed any more than Sunday, without reservation, I mean. August has that "it-won't-wait-for-you" feeling as you resent the five-and-dime stocking its forward shelves with back-to-school supplies when all you've come in for is reduced Coppertone and half-off sunglasses, and you mutter under your breath, "Jesus, couldn't they wait till September 1st?"

But they never do. Reams of binder paper, stacks of Pee Chees, Magic Markers, pencils and protractors are the hot items the sun lotion and shades sucked you in for. It's just plain devious. Get enough Augusts behind you and you know what to expect, though. Then even the season seems to go along. The sun begins to pale. Oh, it heats up plenty in August, but the slant of the sun is different and its color sapped.

August has a holyday but that's no holiday, not by a long shot. In fact, the rest of the holyday phrase says it all—of obligation. A holyday of obligation means you've got to drop everything and go to mass or go the mortal sin route. There are thorns in the side and pains in the ass, and the Feast of the Assumption, for my family, invariably turned into the latter. See, we tried to rig August, taking our vacations then, creating our own holidays, bleeding summer into September even by extending a week after school took up. It p.o.ed the nuns, but the Jesuits flat wouldn't let us.

Being away on August 15 meant we had to advance-check churches and mass schedules or arrange a dispensation before we left. Mary's timing on the Assumption was singularly off.

Boulder Creek had a mass all right—at 11:15—so it cut right into whatever you wanted to do. Evans' Rest, our resort on the creek, served as my family's transition from Santa Cruz proper to eventual Sierra campsites. Not that Evans' Rest was a campground; it wasn't. But it was rustic and wooded—dark cabins that listened to water spill over boulders to a wide spot with unplumbed depth. Blue-tiled Forest Pool was a two-mile drive and always crowded. Most times we waded the moss-slick brook catching up with the creek and spread our towels on the coarse slope that gave you a run at the swimming hole.

The Evanses were an English couple who timed-out from grounds chores to chat with guests on yard stones. It was a time when accents weren't common in California, so you noticed theirs.

Allen could imitate their clip so's you wouldn't know he was ours if you were another guest. He was also the age when guys begin body hair and when being hung takes on importance. He was doing diving-board pull-ups for some girls on the beach one day when his Bellarmine ring hooked a nail and nearly ripped his finger off when he let go. God, he passed out when he saw what hurt so bad and had to be rushed to emergency. Emergency fixed his finger, so now it's just kind of a famous memory when you talk about old times.

That old swimming hole's where I learned to float, looking up the leg of a guy's trunks as he sunned himself with no jock strap and wobbled a foot that jostled his balls in the shadowy arch. I was so cold I was blue by the time he crossed his legs, but I couldn't get out of the water for another seven minutes.

All kinds of guys looked like him that August—like the one in Levis, tee shirt and loafers who kicked sand on us chasing whoever called his girl a name. The name caller belly-flopped, thrashed to the really green part, spat water and yelled, "Fuck you! She is a slut!"

That did it, of course. The gallant hauled off his tee shirt, kicked off his loafers and stripped off his Levis. My father was off the beach blanket by then, yelling, "What's the matter with you? Can't you see there's women on this beach?" My mother, shielding her eyes from the sun, said, "Hush, now, Axel. Don't you get into it, please."

The youth scowled magnificently ... with his whole body ... fists readied at his jockey-short thighs, genitals nested in a pouch well enough worn to dangle and show. I would think of him later, reading of Caesar Augustus, and remember how proud defiance made you look, and I realized that that was a majesty too that made a body august.

His aggrieved girlfriend talked him down from provoking my father, striding barefoot toward his nearly naked, though hardly less modest than most of us, body. He pulled on his pants finally, not bothering to turn as he buttoned them, slung his shirt on his shoulder and hooked one finger in each heel of his shoes. With his free hand he jammed his finger at the villain treading water then left the beach hugging his girl against him.

That incident aside, the Evans' Rest taste of the woods whetted my father's appetite for hardcore forest, and Triple A drew up next year's triptik to the Sierras.

Housekeeping tents initiated us to Yosemite during an electrical storm that turned midnight into noontime and thunder like a cannonade that rattled the bed frames. It was terrifying with an odor like primal soot. But the morning was pristine as if the earth had just been pitched from the hand of God—a freshness authentic enough to smell even through damp canvas. My father stepped out on the sun-stricken pine needles, and his conversion was complete.

The following August, we towed a two-wheeler into Awahnee Valley packed with tents, propane stoves, Coleman lamps and cots ... something of everything Mel Cotton's had to offer. My father, I think, felt a little like a feudal lord, encompassing in canvas his own little fief. Rising at dawn, he fanned each night's embers into next morning's flame then dropped on proper logs. Brewed coffee was the antecedent to his call as he shredded potatoes to complement Spam and eggs and pancakes. Breakfast, he believed, was the day's most important meal.

Waking there was a steeper transition than at home ... the plunge of cataracts, unwatched yet relentless under the pierced sky, powering the pace in my own veins like wet dreams pushed from the psyche's precipice, coagulating on my belly; subterranean forces that gave passion its impetus for domed monoliths on which another sun crested.

Sound was sharper, the contained fire licking unconstrained at the limitless air. I'd heard wind in palms all my life on Fifth Street, but wind in the forest meant hearing the earth inhale. The word august took on vaster dimension in that waking. It was impossible to stir in those granite environs and not sense the dominion of elements over us. My thighs ached with Eden ascents, a mist trail eking the margin of power in ageless springs and, even supine in reflection, my head reeled with a sparrow's swoop into the vaginal abyss where eons of ice had lodged like a phallus, my hands fastened to railing sunk in the eroded labium 3,000 feet high.

I knew then, even as the bite of matted pubic hairs defined my moving, that august means a place where you wonder whether you can possibly matter and where your fingers go white with wanting to; that august means you can't be an atheist, but you might be agnostic because behind it all you want someone who cares.

My father's campfires were the wheres to wonder, places to process. They rewarded us for dressing in skin-stung chill before the sun recalls that Tenaya Canyon has a floor. They tamed thoughts out of privacy the way marshmallows toast on whittled sticks. He poured steaming Hills Brothers into cups you had to wait to drink from, so I mulled great thoughts begun in my sleep or examined fragments of last year's learning—Was it Thales who said you can't put your foot in the same stream twice? I'd remembered that just yards away in a tributary of the Merced, my own foot shimmering with the flux of Grecian truth, and had been humbled by the itsy-bitsiness of my being compared at least to the riverbed where infinite approximations of a stream had flowed. And I wondered how august could ever apply to a person—even a caesar like the kid in worn jockey shorts. And it occurred to me that we seek ourselves in beauty, in majesty, in grandeur and that we want very much to dazzle the world with our living ... if only for a bit.

And that was the rub, the "What does it profit a man...?" bit. Ambition conflicted with virtue. The message among the Jesuits had been the same as among the nuns: subdue and submit. "Lord, make me an instrument ..." Dazzle you earned in the hereafter crown by putting aside yourself in the now. In the August that breached my exit from Bellarmine and entrance to the novitiate, I struggled endlessly with the enigma of my own being. Seated on an upended log at those final family campfires, I turned my lurking difference into desperate vows of celibacy, repeating my commitment to be a priest as orgasm after orgasm addicted me further to my sexuality.

Expectation did not fit. Dating I'd endured because the sophomore hop, junior prom and senior ball were events in a young man's life. You were expected to go. That I needed no external restraints in matters of intimacy was attributed to my latent vocation. I nearly ruined Allen's reputation and Kathleen's standing at St. Pat's youth club, however, where the popular priest-proctor roamed the dance floor, flashlight in hand, whistle in mouth, reminding the lax and the lapsed of their duty. With my hand stamped, I sought dark-walled obscurity, hoping to avoid girls whose loyalty to my brother and sister prompted them to dance with me. One of these, doing duty for Allen, earned a "poor fish" from a co-ed wrapped in jock's arms one night, and I excused myself to the lav as soon as the music stopped.

I walked in on a junior named Gabe sprawled on a commode in an open stall, his pants collected at his shins, his shirt hiked to his belly. His reach to slam the door said he was drunk. Brief as it was, my glimpse memorized the flat of his navel and the furred drape of genitals I'd only seen bunched in his denims as he mounted the #10 line at First and Santa Clara for the remainder of my commute to Bellarmine. Gabe was the first consenting partner to male-male sex that I'd ever seen, and it happened in the guise of a game in Jug one afternoon. Jug was the Jesuits' after-school detention and happened, usually, in perfect silence for a solid hour under the eye of a dour-faced prefect. On the day of the sex play, the prefect had fallen ill at the last so that the vice-principal crowded us into the foyer beside his office for modified supervision. Gabe, again, managed a sprawl with one leg bent locust fashion on the bench, the other buttressed against the floor. His crotch bragged beneath his fly so that even the most deft at pretense could not ignore the fact of it. Ironically, I'd done nothing to warrant Jug but be where the culprits were.

Mass punishment was rife among the Jesuits, the ethic seeming to be that everyone would be taught a lesson, or that the innocent would make the guilty pay later, or that the guilty would feel guilty enough not to make the innocent suffer again. It never worked. What did work was the temptation I'd been imprisoned with. The kid beside Gabe was a pasty-faced son of a judge who grinned candidly at Gabe's endowments, reached out and snatched a grab. Venal chuckles from the truly guilty encouraged the sport, Gabe's raised thigh crashing down to protect his prize which all the while increased in size and definition. What might have happened the vice-principal spoiled, emerging from his office with racket enough to warn us and snarling, "What's going on out here anyway? Keep it up and your time is doubled." They didn't, regrettably.

Anyway, getting a glimpse of Gabe exposed made up for the sting of an indirect slur.

One or the other of two close friends occasionally accompanied me to St. Pat's. Both I'd met at Bellarmine, and both also intended to be priests. Daniel's excessive desire in that regard gave the whole bumping-bodies youth-club scene a futile silliness. "Why bother?" he would reply finally to those invitations. His flamboyant levity endeared him to us but persuaded us he would never survive in religious life. When the mood struck him, Daniel "blessed" whatever lay in his path—roses, dogs, parking meters—and always a benediction in triplicate, an episcopal see being his long-range goal. While he never acquired the crosier and ring, he seemed to thrive in religious life till decades later he left and married.

Ken, on the other hand, was the pragmatic opposite of me and played devil's advocate whenever the opportunity arose. Often I was thoroughly worked up over a position he'd taken before realizing he didn't believe it at all. He had a sharp, quick intelligence that honed itself on argument. To everyone's surprise, the Society of Jesus asked Ken to reapply in a year ... a thing he refused to do. The Jesuits lost a man with a mind in him.

We ate together, sack lunches on the lawn at the feet of the Fatima phallus, discussing the world, the Jesuits and God. Platonic love raised itself from classroom issue to personal consciousness in those noon sun sessions in which we tested what bound us together. That there had been physical dimension to Plato's loving we neither allowed nor alluded to, agreeing only that men could love one another for their minds and personalities, and affirming that it was so with us. We felt quite advanced ... a little dangerous even.

The hop, the prom and the ball we got through together because they were there to be done that with. They were milestones of the cultured class, earmarks of sophistication. They were rites in becoming a man—a taste of tuxedo and corsage, bands and rhythm, grand ballrooms and costly dining. If the shield of avowed vocation explained my lack of sexual aggressiveness prior to the seminary, it worked less well afterwards. I could see girls question behind their compliments exactly why I was such a gentleman. One of my former Bellarmine teachers tapped the truth in a Boardwalk restroom about that time during Santa Cruz's off-season. I'd bought a bathing suit that laced up the exposed thighs and couldn't get it to fit, I was that excited. He'd come in barefoot so I didn't even know he was there till he cleared his throat and I looked up startled from the open door of my stall and there he was ... no Roman collar, no anything but his pulled down bathing suit ... angled away from the urinal, watching me.

But nothing equaled Yosemite restrooms. I'd discovered that on that final family vacation taken early in August because of the novitiate's entry date. Curry Company quartered its employees in housekeeping tents between our campground and the lodge at the base of Glacier Point. Every evening Camp Curry staged live entertainment climaxed by a fall of embered bark shoved from the precipice 3,000 feet overhead. A fragile rendering of the Indian Love Call cut the dark below with the first gash of sparks above, then caught the audience in a collective gasp at nature upstaged. A great bonfire returned light to the valley floor as sing-along sorts huddled onto benches and worked the kinks from their necks. Sing-alongs, like county fairs, depress me, and I still don't know why. I checked out of the program often at that point and went back to our campsite to light the fire my father had readied for the end of our day.

Short-cutting through the employees' camp that last night of our stay, I realized that distinct shifts of energetic collegians staffed Curry Company's facilities. I'd seen many of them basting on the banks of the Merced by day; watched as they intermittently dove into the crystal depths to refresh themselves, then return, as if they didn't know their clinging suits showed everything, to their towels and let the sun coax more of their beauty to the surface. My father asked one of them who bussed our table the time we ate out, "What do you kids do for entertainment at night?"

The fellow, who looked good even in his uniform, flashed a grin. "Oh, we make do," he said, and my father chuckled.

Lights here and there, as I walked, caused the little canvas houses to glow, and the flaps, tied back for ventilation, gave me a passing view from the dark till one blond fellow in jockey shorts confirmed me as a peeping tom. I took no time to think. My body knew what to do. I dropped to a kneel, reflexive as a genuflection, attending to a shoe that needed no lacing in the event anyone watched my watching. The off-shift collegian examined his even features, checked his smile in a mirror mounted on an old bureau. Pressing his fingertips against his chest, he withdrew them quickly to test his tan. Yanking a towel from the bureau, he tucked it about his waist, grabbed a shaving kit and stepped thonged into the night. I held my breath. If he noticed me in the dark, he gave no indication. His white towel was simple to follow. Besides, he whistled as he walked.

At the door of the lavatory, I heard his voice acknowledge another as he entered and I plunged, past caring, in after my need. The callow banter continued as I glanced toward the sinks where another finely built collegian cut swaths in the cream coating his jaw, naked but for one towel-draped shoulder. The object of my pursuit stationed his gear on a bench by the showers and balancing on one leg, then the other, stripped off his shorts. Seeing no feet beneath the stall doors, I yanked open the one I hoped had a view. My breath, as I latched the slender panel and checked the settled jamb, competed with running water and resonant echoes. My entire body, as I squinted to that vertical peek, felt whittled by this last night's vagary ... this shortcut with such a bountiful yield ... and my throat swelled with luck cursed. Tomorrow we returned to San José.

I tore at my belt and zipper, struggling to muffle my already peaked condition. Pants shoved to my ankles, I fisted my phallus and sweated at the narrow portal for a glimpse of flesh. Definition, like a quadrisyllabic migraine, battered my conscience. Aunt Millie's American Pocket Medical Dictionary had been succinct: masturbation—self-pollution. I watched the pre-coital fluid seep from the mouth of my swollen phallus and thought of the dominion of elements over us and remembered that, God, I was a week away from entering the seminary. Desperation shoved another cry after the curse still blocked by my tongue. Even as I strained at the crack in the jamb for slivered glimpses, I denied that theirs was the shape of desire for me; that what shoved itself straight up through my innards like a giant erection poking my conscience was need defined by toned muscle and tight ass moving at the sink ... Jesus, within reach ... and I raped my cubicled quiet with my lie: "I ... don't ... need ... this!"

But the shaver asked, "Wanta climb up a nice tight butt?" as he rinsed his Gillette in the basin and I went over the brink. My fingers squeezed against delirium's exit, and I scarcely heard the answer.

"No, thanks," said the fellow I'd followed.

Projectiles of sperm leapt from my penis, striking the door, dribbling down names and numbers scrawled beside skills and needs and sizes.

"You'll never go after any more pussy," the shaver persisted, but the shower turned on leaving the argument moot.

The cleansing sweep of aftermath had no time to endure. Guilt was an undertow that never let it surface. My throbbing organ remained hard as I tugged crisp sheets from the tissue dispenser. Tomorrow I must pedal early to the nondenominational church where the priest with the brogue heard confessions on just a chair with you at his side in the light, making his mass late.

With the toilet flushed, I popped the latch on the stall door, positioned my hand in my pocket and bolted out. Against my will I glanced at the guy with the offer, his penis curled on the porcelain as he dabbed a nick on his chin. I hurried on out lest his generosity extend to me.

I was disoriented in the dark. The precise sprawl of stars supported by pines confused me with its beauty and the fact of God, and I stumbled past the tents into what I hoped was the direction of our campground. I tripped on roots and then what I thought were roots till a thickened, "Jesus Christ!" startled me in the undergrowth, and I went down, forest loam cushioning my fall, ferns scratching my face. A feminine titter robbed the first voice of anger, turned it to belly laugh and suddenly there were voices all around me—on the ground, against the trunks, among the ferns. Cigarette tips glowed like fireflies, and my still-pocketed hand worked my erection crazily. Stupidly, blindly, I crashed on through the woods toward lights in the distance, sweating, panting on reaching, finally, our canvas encampment. My lips quivered, the Sierra night like blades in my throat as I untied the tent flap, lunged in and roughed out a second orgasm, eyes stitched shut, hunched on the edge of my cot over seed spilling in my pants, begging God for an end to this need. The sound of my own sobbing made me still. Kicking off my shoes, I zipped myself dressed into my sleeping bag and listened, shivering, to my heart against the pillow. I wanted to sleep but my eyes wouldn't close, not till familiar voices threaded the dark:

"Where's Ronald? How come there's no fire?" and someone said, "Check the tent," and a flashlight felt my face and someone said, "He's asleep," and someone said, "Poor guy, it's been a hard day for him—last day of his last vacation with us," and someone said, "It's been a hard day for all of us," and started to cry. And I should have known who said all of those things but it was as if they were all said with the same voice, and I didn't, and finally I fell asleep.

I stood, a week later, under the Novices' Tree, a venerable oak, meditating on Santa Clara Valley from the Los Gatos slope that climbs from Sacred Heart Novitiate into the Santa Cruz Range. Young men, handsome as the pair in Curry Company's restroom, milled about, only these were clothed in cassocks and reversed Roman collars. Second-year men now, they were "angels" to us, the incoming postulants, and enthusiastically worked acquaintance toward trust. It was the eve of the Assumption. I would, on the eve of the Virgin's next feast, call my parents to come for me, though, on that August 14, I'd thought to be gone for good from the family and home I so loved. My eyes examined the close-shaven grins of this new all-male family, then drifted across the expanse of diminishing orchards and proliferating tract homes to the nest of lights that was San José, and I remembered that a week ago I had not lighted the logs for my family's return to camp...

A finger jarred my chest suddenly. I looked at Daniel, my friend, my connection with home, and heard his voice choked with happiness. "Stop looking so glum, Brother Schmidt," he said as easily as he'd ever called me Ron. "You're going to love it here!"

My sternum hurt with his repeated jabs till two second-year novices simultaneously intervened. "Rule 32, Brother!" they exclaimed to Daniel. "Rule 32!"

Daniel looked at me, admonished, both of us puzzled. "Rule 32?" he said, finally.

"Yes, we are not allowed to touch one another. That's Rule 32."

Daniel started to say, "That's stu...," then stopped, thinking better of it. Our eyes met briefly, and I looked back at the valley and Plato beside the phallic Fatima and the bare-butted proposition I'd wished had been mine—and I swallowed with the implication of Rule 32. Tomorrow would be a holyday of obligation—not a holiday—and I knew that all the days of my life must be thus.

CHAPTER 15

THE GUISE OF INNOCENCE

What I said to Jolayne was this: "Reed is a saint. I honestly believe that." I remember she looked at me across the garlic cloves and onion sliced on the cutting board, her fingers oblivious to the steaming coffee mug I'd just handed her, a quizzical smile on her Slavic features. She was a big girl, large boned. She had called to us from across the university pool a week earlier as we stood toweling ourselves, dove in and surfaced at our feet like a kind-faced seal in chlorine-thinned waves.

It was that afternoon with our sun-stung chests still expanded with the exertion of endurance laps that I watched Jolayne making too obvious a play for my best friend and roommate, Reed Pollock.

Seven days later, when she called, she made no bones about why she needed to talk to me. "I want to talk to you about Reed, Ron. See, I think I'm in love with him, but he doesn't pick up on any of my cues. I need to know how serious he is about Sharon ... or if there's anybody else?

"Last Saturday at Santa Clara's pool he mentioned that this was his National Guard weekend, and I just thought, if you're not busy ... Say, is your fiancée over?"

I smiled. "Felicia went home to Merced this weekend, Joly. She's trying to convince her folks that she should move into an off-campus apartment in Belmont. The good Sisters of Notre Dahm tend to cramp a girl's style."

Jolayne laughed. "I wondered when that would happen. Have you two set a date yet?"

"Not exactly. Probably a year from this summer. She'll have graduated; I'll have my credential and be marketable, so she can go on for her masters. Her folks sort of made that a contingency to consent."

"Hmmm ..."

"I know, but ..."

"Well, then, can I come over and talk?"

"Hey," I told her, "besides cramming for an ed psych final for the last three days, I've been creating a term paper masterpiece on English poets of the Contemporary Period and, lady, I'm ready for a break. Come ahead. You remember where we are?"

"Still on Bellomy?"

"Nine-thirty ... the white stucco with the bougainvillea growing up the side. The rear apartment. Park in the driveway. Shall I put on some coffee, or would you rather have beer?"

"Coffee. My new diet ... Just coffee."

"Great! I may even try out my term paper on you."

"On second thought..."

"All right, scratch the paper. How are you at meatloaf? It's my night to cook, and meatloaf is what my roommate's distinguished palate likes best."

"Palate my foot. That's what your undistinguished budget likes best."

"Jolayne, you leave a guy no dignity."

She laughed again. "Okay, about meatloaf I'm knowledgeable but no term papers, promise?"

"Promise."

"A saint?"

"Yeah, and I mean that, Joly. Go ahead and laugh, but I'm convinced of it."

She thumped a pack of Kools against the fatty base of her palm till a pair of white cylinders slid unevenly forward. She took one out, tapped one end against the oilcloth covered table and let it dangle between her parted lips. Her thumbnail spun the flint on her lighter, and her eyes narrowed as she leaned toward the flame breathing the tip into embers. Picking a tobacco shred from her tongue, she phased her blunt nails into an exhaled cloud and said, "That's a new one. Being turned on to a saint is a little threatening. But then maybe it's a matter of definition. What do you mean by a saint?"

I grinned as I peeled the butcher paper from the ground chuck and dropped the raw mass into the Pyrex dish. She couldn't get it. She didn't live with him. She didn't know him. No one did ... not the way I knew him. I diced the onion, sprinkled it into the beef and began mincing the garlic.

"Reed Pollock is the finest human being I've ever known, Joly. It's that simple." I felt the fervor rise in my chest and in the rims of my eyes. "He's the most genuinely good person anyone could hope to know—absolutely guileless. He's kind to a fault, sensitive to the needs of others, often to his own detriment."

Jolayne's hand waved to disperse the smoke. Her pageboy clip swung against her cheeks as her head shook. "Wait a sec..." she said. "You sure we're talking about the same blue-eyed blond hunk here?"

The garlic dulled the onion reek.

I nodded cautiously. "I guess that would be a fair assessment from a feminine viewpoint."

"The same Reed Pollock who can't keep his eyes ... and probably his hands ... off Sharon's black-sweatered boobs?"

"Hey, come on, Joly ..." my voice cracked, "that's not a fair assessment."

"Sorry! Sorry! But the Reed you're describing doesn't sound human."

"He's human all right, but when he stumbles he gets up and back to the sacraments. And that's what it's all about, isn't it?"

Jolayne arched her lips. "For some of us, I guess."

I shrugged. "We all make mistakes, but some of us wallow in them. Not Reed. He's a model for me, Joly, he really is. I've never wanted to be like ... to emulate anyone ... as I want to emulate him."

And that was true also. There had been Bro. Patroclus, a fellow novice at Sacred Heart Novitiate during my brief stint in religious life. He too had a spiritual aura that filled me simultaneously with a sense of devotion and my own unworthiness. I battled temptations against purity as much in those sacred environs as I had on the outside, but Bro. Patroclus seemed beyond temptation, whether silently vigiled in St. John Berchman's chapel or combing the vine-skewered hills above Los Gatos, his fingers probing blood-thickened leaves for vintage Black Muscats in September's novice harvest.

His eyes shone with a calm I'd never experienced, clear-blue innocence between wide-set ears that made him seem vulnerable. But his features were strong, the bones prominent, the skin taut and white as the sun on his ancestral Aegean. Kneeling in the presence of the Blessed Sacrament, his whole demeanor articulated control and vigorous self-discipline. To watch him thus was to view rapture in progress, his every motion compatible with the will of God. He had that in common with Reed Pollock ... but I had not been close to Bro. Patroclus as I was to Reed.

When I confided to the Master of Novices my struggle with impurity, he listened attentively, but when I detailed my admiration for Bro. Patroclus, his left eyebrow lifted. He leaned forward, his splendid fingers spread against the varnished desk, and said, "Bro. Schmidt, in the Offertory of the mass each day, the priest recites the Twenty-fifth Psalm as water is poured over his fingers, "Lavabo inter innocentes manus meas ..." Do you remember the English translation?"

I nodded. "Yes, Father Master: 'I wash my hands in innocence ...'"

Father Master inclined his head. "That's correct, Brother. 'I wash my hands in innocence.'" He shifted in his chair, leaned on the arms and interlocked his own arms across his black cassock. The imprint of his fingers on the varnish faded gradually like unsustained images from the Shroud of Turin.

"Let me ask you, Brother, exactly how severe was your problem with masturbation before entering Sacred Heart?"

I hesitated.

"How often, approximately, did you ... abuse yourself?"

I looked away from his direct gaze. The Roman collar constricted my breathing. My voice was barely audible. "Five or six times was usual, Father. Sometimes more."

"Please speak up, Bro. Schmidt. Five or six times, you say? Was that per week or per month?"

When I did not answer his other eyebrow raised as well. He cleared his throat. His voice came from a great distance. "For some reason, Brother, God, in His infinite wisdom, equips some of us with a stronger sexual drive than others. I have come to see such a need in a novice as a sign that a priestly vocation is not present ... Do you understand me, Brother?"

I listened in disbelief as he went on quoting, "'But I walk in integrity; redeem me, and have pity on me ...' That is also part of the Twenty-fifth Psalm. You see, Brother, most men attain salvation as laymen, in the secular life. I think it is God's will that your walk in integrity be on the outside."

I cracked a raw egg into the hamburger mix and began kneading the ingredients together. Sun spilled through the white-curtained window panes raising the late afternoon temperatures in that spacious old kitchen. Jolayne had begun to perspire. She studied a spiral of smoke as she rounded the tip of her cigarette against the Harrah's Club ashtray. Her moist brown eyes narrowed again.

"What're you telling me - 'when he stumbles'? You telling me he's making it with Sharon?"

Anger convulses, causes spasms. I know it does because I felt it right then—my whole chest squeezing tight—and it was clear to me that I didn't much like Jolayne. My cheeks smarted as if they'd been backhanded. I scraped red flecks from between my fingers, then rinsed and shook my hands over the sink. Picking up the garlic salt, I tried to smile.

"'Course not," I said. "I think I know Reed well enough to say that he would never go all the way with a girl he wasn't married to. I know I can say that."

"Hey, no offense. Look, Ron, when it comes to snug black sweaters, I've got it all over old tight-tits Sharon, so what is it? The red hair? Would it make a difference if I became a Clairol redhead? ... Uh-uh. Know what I think? I think she is putting out for him. Tell me he's committed to her spiritually, and I'll tell you you've been sheltered a lot."

Her eyes lost their predatory slant. "God, go easy on the garlic salt, will you?" That was her sole contribution to the meatloaf. She was a kind-faced seal again.

My smile stiffened. I shook my head remembering. Felicia had announced our engagement at Notre Dame just before spring break. In the traditional candle-passing ceremony at dinner in the Ralston mansion one evening, she watched the slow approach of the flame from hand to hand till at last it reached her and it took her three breaths to blow it out. We invited Reed and Sharon to drive up to Merced with us that weekend to celebrate with Felicia's family and show them the ring. Our plans included a day trip up to Yosemite and back to Merced, and it was one of those exquisite days whose exhaustion is inherent in its beauty—the awesome climb up the Vernal Falls mist trail lingering in our joints, the drive out of the park mellowed with Debbie Reynolds crooning "Moon River" on the radio of my old Chevy coupe.

But as dark fell, so did a deep silence in the back seat. Felicia's head rested against my shoulder, and we began getting knee-nudged through the seats. I looked in the rearview mirror. Reed and Sharon were really getting into it ... French kissing and stuff I couldn't see. The Jesuits had warned us about how easily a guy could lose control if a girl was willing, so I decided to help him out. I lowered the window. The Sierra chill fluttered into the car like winged actual grace but was summarily rejected.

"What the hell, Ron! ... Close that window!" Reed's voice was clotted.

"You haven't noticed how hot it's getting in here?" I said, but he didn't bother to listen. The knee-nudges had already resumed, and their reflections locked mouth-to-mouth again. When Felicia's breathing deepened and her head inched onto my chest, I switched off the radio, fumbled in my pocket for my beads and said, "Let's say the Rosary."

Well, it was like a good old ton of bricks wiped out the back seat. Reed and Sharon sat bolt upright as I began reciting the Apostle's Creed, and Felicia hung her head as she rummaged in her purse for her prayer beads. Participation was muted, grudging even, but at least it was participation. I knew that Reed would be grateful in time; in fact, he would have done the same for me had I let myself get that far.

"Why do I get the feeling you're not going to say anything else about my suspicions ... about Sharon and Reed, I mean?" Jolayne lit another Kool with the remnants of a predecessor, then snuffed the stub against the casino logo sealed in glass.

I shrugged. "Joly, I've already told you I know Reed wouldn't do what you're suggesting. As for long-range plans, if he and Sharon have any, he hasn't discussed them with me ... and I think he would if he had. Of course, if it were a confidence, I couldn't tell you anyway, huh?"

"Rat!"

"Come on. Reed's in control of his own destiny ... more so than most of us ... me, anyway. If you want to know, ask him." I molded the meat into an oblong shape.

Jolayne cocked her head, studied me with those narrowed eyes. "You got a crush on your roomie?"

"Not funny!" I said, my voice twisted.

"Sorry," she said immediately. "You do have rather a bad case of hero worship though, you know?"

I searched her eyes for a motive. Finally, I said, "I've learned from Reed, learned a lot. Leaving the novitiate set me off kilter, Joly. All I'd ever wanted to be was a priest, and I couldn't seem to gain my footing, my secular legs, so to speak. Reed taught me that, modeled for me how to stride with confidence in the world. Not a day goes by that he doesn't measure that stride with integrity. That's what's so special. He's a good man, Joly. And maybe you're right about the hero worship thing. So he isn't a saint ... yet. He's a genuinely good man, and that's just a step or two away."

"As long as he stumbles, there's hope for me. You've admitted he does that. But if it isn't Sharon who trips him up, who ... or what does? Want me to guess?"

"Hey, all you need to do is look at the scuffs on my own shoes to know that I'm not even remotely justified in discussing Reed's or anyone else's shortcomings."

"Are you overrating ... or just being too hard on yourself?"

"Being realistic. In fact, the subject of my own scuffed shoes is what led me to Francis Thompson's "Hound of Heaven" for my term paper. Ever read it?"

Jolayne exhaled a double jet of smoke through her nostrils and shook her head. "Ron, I'm into light romances—the kind you don't have to concentrate on. I can safely say I've never read the "Hound of Heaven" and I've never even heard of Francis Thompkins."

"Thompson," I corrected. "Too bad, he's great! It's great! And it is a romance but you can't help keeping your mind on it. It's an abstraction of spirit in flight. The chase between God and man with God in pursuit. Here, let me show you."

I wiped my hands on a towel and lifted my Baugh and McClelland tome of English literature from the end of the table where I'd been working when Jolayne called. I opened to page 1376 and a clip of jotted notes.

"You did promise you wouldn't do this ... Oh, God! It's one of those long buggers."

"Look, I'm letting you off easy. I won't make you read my paper. Just read the first verse of the poem. It's Thompson's spiritual autobiography ... but it's mine too, except that I'm a far cry from where he finishes. But Reed's not. Reed's there already."

I felt her eyes on me. "Do you suppose Reed has ever been where you are?"

"Here," I said, hoisting the volume. "I'll read it to you." She started to protest.

"Just listen:
'I fled Him, down the nights and down the days; I fled Him, down the arches of the years;
I fled Him, down the labyrinthine ways
Of my own mind; and in the mist of tears
I hid from Him, and under running laughter...'"

The exalted images inflated my senses. I glanced quickly at Jolayne, then went on reading:

"'Up vistaed hopes I sped;
And shot, precipitated,
       Adown Titanic glooms or chasméd fears,
From those strong Feet that followed, followed after. But with unhurrying chase,
An unperturbed pace,
Deliberate speed, majestic instancy,
They beat - and a Voice beat
More instant than the Feet -
'All things betray thee, who betrayest Me.'"

I closed the book. "Powerful, isn't it?"

She smoked, unimpressed.

"You must be on pretty good terms with yourself," I said, "not to be moved by it, I mean."

"Just stupid."

"Hardly that. Maybe that's what attracts you to Reed."

"I don't follow."

"Well, he doesn't really feel this poem either but then, as I say, he's already there—where the poem wants to get you."

"What makes you so sure you're not?"

"I hear the beat."

"What?"

"The beat. Of the Feet and of the Voice. You know the sound your heart makes when you lie with one ear pressed to the pillow? It's like that, a steady tramping like someone walking through leaves—only, a lot of the time I'm up and about when it comes to me. That's what it is, though. But, see, I keep running ... adown those Titanic glooms and chasmed fears ... Titanic glooms speak to the Irish in me."

"You're weird, you know that?"

I smiled. "You see then, were I to tell tales on Reed, I'd be a lesser man than I am."

I'd picked that phrase out of a recent conversation with Felicia's dad. He was on a business trip to San Francisco and dropped by the College of Notre Dame on his return to Merced. He called with an invitation to join them for dinner at the Lanai up the peninsula. "Bring Reed along too if he hasn't other plans," he added.

It was another of Reed's National Guard weekends, a full-dress occasion for a visiting I.G., and he came to dinner in uniform.

During a study break that afternoon, I crafted a lei out of the magenta blooms climbing the cracked stucco side of the house. I'd made a habit of bringing Felicia at least a single flower whenever I took her out and, though it crossed my mind that a lei was probably a bit carried away, I persuaded myself that the Lanai's Polynesian atmosphere warranted the excess. Besides, she liked my bringing her flowers. "It's one of the things that sets you apart from other fellows I've dated, Ron. You're not afraid to be gentle."

Felicia's dad, by the time we joined them, was on his second Kamehameha, one of those fruited rum drinks resembling a stagnant pond. Each of us took turns dancing with Felicia and, while she was on the floor with Reed, her dad kept watching the pair of them dance. Most guys in army issue look like most guys in army issue but not Reed. His uniform fit as if the Hedding Street armory were his personal tailor—trim O.D.s with gleaming lapel brass. Reed fit Felicia with equally impressive form, graciously close, his scrubbed Polish lineaments mellowed with rum. He was crushing my bougainvillea lei. My future father-in-law was braced against the woven wicker nimbus of his chair, poking in his pond with coral straws. Candle light muted his hair, softened his ambition.

"He makes one hell of a smart-looking soldier, your friend Reed. Clean face, broad shoulders, solid chest, trim waist and narrow hips. Damned if some men don't look good even in fatigues, know what I mean?"

I nodded uneasily.

He was a caring but tired man. He'd begun his own security business in his late forties and worked hard to make it go. The rum tempted his exhaustion. "Naw, your friend Reed's one of those men who has a natural grace, know what I mean, Ron? Not that spiritual B.S. ... Oh, dammit! I'm sorry. I know that stuff's important to you, your having been in the seminary and all."

"No, look, you don't have to ..."

"Well, I am apologizing. What I mean is an animal kind of grace. It's an ... an ease a man has for fitting into any kind of situation. Yeah, that's what it is, and Reed's got it. Makes the most of every situation and consequently enjoys life to the hilt. A lesser man ..." he looked at me across the pond, "couldn't do that. Self-consciousness gets in the way. Know what I mean?" He sucked half an inch of Kamehameha through the coral straws. His eyes fondled my fiancée in the arms of my best friend. "Yep, your buddy is totally unselfconscious. Know what I mean?"

I knew all too well. Envy of that very quality in Reed had plagued me with feelings of disloyalty more than once. But it was strangely awkward hearing it voiced by someone else—especially the father of the girl I was going to marry. I was keenly aware as I followed his eyes that they never shone when he looked at me. I think he honestly believed that Felicia and I would never truly happen to each other. In fact, he as much as said so in a scarcely audible appendix to his earlier remarks, "I was you, I'd watch him."

"What?" I said.

"Nothing," he muttered and went back to his straws.

The evening hadn't gone well from the moment we'd arrived at their table, and I raised the magenta chain toward Felicia's head. Felicia, who couldn't hold her liquor at all, asked, "Oh, Ron, are you going to lei me?"

The three of them laughed. I surrendered the effort to embarrassment and resolved never to repeat the error. Felicia was an attractive, self-confident young woman ... except when it came to me ...

I checked the stove clock as I turned on the gas oven. "I don't mean to rush you, Joly, but Reed will be home from the armory within thirty minutes. If you don't mind being here ..."

"No ... No ..." She gathered her Kools and keys from the table and handed me the souvenir ash tray to empty. "Get your meatloaf in the oven." She stood up. "I really care for him, Ron. Understand, I don't plan to light any candles to him, but I do plan to keep tabs. If I know Sharon, she's bound to slip up. Meanwhile Reed's going to know I'm around."

Her warm hand touched my arm. "He's lucky having you for a friend," she said. "I really mean that. You're a genuinely nice guy. A bit weird, mind you, but nice." Her lips grazed my cheek.

Reed was late. I heard the door of his Karmann Ghia slam—and then the other one—and his easy laughter growing distinct against an unfamiliar voice. The meatloaf and potatoes were on a low bake, the salad chilling in the fridge. I was proofreading my "Hound of Heaven" term paper.

The screen door wheezed. I looked up to find Reed holding it open, his thin hair gold in the dying sunlight, his face ruddy with beer and camaraderie. Felicia's father was right, Reed looked good even in fatigues. His free hand slipped warmly onto the shoulder of a round-faced fellow with red cheeks and short-cropped hair whom he ushered in ahead of himself. "Toby Frantz, meet Ron Schmidt."

Reed grinned at me as I rose to shake hands. "Toby transferred into my unit this morning, and already I feel like I've known him all my life. How 'bout a beer, Tobe?"

"Oh, you betcha!" Toby said. His eyes suddenly blinked like rapid-action lenses, and his head lurched to the left. Neither he nor Reed seemed to notice. I sat down again, but Toby remained standing, both fists plunged into his denims as Reed opened the refrigerator, took out two Olys and said, "I don't know when I've laughed so hard. Toby here is the natural man, Ron. You gotta hear his philosophy on being yourself." He punched a pair of triangles into each can with the church key, handed one beer to Toby and drank thirstily from the other. Sighing appreciatively, Reed wiped his mouth on the back of his hand, looked at me and said, "Mmm, you want a beer, Ron?"

I shook my head, which had begun to ache. My cheeks had gone tight, the rims of my eyes begun to burn. "No thanks, not right now."

Reed shrugged. With his free hand he loosened his brass buckle and yanked his starched fatigue blouse out of his pants.

"Anyhow, Toby don't believe in after-shaves, deodorants or camouflaging body functions, right, Tobe?"

Toby nodded, licking foam from his lips.

"Show him, Tobe!"

Toby obliged by expelling an enormous fart, then grinning like some guru who had just enunciated a transcendental truth. Reed laughed and said, "What'd I tell you? And you know what? He can do that whenever he wants!"

"God, Reed," I said, "that's really great. Congratulations, Toby."

Reed frowned. "I knew you wouldn't like it. Didn't I tell you, Toby?" Reed leaned toward me, his radiance dulled, his index finger poking my chest. "You need to lighten up."

"Do I?" I said, a smile carved on my face. It struck me as little wonder, following Toby's feat, that so many of us work so hard to overcome our natures.

"Know what else?"

"There's more?"

"He don't apologize for it neither."

"Double negative makes a positive, Reed."

"What?"

"Don't plus neither—that's a double negative. Screws up your intent."

"Goddamn!" Toby muttered. "Is this guy for real?"

"I'm an English major. I live my work."

"Bullshit on your double negatives; Toby understands me."

"I hope you two will be very happy."

Reed was angry. "Like I was saying, he don't apologize for bein' human. Right, Tobe?"

"Hell, no! Apologize for what? Anything I can't stand, it's these wimps who excuse themselves every time they sneeze. Don't make sense." He blinked thirty or forty times and jerked his head to the left. Turning a kitchen chair around, he straddled it and leaned his arms across the back.

"Somehow passing gas hardly seems in the same league with sneezing," I said fanning the befouled air with my "Hound of Heaven" carbon. "Actually, this is a moment of marked change for you, Reed. You've done nothing but bitch when the wind wafts in from the dumps at Alviso."

Reed laughed grudgingly as he moved toward the bedroom. "Tell him about the Kansas farm boy and B.O., Tobe. I can hear you while I'm changing." He aimed his finger at me. "Now you listen 'cause this is good—and it's true, right, Tobe?"

With that he abandoned me to Toby's tale of a virile Kansan who sweat profusely and kept a big red handkerchief wadded in his armpit when he went to barn dances. Every time he got a girl warmed up, he'd pull out his handkerchief to pat her brow, overwhelm her with his musk and have his way with her. Every time.

The ache in my head picked up the pace of Toby's narrative, dull and persistent.

When I was a child, I'd seen a futile attempt to revive vaudeville at San José's old Victory Theater on North First Street. That's what came to mind as Toby Frantz performed. All the world was his stage, and the curtain was always up. He talked compulsively, joked compulsively and had that compulsive blinking quirk punctuated with head lurches. He paused at self-appreciative intervals to cue his audience, and Reed responded to every prompt. Toby was a perfect vaudevillian.

Reed reentered the room tucking the tails of his button-down plaid into his unzipped polished cottons. As I watched, the pace between my temples thickened.

I smiled from time to time in an effort to be civil, but Reed doubled up at punch line after punch line. Maybe I needed a few beers too, but I knew at once that I did not like Toby Frantz. I hadn't particularly liked the Victory vaudevillians either. Toby depended on vulgarity for laughs, and it offended me that Reed found him amusing. This just wasn't Reed's style. In fact, Toby Frantz had no style. He was, purely and simply, base.

When Toby doubled up his beer can with one hand, Reed reached for the refrigerator. "Want another beer, Tobe?"

Toby's cheeks ballooned with a belch. "Naw, hell, let's go. My gut's growling." Getting up, he tossed me a mock salute, "Nice to meetcha, Rob."

Reed laughed, giving him one of those good-buddy shoulder punches. "His name's Ron." Toby shrugged and pushed open the screen.

"We're going to Vesuvio's for pizza and beer, maybe a flick later ..." Reed paused. "You wanta come along?" Throbbing stuffed my ears. Toby double-octaved a belch.

"You forgot, Reed, it's my night to cook. Dinner's in the oven."

Reed puzzled a moment. "Mmm ... That's right ... What're you fixing?"

"It's fixed. Meatloaf. Just keeping warm."

In the background Toby muttered, "Meatloaf?"

Reed's nose wrinkled.

"You really ought to like it, Reed," I said, my voice studiously level, "by now it should taste like warmed-over fart." Reed pivoted, scowling. "See you later."

"What'd what's-his-name say?" Toby's voice echoed between the houses.

I listened to the drift of voices down the driveway, my breathing knotted. The throb in my head beat the backs of my eyes. The symmetry of Reed's voice, beveled with laughter, jarred me—a warmth I was used to, withdrawn and redeposited. The Ghia's doors slammed like paired exclamations.

I knew what would happen next—the Irish edition of Thompson's Titanic gloom, the legacy of my mother's people, would descend. And it did. Swiftly. Swoop-winged. Things always got to me that way.

"You wanta come along? ... You wanta come along? ... You wanta come along?" So? I had no strings on Reed Pollock. What right had I to feel like an afterthought?

Threads of the afternoon's emotional patchwork unraveled.

"He's the most genuinely good person anyone could hope to know," I'd instructed Jolayne, "kind to a fault ... sensitive ... to his own detriment ..." I sat with all those comfortable stuffings come loose and a puff of Ghia gas in the growing dusk.

"Yeah, Jolayne," I said to the silence, "we were talking about the same guy." My voice had the earmarks of its very own echo.

Between my temples the tramping began. Squashed leaves. I needed something to soften the descent, but beer wasn't it. Beer bloats, as Toby Frantz had so graphically demonstrated, and I wasn't into satisfaction by gas emission. We had a bottle of Ten High in the cupboard over the fridge. It was that I reached for and poured half a tumbler of over ice.

Boxed in. I felt completely boxed in ... and betrayed.

Felicia was in Merced. I drank, wincing, added water, drank deep. Expansive, the boundaries of pain wavered. Needs would ease. Blunting should be comfortable.

Had she stayed in Belmont, would it have mattered? Could I have driven up and complained, "Felicia, Reed hurt my feelings. He went out with another guy ..." An oscillating shrill pitched between my ears. The room swam. I lowered my head against my hand, the bite of garlic and onion remote on my fingertips. Tears burned like stifled rights, and I swallowed greedily from the glass. Reed's hand on Toby's shoulder ... the pit of my stomach burned too. Did other people's feelings get out of whack this way? Was I the only one who had to order his sexual priorities? Hardly. Besides, when I really let go with a fantasy, wasn't there always a girl involved? So, it didn't start out that way. That was because I resisted temptation. What the hell! Obviously, I knew what men's bodies were like, and what's familiar comes first to mind. It wasn't as if that was a turn-on. Men were involved because my fantasies peaked on couples. Males were the aggressors. They were on top, their rutting, squirming muscles simply more visible. That wasn't the positioning of my desires, that was a biological fact. I always got a woman in there ... Always. I needed women as much as the next guy. To hell with my sainted roommate! I didn't care whom he chose to go anywhere with. He could screw Toby Frantz for all I cared! ... My control crumbled, my mind reeling with images of Reed and Toby Frantz doing exactly that. Together. Mouths locked. Butts jamming. Fucking. My eyes clamped shut. The wind tunnel of my chest shoved the bolts on my breath. "Put a girl into it!" I told myself. "Jesus, not Felicia! Not the girl I'm going to marry!" The frenzy of knees against my back. That was it! Sharon! Old tight tits, used to having her black-sweatered mounds mauled.

Things stopped. Just like that and I looked up. Toby Frantz grinned above the chair he'd straddled, blinking, jerking, his mouth in diarrhetic flux. I raised my glass. "Fuck you, Toby Frantz! I wish I could forget your name. I wish to God I'd never heard it." I tipped the glass to my lips, letting the dregs anesthetize my upper body, then poured more whisky. Easing ... Easing.

Last night as I sat at my desk typing the final draft of my "Hound of Heaven" paper, Reed came in from a date with Sharon, stood beside me and asked, "How's it going? Almost through?"

I nodded as he leaned into the glow of desk lamp to read, his lips parted, his warm fingers clutching my shoulder so that the hair on his forearm was a tangle of rainbows spilling peripherally into my vision. It was a caring gesture that sanctioned my hours of labor and filled me with a confused happiness. Reed was good. Reed was sensitive. Within, the beat was a mere tiptoe. I admitted nothing to myself.

Inches from my elbow I felt the warmth of his loins, that vague prominence, and I knew the ache of the unfulfilled—the desire to move my arm against that prominence and gentle it out of obscurity. God ... to touch him in that privacy. My lower body was concealed by the desk. The chase had begun.

Reed was not given to nudity around the apartment. When he showered he always strode to and from the bathroom with a towel slung on his bare shoulders and wearing boxer shorts, an inevitable undone snap winking dark velvet with each stride. Those times I'd viewed him naked were in the locker room of the university pool cleansing his sudsed limbs, lathering his impromptu length centered among the solid and shadowed contours of his body—stolen moments with his eyes shut against the soap sting. He would stretch naked, relishing the hot surge darkening his crown and rushing over his flesh. Thumbs latched overhead for a mock dive, he would bounce softly on his toes, tendons alerted the length of him; freshets tugging the dark froth of his armpits, rinsing the oils from his glistening, sun-baked skin. Flexing tapered his limbs like a Sistine fresco.

And each time I had forced on that vagrant joy the shape of a woman to justify its presence in the gnawed parts of my conscience and make confessing tolerable. But the imprint of Reed's open-pored suppleness moved beneath the surface of memory and expelled itself in nocturnal torment.

The Titanic gloom led me to my desk again in the now-dark and cornered silence of the living room. My fingers pulled the beaded brass, igniting iridescently the remnants of my intellectual striving—scattered notes coarsely dusted with erasure filaments; pencils snubbed at both ends; the parade-rest Smith Corona Clipper; legal-sized first draft scarred with revision.

Sinking into the swivel chair, I garnered the fragments of the previous evening's mood and, coaxed with whisky, memory obliged ... the strength of Reed's fingers radiating from his shoulder grip across my chest, his energy healing and wounding at the same time ... slow, rapturous. It was true. I had struggled with the desire to roll back my chair so he could witness my need. His weight shifted from one foot to the other, and the relaxing thigh captioned his polished cotton crotch with a taut wrinkle, pronouncing the mound with the length of his shaft, closer to my shoulder, inches from my face; the scent of his musk widening my nostrils, searing the Feet faltering in my brain.

His fingers squeezed, then patted. "Good stuff, Ron. I don't see how you can think of so much to say about a pome."

"Thompson did all the work," I said, hoping to prolong his touch. "Look at that imagery: 'the arches of the years ... the labyrinthine ways of my own mind ... Titanic glooms ... chasmèd fears ...'"

But his fingers had gone to the buttons of his plaid shirt and begun easing a swath into the coiled grace of his chest.

He listened as he worked, my voice edged with his nearness. His knuckles flexed white above his belt as he pulled the shirttails free, emancipating his odor, and continued unbuttoning. The firm lobes of his man breasts glowed in the verdant aura of the lamp, the nipples gnarled and shining with the saps of his twenty-second year. The dark coils rising, falling with each breath, spilled from his chest in a narrow descent, a low and dusky taper brushed flat upon the navel and fanning out, thickening for further descent ... The beat in my head stopped, caught between the temples, breathless, still.

I forced no female upon these reflections, not even a black-sweatered Sharon, to amend the character of temptation; and I conceded to Reed's absence ... and the knowing silence ... that there had been none last night either, except after the fact and consciously imposed. Desire braised my skin with the residue of his touch. Unselfconscious. That was Reed. Unaware of my need to touch him, to open my mouth against the flat of his belly and stoke that quiet cavity with my tongue, to undo his belt and go down. My denials could not stand against my need no matter how I Act of Contritioned it away.

Even my affinity for Bro. Patroclus, I admitted now, had been not the motive of the spirit but the design of my flesh instructing the spirit in the stride of integrity—my integrity. The Master of Novices had intuited the guise of my innocence. Bro. Patroclus had not been beyond temptation; he was temptation. Those strong Feet that followed, followed after belonged not so much to God as to the nature God had bestowed in me.

I could never again mean "a firm desire to sin no more," if this be sin; its claim upon me was complete. There was nothing left to deny ... My Hound was still. The truth of it washed like cheap whisky into my system, cleansing but harsh, and I felt as if I had myself been sucked through coral straws and survived. Ice rattled faintly as I nudged the glass away from the desk's edge. I moved from my swivel chair into the darkened bedroom and toed one heel after the other out of its shoe. A breeze billowed the curtained stillness as I examined the pale discards tossed between the beds—Reed's socks and boxer shorts—and, for a moment, I felt Felicia's father smirking across his stagnant rum.

Easing onto the rug, I stretched supine, and it seemed the most comfortable I had ever been. My fingers tested the fabric of Reed's things, closed on the rumpled shorts still humid with the press of his flesh, the intersection of seams soft from the rub of his low-slung, dark velvet privates.

"Let him smirk," I said, curious at the thickness of my voice, and I wondered how I would tell Felicia when she returned from Merced. I wanted to be done with lies, especially to myself.

With tempered reverence, my fingers dragged Reed's shorts across my own engorged midsection, up my chest to my lips and I kissed that stale garment ... inhaling its sweet reek. Toby Frantz, I guess, wasn't a total ass. As my other hand worked my zipper free, I remember thinking that afterwards I must not fall asleep that way ... and, Oh Christ! I had to turn the meatloaf off.

CHAPTER 16

DAY OF WRATH

The power that forged me to the man behind that door, a man I had never met, severed the links of my resolve about that room, and I would go in. Something of him was in me.

None of my duties required contact with that room. Of that I'd made certain when I'd agreed to the arrangement. In exchange for my quarters upstairs, I must answer the night phone. Beyond that, my time was free to study. But that call about him ... in there ... had changed all that.

Dies Irae ... the chant from the Mass of the Dead tolled in my mind. I stood before the unmarked door, staring, sweating with my need to go in, to see him, to be near him. My temples throbbed ... Dies Irae ... Dies Irae ... Dies Irae ...

I had stayed upstairs when the grinning hearse arrived, watched from behind my arched windows till they'd brought him in and then left to resume roles among the living. Quickened with swollen memories, I was disheartened. I'd thought them healed, but they were fresh as the wound in his mouth where he'd laid the muzzle. Dies Irae ...

His presence there, in that room, when the others had gone, shouted for me, and I rose in dread, the tolling amplified with each beat in my breast. In my mind I saw the priest in his black chasuble, his face grim and pale with the ritual that was useless to perform. Incense on burning coals pierced the air. Final impenitence was the unpardonable sin. Dies Irae ...

Therein was the core of my answering cry. I must go there so that any lingering fragment of soul, any shred of that shattered man could know that I forgave him, I understood.

The odor leaked into the anteroom, chemicals and the decay they would forestall. My grip on the doorknob steadied me. I dared not breathe as I pushed the door noiselessly open. My eyes stung. There is no silence like that which the dead sleep.

Only his foot, gracefully arched, thrust free of the sheet, a stark and final verse in the poetry of sun and sweat and sinew. This was the end I had myself come so near, and my thoughts etched his epitaph on the silence: "This is not fair!"

The words convoked my old rage, and God stood accused again between the silent corpse and my reawakened despair.

"Young guy," the embalmer had said when he called to confirm his pickup, "twenty-five, twenty-six. Blew his brains out and shattered a hole in the wall of his mobile. Seems his wife was makin' it with a friend of his couple of trailers away. Came runnin' when she heard the shot. Little chippy 'bout went out of her skull when she looked in, they say."

The surge of strength gone dormant ... No ... to waste, bled into the wall-to-wall carpet of a modest beginning. Irretrievable. Such a statement. The pressure of a warm finger on a cold trigger. And would she know, really? Could she know what she had to live with? Or would she bury it with him with the first thumps of earth on the coffin lid? Because, in the end, it could only be his.

Dies Irae ...

It might have been me. Dies Irae ... Dies Irae ...

"Was your roommate troubled?" the officers would have asked Reed. "Do you know what about?"

And he wouldn't, of course. Not consciously. Not for sure.

"He recently broke off his engagement," he'd have told them and stopped there. He wouldn't have added that it was because of him because I never told him flat out. Rejection would have profaned what I felt, made him less than I hoped he might be.

The priest in whom I confided that sat up and said, "Reed Pollock? Why, he's not that way. He's a fine young man." And he sent me to a psychiatrist.

My outrage against God was complete. The worst of all possible labels applied to the expression my sexuality sought: debased, degenerate, perverted. I craved sex with another man. I had come, in spite of myself, even to love one. Was I crazy or was I damned in advance? The latter conviction sucked the marrow from my soul. Hope was gone.

I became terrified that I would suddenly become a menace to little boys; terrified that I would become the ghoul whose unsuspecting victims, all male, would eventually resist the spade in shallow graves; terrified of terror and of my own ignorance. I would have no more of God or of His Church.

He could take His grace—actual, sanctifying and efficacious ... and shove it. I had not sold my soul to the devil; God had issued the contract on it. There is no honor in such arrogance. Let God count falling sparrows; I would survive without Him. When I was done He could do with me what He willed, but until then, every breath that I drew declared my independence.

My need for Reed sent me in search of surrogates, and I made quick, furtive, frantic trips into the corridors of sub-identity where age was entrée and anonymity a frozen hope. Adults Only. Fast-buck books, quarter peeps and squalid porn flicks. No questions asked but my own. Satisfaction cradled guilt in spent arms.

The need for Reed altered with absence—distance and time—but not the essence within that need. It would draw me, eventually, into the further reaches of brief encounter, allow me to linger instead of loiter. I would reach out among exiles and find those who reached back, not repulsive, but tender, needing as I needed, searching as I searched. And terror would withdraw. In the bars and in the baths would come those like me, whose needs ran deeper than surface lust, constant with meaning. I would begin, among them, to sense acceptance, tentative but willing; partners seeking satisfaction, yes, but identity as well and more than that ... validation. By degrees they would move me from the edge of despair into a wisdom my Church had cluttered with qualification ... "and the greatest of these is that you love one another."

On the other side of anger, some believe, is a God anxious to sanctify my self-acceptance. But there or not, with or without Him, the fullness and goodness of the being I am is my emergent truth, my existing reality.

It is not fair to value oneself so little as the crisp-sheeted man uniformed with death.

A nun, faceless against the tapestry of identifiable doctrine, had taught me that death should be a beautiful thing and, if her faith be any measure of that beauty, then I do not doubt hers was. But beneath that sheet only beauty's remnant lay.

John Donne wrote, "No man is an island," but here lay one who believed he was, and who now could prove him wrong?

"Any man's death diminishes me," Donne continued, and it was this that I would have had him know that man with the gun-blasted head. I understood ... Dies Irae ...

CHAPTER 17

FIRST PERSON, SINGULAR … ONCE-REMOVED …

When the lights went on, we were both undressed, stark naked, and in that little car. "Start the engine! Get us out of here," the other fellow said. I didn't even know his name. I tried but the Morris only coughed and rolled a couple of inches. The policeman called, "Halt or I'll shoot!" We halted. The lights glared, merciless. We grabbed for our clothes but there he was looking in at us from my side of the car.

"The arresting officer says he saw the other fellow's head coming out of your lap, Ron," my attorney counseled. He raised his hand. "Whether he did or not may be influenced by his own sense of outrage." He shrugged. "They're only human, cops."

"Don't arrest us," I had pleaded. "I've never done anything like this before." (That wasn't true.) "I won't ever do it again." (Neither was that.) "I promise!" (I never meant anything so much in my life.) "God, listen to me! I'm engaged to be married! I'm about to get my teaching credential!"

"You should've thought about those things before you decided to get into this mess. Get dressed and stand outside the car."

My partner in crime seemed far less disturbed than I. The officer radioed for another car. The vacant lot spun with the red-and-white remnants of a neighborhood—disengaged foundations and yard trees no longer pruned. Porch lights snipped the night from the periphery. The maples we'd pulled in among had refused us privacy as if eminent domain had been our fault, as if we had jacked up the homes and towed them away instead of a council vote to access a freeway.

Handcuffed, in the back seat of a black-and-white, I watched the City of San José pass through meshed metal. My rights still echoed in my ears, though I no longer felt that I had any. The officer was in no rush now, pausing for stop lights and listening to the dispatcher's crackle. I strained backward seeking the custody of shadows against the street-lit stares of passing motorists ... and weighed the outcome of my wanton behavior. I thought of my mother and father, and of Allen and Kathleen. I thought of Aunt Millie, who'd grown old. I thought of Felicia, my fiancée. They had done nothing but love me, and for that association they must shoulder my sin and bear my disgrace. Yes, Felicia knew our engagement was in trouble but not the reason why. I had spent the weekend at the ocean alone, sorting things out, and come home to this. Some sorting. I closed my eyes ...

"If thy hand is an occasion of sin to thee, cut it off." How many times had I considered that admonition regarding the part of my flesh that occasioned my sin ... and now it was too late. I had no defenses equal to the tyranny of my own genitals, and God Himself had reneged on His alliance. "Knock and it shall be open to you," had proved a hollow promise. My prayers and entreaties ran battering rams against the indifferent doors of heaven until praying no longer mattered.

In the holding cell, as we waited to be booked, another captive asked, "What'd they get you guys on?" and my accomplice actually began to tell him.

"Don't say anything," I pleaded, shaking my head. "Don't say anything." And he didn't ... for a while. I could tell he had later when he came into my cell during a post-supper rec session. A couple of other inmates were with him, and all they did was watch me as he chattered about getting my attorney to defend him too. I hadn't gone to supper. I was terrified of being seen, having it known what I'd done. I said I would ask my lawyer when he arrived in the morning. Satisfied, he left taking the watchers with him.

My cellmate was Pop, a wooly-haired man about sixty who sat in a niche he created between the bars and the metal table on which he played solitaire ... and smoked ... and lamented the woes of his involvement with women. He was curious but respected my lack of privacy and my youth.

"You wanta talk about it, son?" His voice climbed into the top bunk with me, my hands caught on the cold bedstead.

I turned my face to the wall. "I can't talk about it," I said.

I could feel him nod as he shuffled the deck. "My old lady's the reason I'm back in here. Onriest goddamned woman alive. Like they say, though, I can't live with her an' I can't live without her ... 'cept in here.

Only way I get me a minute's rest." He dealt the cards as if he knew their face value—some randomly, others with a thump.

One phone call and that to a priest who'd taught me English at Bellarmine. He called another Jesuit product, a young attorney named John Vasconcellos to come to my aid. I could only wait. I pleaded to make one more call so my family would not worry. After all, I reasoned, should they report me missing, the department would be out much more than the cost of a second call. A husky officer wavered, then shrugged. "Make it fast," he said.

Jails are noisy places. Hugging the mouthpiece, I called home. The Morris Minor had stalled outside Monterey. They were not to worry. I would get a room and drive home next day when the car was fixed ... I hoped.

That lie bought me a little time. That's what life was becoming, segments of time bought with lies. But what kind of lie bought off a news item? Would the neighbors cluck about poor odd Ron as we had done about poor odd Claude when they shook the wrinkles from the morning Mercury?

"Depends what kind of day they've had, Ron," my attorney advised, "how much news there was and how much space needs filling. Item like this, if you had a name, would be all over the morning edition. You may have nothing to worry about. Tell you what. I know one of the fellows assigned to the police blotter. He owes me one. Let me talk to him."

Inmate denim is harsh against the skin. Underwear is not part of the issue. I'd had to shower in front of a guard and bend over to be searched, items which, if he knew the charge against me, he must have thought turned me on. Dante's Infernal Judge at the entrance to Hell's second circle, he watched, "Grim Minos ... that connoisseur of all transgression."

The metal bedstead was cold in my grip. At home Ed Sullivan would flicker across my mother's slow fret. My father, picking rig grease from beneath his nails would scowl at Aunt Millie, "Pssst! Dammits, Millie stop that everlasting racket!" and the dramatic monologue would descend like an underground stream to a secretive whisper. At Belmont, Felicia would divide her concentration between her ethics final and me, fingering the little diamond that pierced the eye with light and evidenced my faltering commitment to a wedding band—assessing my silence.

The stomach truly does have a pit—the vessel of despair and basin to the soul's rock-bottom descent in unamended loneliness. I covered my face with chilled hands. What had I done!

What I had done was to contract with another man to relieve each other sexually. Contract? What a timid word. It was compulsion. No question about it. The maximum liberty I'd ever taken with a woman was to fondle the back of Felicia's neck, whispering, "Stop me ... Stop me ..." like some satyr bent on reform as Felicia puzzled, "Stop you?" in reply. Catholic girls were supposed to insist on no liberties. I had counted on that. Didn't she know fondling her neck was a liberty? Unabated need forged my contract to that other man, and had it not been him in particular, it would have had to be another with equivalent adornments between the legs to bulge the pants and insult the conscience and curve the jaw with textured lust. Regardless of religious indoctrination and the opinion of a preponderance of otherwise good people, I had to be relieved, and it had to be by another man. The black-lipped memory of my first experience muttered its message in my blood. The simple, incredibly complex biological need to touch and spend one's flesh in the stark naked, ravishing union with another's was the summons I had answered. That it was not subject to the same tongue-in-cheek reproach that sanctioned my brother's summons made the call no less clear, the need no less demanding. If anything, it increased the frenzy as partners in any illicit liaison can attest.

We had stood next to each other in the Humidor Shop on South First thumbing through muscle magazines. I'd waited for him, when I left, in my little Morris Minor, motor idling, and he'd looked at me as the smoke shop door closed behind him.

"Want to go for a ride?" I asked through the lowered window. Then he was beside me in the car.

"Why don't we get a room?" he asked, experienced, as I pulled out of the parking space.

"I don't have enough money, do you?"

He shook his head. "Let's just drive till we find some place we can pull off and be alone."

We were alone too till the black-and-white crossing the overpass picked out the Morris's bald dome among the maples and made us public.

"They could send you to Atascadero, Ron," my attorney told me, "the state facility for criminally insane sex offenders. The fact that you've been voluntarily undergoing psychotherapy could be a big factor in your favor. Look, I'll have you out of here in a few hours. See if your psychiatrist will write a letter estimating your chances for a cure ... especially if you're allowed to continue therapy without incarceration. The court may be swayed by that."

And it was. I did not even have to appear personally. The charge was dismissed on the grounds that I had already sought therapy and was making progress. Progress? The old theory that things have to get worse before they can get better, perhaps. The psychiatrist obliged with a 50-50 chance of conversion. That was apparently better than in-house odds for Atascadero. The court had no wish to interfere with the effort to correct my deviant sexuality. Besides, I was paying for it. In the long run, the state was getting a bargain.

I was spared the humiliation of publicity. Both the Mercury and News had more pressing fillers, or my attorney was persuasive with his connection. I was out of jail by early afternoon of my first meeting with legal counsel, and he drove me to the scene of the crime before returning to attend to my co-offender. My car had not yet been impounded. I was not spared his glance as Vasconcellos surveyed the size of the vehicle for activities such as I'd been arrested. But he was a compassionate man, even in his youth, and he would, in time, project that compassion into the California State Assembly, a Kennedy democrat who carried the flame from Camelot to Sacramento and personally nourished it. His living moves me.

I had the psychiatrist to help me redress the wounds to my ego, and I got on with the business of effecting a cure. I also had two skeletons in my closet.

In the semester prior to my arrest, the junction of seventeen years' education and energies required to focus on psychotherapy dictated a detour in my career plans. Dealing with the loss of faith, the psycho-trauma of attempting to alter my sexual orientation and the pressure of impending marriage left me no reserve for the commitment to completing a credential. My grades had fallen off miserably and my interest in education per se, even more than that. I dropped out of the postgraduate program at San José State with only one semester left. At that point I cared nothing for being in a classroom. Indeed, if the rumors I'd always believed about people like me were true, I didn't belong in the classroom.

An English major, I'd run the gamut of conjugations in my own tongue as well as Latin, Greek and Spanish and I felt, for all that, confused in the person and number, not to mention the gender, of my own being. The nominative assertion for the verb to be was still a freshly undone presumption for me because the phrasing belonged to God ... "I am who am" ... and none of us, I'd been raised to believe, took a breath or moved a muscle without His awareness and even His leave. My complete reliance on an omnipotent, all-loving Creator had brought me to the brink of suicide, prison and emotional collapse, so my own legs were understandably uncertain when finally I stood, took a breath and shouted, "I AM!" That's first person, singular. The tense is present, but it could as well have been future. I'm still catching up with the past. Only the gender remained in doubt. Were homosexuals some sort of mutant third sex? The cure would resolve that.

Pronouns are supposed to agree in person and number with their antecedents, but I seemed not to agree with any of my antecedents at all. All of them wore the mantle of heterosexuality or, if they didn't, they goddamn well carried off the pretext. St. Paul, in his much-quoted letters to the Corinthians, elevated lifelong frustration to the rank of virtue: "It is good for man not to touch woman. Yet for fear of fornication, let each man have his own wife, and let each woman have her own husband." To St. Paul, sex, even between straight people, was a necessary evil at best. He saw no beauty in it.

The singularity of I was frightening to me. It echoed against the future, and I ached at least for the capacity to become we, the focus of my years telescoped into those fifty-minute hours in the scheme of transition.

Aunt Millicent, in those days, ran the gamut of relationships as I had the conjugation of verbs. Longevity made her more and more the family historian. She knew who among us were first, second and third cousins as well as who were once, twice and thrice-removed. She loved that word thrice. Once-removed has always seemed the fit for me. Therapy cleared up the question of gender, but the reasons were wrong. There is no cure for sexual orientation. It would take me another sixteen years to gain that perspective. Therapy had merely colluded with deception. Late to the reality, I am proud finally of the fact: I am a man in love with a man, and I would have it no other way. Yes, acceptance of what is innate and natural to me has once-removed me from others' expectations of maleness, but I am not responsible for that lack in them. I work to instruct that ignorance because I would delete the distance the qualification imposes. Homosexuals are simply humans whose love relationships find fulfillment in their own gender. No one who thinks need be bothered by that. Respect of person is the antecedent of any law. I need no one to tell me that what violates the truth of my person—be it the Old Testament, the New Testament, the Koran or the Supreme Court of the United States—is wrong. John McNeill, S.J., in The Church and the Homosexual, has written: "We can conclude at this point, however, that a general consideration of human sexuality in the Bible leads to only one certain conclusion: those sexual relations can be justified morally which are a true expression of human love." And John McNeill has been silenced by his Church.

Truth of the first order lies in the heart. All the posturing and all the lofty extrapolation about literal and figurative interpretation is meaningless beside that perfect simplicity: Listen to the heart. I am more fully masculine because, secure in the person my particular manhood makes me, I have returned anxiety to the shoulders of those who make expectations. Correctly computed, my I reads out as: First Person, Singular, Masculine and, for the present, Once-Removed ...

My diploma as a straight man, however, a bona fide heterosexual, came in the form of a marriage certificate two years after the arrest and it was a degree I truly believed I had earned. Felicia belonged to an us that neither she nor I any longer was and indeed never had been. Colleen McNaughton was the love of the emergent me, the promise of an after-all future. She had not known me when. Colleen called me to a world I coveted, in which I wanted desperately to believe I belonged—husband and father. Colleen became my wife.

What rocked the cottage of our early bliss was the rattle of the second set of bones in my closet. Our first son, Drake, was newborn when renewal of my security clearance at the printing company for which I worked was denied. I sat outside the post office one late Tuesday in my '57 Ford coupe, the blatant contents in my fingers braced against the steering column. "Clearance denied." The reason was boldly typed: "Lewd and lascivious conduct."

The pit of my stomach was there, but sense had abandoned my extremities. It was the first gathering of echoes over our marriage.

I appealed the decision to no avail. My employer was confused, knowing me but not the details. I had come to him straight from Sacred Heart Novitiate and, but for Air Reserve interludes, remained part or full time for ten years. He found no risk in me.

Odd that in all of San Francisco it is possible within the perimeter of a single intersection to come across the one person you had feared ever to see again. But there he was, running kitty corner across Fell and Laguna as Colleen and I exited the San Francisco freeway en route to her parents' home out the Avenues. Our eyes met for just a moment, his and mine. There was no mistake. The same lithely handsome black man, who had gently taken my hand in his before unburdening me of my innocence in that little theater on Market Street five years earlier, trotted past the Ford against a caution signal. The warmth of his lips revisited my crotch.

I touched Colleen's hand in the silent ascent of Fell as the light changed. She had seen nothing, and if she was aware of any change in my manner, her manner gave no indication of it. I can only think she was not. We had been insular in our relationship; our circle of friends was small. We had shaped an island of our lives like the physical one on which we'd honeymooned in Puget Sound, and ... I stopped ... backtracked. Puget Sound. Was that the way out? I had kept my denied security clearance from Colleen while I rummaged through options for jobs. I could say nothing of the risk I was deemed without the reason. I had left Puget Sound out of the options completely till now. We had determined during those golden October days to return to that tapestry of salt-water channels and shimmering forests one day to live.

"Why wait?" I suddenly asked.

"Wait for what?" she replied. Light glanced off the yellow hood as we nosed into the sun's descent.

We both lowered our visors. Drake sputtered in his car seat in back.

"To go back to Puget Sound. We'll keep finding reasons not to unless we just make up our minds and go. It would be a perfect place for Drake to grow up."

Her fingers turned upward, clasping mine. She smiled as only she could do, with her eyes more distinct than her lips. "You're serious, aren't you?"

"I'd have to send out feelers for a job. I'm really ready for a change in that department anyway."

"Well, see, I've been thinking about that. You're wasting your talents in that print shop, Ronald. You belong in the classroom."

"But I ..."

"I know, the credential. But if you teach in a Catholic school for the archdiocese, you can complete your course work in the summers. I know you can do that because I did. After that it would be an easy move into the public schools. We'll just address your application to the Archdiocese of Seattle instead of San Francisco."

I glanced at her, grateful, relieved.

"By the way," she added, "my answer is yes."

Marrying without revealing my past had been a risk. I had now to risk again to protect that marriage. The Archdiocese of Seattle hired me sight unseen on the basis of my seminary experience and B.A. from the University of Santa Clara. I was to begin teaching in September despite my lack of a credential, a problem resolved in time through the good auspices of an enlightened, compassionate official in the Washington State Department of Education. He listened to my confidence in the long-shot effort to seal off the past. Another letter from my analyst cinched the balance already in my favor. Throughout these maneuverings Colleen was unaware that anything other than first-year teaching caused my anxiety as we established ourselves in Tacoma. All that secrecy to ensure that we-ness, that condition of first person, plural ... but I'd done it without her ... and so kept my singularity.

In philosophy I had learned about intrinsic contradiction, and it was that that undercut my effort, the intrinsic contradiction. But how could it have been otherwise? I loved her, and if I would keep her love, I could not let her know me. Once-removed ... Distanced in an ambiguous context. Even in those earliest days of husbanding, I dealt at a distance with homosexuality. My brain kept its vigil. Same-sex attractions, I had learned in therapy, were not uncommon even among heterosexuals, and I experienced those at least inversely. There were those men at whom I made it a point of not looking. More than that, I kept the issue at bay with the point of my pencil. I had begun writing a book in which I was the thinly disguised central character. The homosexual element was written into a separate but sympathetic, supporting character named Father Joe. Father Joe I spent many hours learning to like as my pencil wove his humanity through those unpublished manuscript pages, absolving partners to whom he'd just administered blow jobs. I did not know it then, but the writing vented still-existing needs that therapy had merely bound and shackled. Yet even with that false security, I relaxed my vigil enough to appreciate the person whose pain I had suffered and would suffer again. Indeed, the bonds were loosening.

Meanwhile, Colleen exhibited symptoms of a fresh bout with morning sickness.

CHAPTER 18

PHANTOM BRIDE

Tahoma—dwelling of the angry god—a name befitting the power and presence of a slumbering volcano. It was an Englishman, Peter Puget, sailing into the sound that would eventually bear his own name, who set aside the tradition of ancients and renamed the mountain for a British admiral who never would see its grandeur.

We had an imposing, if distant, view of Mt. Rainier from the dinette and living room windows of our Tacoma cottage. I say cottage. It was a cozy story-and-a-half, actually, and from the southern exposure between the roof's peaked halves, we enjoyed an even loftier view. Our bedroom, Colleen's and mine, was up there, and it filled one morning with so wild a radiance that I woke before the Baby Ben. Heir to my own early fervor, my mind leapt at the imminence of something celestial, a vision at very least. God, perhaps, had come to make up for the past. Throwing back my side of the quilt, I grabbed my robe and penetrated the vermillion ether, padding barefoot to the south window and the glow's exquisite inception.

My breath catches even now as I recall the shafts of shadow and light converged in the mountain's eastern thrust. The Indians were right. I recorded the proof with my mind's eye and, for nonbelievers, with my Argus C-3.

Had I been one to lend credence to omens, I should, I suppose, have sat out that day in trepidation, but I resisted the nag of superstition. Besides, the mood of that brooding peak, for me itself a god, demanded awe of its viewer but not fear.

Anyway, share it I could not. I tried feverishly, but Colleen rolled over and that was it. She would not be roused anymore than Drake, whom I carried from his bed downstairs, determined that he should have this supernal spectacle to enhance his wonder of the world. Squinting at that prehistoric hosanna seat, he scolded, "Da-a-AD!" and slumped into the crook of my neck. Cursing the Sandman who nightly received my benediction, I returned my son to the nest of his unfinished sleep.

Drake, perhaps, was too young, but Colleen was not too old. A moment so rare needs sharing, unless I am alone, or the ecstasy pales. Having the slide isn't the same as having someone who saw it too.

I came home from school that day to Colleen's first inkling that I'd held things back from her. She was distant, moody as the mountain she wouldn't rise for, brooding as it had been that morning. Washington's weather afflicted her as it did me and, indeed, countless other Pacific Northwesterners. Seattle, forty-five minutes north of us, ranked as a national contender among cities with highest suicide rates. That eight-day honeymoon on Harstine Island three-and-a-half years earlier had been cast in gilt from the sun's slant to the fawn-bent hay—and equally misleading. Exceptions, they were eight rarities in the bleak and leaden format of an intrinsic beauty hard to parallel ... when the sun shines. Important qualification, that.

Finally, she said, "I was looking in your desk for long envelopes, Ronald. You wanted me to mail those copies of your transcripts and credential to your U Dub Placement Office file."

"Yes?" I said, kissing her forehead. A cry was mounting in her flawless brow. "What is it, Colleen?"

Morning sickness troubled her only slightly; she had easy pregnancies.

"Ronald, why didn't you tell me you'd been to a psychiatrist?"

"What?"

"The insurance policy from Phoenix Mutual. It was in the drawer with the envelopes. I decided I ought to know what it says ... and one of the things it says is that you spent two years in psychotherapy."

The brooding burst, and she cried in her hands—heavily for a few moments—then wiped her eyes with a Kleenex. "Aren't you going to say anything?"

The time from our meeting till then had not been bought with lies, but neither had I paid with volunteered truths. How much to say?

"Did the transcript and credential copies ever get mailed?"

"Oh, Ronald," she wept, "I'm your beneficiary; I wasn't snooping."

"Of course you weren't," I said, immediately contrite. "You had every right ... I needed help. I told you about leaving the Church, breaking my engagement to Felicia, then running out of steam on my career goal.

That was a lot all at once ... Does it matter?"

"It doesn't matter that you had psychotherapy. It matters that you didn't tell me." She blew her nose in the Kleenex. "Were you in therapy when I met you?"

"The latter stages," I nodded. "Those appointments in Berkeley ..."

"Why didn't you tell me?"

"The inscription on your wedding goblet. It's on there—'the haunt of past echoes,' remember? You called it the silver redundancy." My heart was still, my veins sluggish and chilled. "Does it matter?" I repeated.

She cried again. "Of course it matters, Ronald. You're my husband, and I love you. If I'd known I might have been able to help you."

"Not knowing and loving me ... that helped most at the time."

She flung her arms around me. My veins surged, and my heart filled. My arms squeezed back with gratitude and love, yes, and fear, as I took stock of what else she did not know ... of that further immanence in the silver redundancy.

Drake tumbled into the kitchen clutching Corky the Cocker by her flagging tail, laughing. Our second child booted the womb Colleen pressed against me, barely discernible but there, and so much seemed so good at that moment that the hope leapt in me that there might be a beneficent God after all.

We lay, later, under the slanted ceiling in the scented after-thrall of lovemaking and listened to the quiet pulse of that house, the throb of what we had. The moon slipped in and out of dense cloud against the narrow north window like a patina of breath, and suddenly Colleen said to me, "Ronald, you won't ever leave me, will you?"

There are thoughts better not voiced. Expression gives them a reality that cannot be rescinded. My arms drew her close against me, naked breast to naked breast. "Jesus, Colleen, what a thing to ask! Of course not."

"Not ever?" Her lips moved with a foreboding weariness against my neck, a prophecy of irremediable fatigue. I searched the darkness for ominous signs—there had been only that morning's sunrise for which she would not waken—and knew that no assurance could be as complete as she required. I cupped her breast in my palm. Her lashes felt damp to my lips. "Never, my darling," I whispered, "never."

There had been another time, now that I think of it, that doubt phrased itself in her voice. Colleen was pregnant with Drake. Deadlines at the print shop ran into overtime most days. The commute to the Campbell suburb of San José further delayed my getting home so that Colleen passed those long days alone among neighbors who kept to themselves. We sat together on the hand-me-down couch looking through hand-me-down lace at the end of one such day. The black walnut across the street was brittle with wind, and we held each other. "Ronald, ..." she asked, "were you ever ... with anyone before you met me?"

I hesitated.

"I mean, did you ever make love to any other woman before you met me? Go all the way?" She regretted having asked but wouldn't stop. "I mean, it's all right if you did and you don't have to answer if ..."

"I never made love to any other woman before or after I met you," I hastened while the qualification was in effect. "Why?"

Her shoulders bounced against my chest. "You just seem to know a lot about it ... what you're doing when we make love."

"I've read a lot," I said, which was true. But truer even than that was the fact that the rhythm of passion does not discriminate in the choice of partners. Gender combinations aside, desire is a basic and common truth.

"Sorry ..." she said, embarrassed to look at me. "Do you want to know about me?"

"Know about you?"

"Whether I was ever with anybody else?"

"I don't think so." I stroked her hair.

"Well, I wasn't."

I hugged her.

"I love you, Ronald."

"And I you, Colleen."

An elderly uncle, when I was a child, used to pass all his boxed National Geographics on to my family. I can remember sitting in the bathroom till the undersides of my thighs went to sleep and the seat left a red circle around my rear. The Geographic was always good for a naked native or two and provided my first clue that the unclothed body had some legitimacy, although my interest in it was strictly illegitimate as yet. My sexual quests inadvertently opened the curiosities of the world to me, and I became an avid reader in spite of myself. The island called Martinique, I remember vividly, loomed large among global curiosities for me. Since the beginning of time, the molten juices of the island's volcano had devoured villages and digested inhabitants on its lower slopes without qualm. Yet, invariably, survivors returned to those slopes to squander hope on new settlements whose destinies were clearly foreordained. What made them do it? It was, it turned out, because the living was so good. The belched innards made the soil the most fertile and arable on the island. Nothing, I resolved, could have induced me to dwell on that warm and unpredictable belly ... nothing. But there it was, in the Tacoma News Tribune, as I poked the crinkle from the front section fold and settled down to my Sunday morning coffee. Scientists were monitoring volcanic activity inside the brooding god that slumbered forty-five miles from my sun-pierced window pane. Was this the revenge of tribal deities for Peter Puget's indiscretion?

"Guess what?" I said to Colleen as she filled Drake's Captain Kangaroo cup with orange juice. She hmmmed, splicing her attention between Drake and me.

"According to the TNT, we're practically sitting on an active volcano."

"MOMMY!" Drake shouted, his small hands damming the stream of juice squirming to the table's edge.

I fretted about having a second son because of loving the first so much. How did one divide love between children of the same gender? A daughter would be different, require affection of a separate sort and make the balance right. I knew so little. Love does not divide, it extends ... encompasses. Tracy taught me that in the summer of 1968 just by being born.

I had heard it said that parents do not love their children equally, that one or another is simply more lovable and gets loved better. While I once feared that, I cannot, on the basis of experience, understand that. I have not loved either of my sons better or more or less than the other. I have loved each with all that my particular being allows, but I have loved them differently, and that difference is the demand of their own particular needs. One responds to another's attributes and flaws with one's own attributes and flaws, and so I have both succeeded and been found wanting. Drake and Tracy bear the plusses and the minuses of our combined assets and limitations.

Colleen loved them both unconditionally. The single qualification was time's intrusion with the onset of illness. She was theirs so short a while. Before Drake was six and Tracy three, insanity had transfigured that gentle woman. Mother-bride metamorphosed before our eyes, became a phantom in our midst.

Tracy, in fact, was four months shy of a year when Colleen experienced her first episode, Drake only three-and-a-half years. I'd come home from school to find her features distorted with fear. The phone, she said, had rung. No one responded when she'd answered it, but she knew who it was. A past presence. A cousin who had hypnotized her when she was just a girl and was trying to do so again by phone. We had seen him at a recent holiday gathering in California. He had noticed the children, and she feared for them. The telephone cord protruded from a drawer stuffed with kitchen towels.

I'd had no preparation for the bizarre. Colleen's intensity overwhelmed my natural caution with the guise of supposition, the what-if syndrome that carries over from the anything's-possible time of the child. I ought, perhaps, to have seen signs of it coming. Retrospect revealed the insidious presence of a third party to our relationship over the previous year—strain. Neither of us recognized its features until they'd become habit and substitutes for loving. Discontented with leaden skies and in-house routine, Colleen had begun to lobby for change—a job that would emancipate her from duties for which education among the Madames of the Sacred Heart had ill-equipped her. Aspirations carved in the Spanish chambers of Lone Mountain—San Francisco College for Women, contrasted sharply with the bulk of unshaped lives in that story-and-a-half on an obscure Tacoma bluff.

My preference for the avant-garde collided equally sharply with my real conservatism in matters of mothering. I resisted her need, opposed the concept of child-care centers and sitters for our sons. Colleen was loosening the pickets in our white fence. Her break with reality collapsed the structure—posts and stringers—and my resistance with it.

Strain altered the expression of our carnal relationship as well, a condition which I viewed with rising panic. Colleen's needs threatened our cozy existence. Predictably, perhaps, I withdrew from spontaneity—uncertain, insecure, yes threatened. The backlog of attractions I'd repeatedly told myself were not abnormal for normal males to experience moved from backstage understudies into the wings of desire, and I found myself creating roles for them. Colleen's transition and my same sex-attractions auditioned with equal vigor, both antagonists on my mental set. Whether one provoked the other to compete and in which order are questions of little relevance now.

What does, in retrospect, seem to be so is that Colleen's assertive ... even aggressive self, was an unconscious effort at ascent in the face of her mind's descent, a compulsion to capture a significant part in the drama that was going on without her. Instead, hallucination played the fragile parameters of her mind until reality became indistinguishable from it. Cars followed her when she drove Drake to child care; the television monitored her thoughts, and she talked with soap personalities. She communed, in fact, with unseen presences in our home, smiling privately.

Aunt Millicent, of course, had been an inveterate, self-contained conversationalist for as long as I could remember and she was, admittedly, eccentric if not peculiar in that. But she only absented herself periodically from the reality in which she functioned. Colleen went beyond. She stopped functioning. She inverted time, sitting in the dark, shade-drawn house—sleeping away the hours of light. True darkness she held at bay with lamps and overheads—chain-smoking, sipping burgundy and riveted on whatever it was her mind was processing. Unresponsive to the children and to me, she ignored even her own legitimate needs. But then, what was not legitimate in her condition? Even her brief excursion into the work force, so highly prized, did nothing to avert the intrusive force of madness.

The friendly grasp of alcohol was not a phenomenon exclusively Colleen's. I was on far more intimate terms with it than she was, stemming from my pre-therapy days of self-contempt, but I would emphatically deny that it was alcohol's grip rather than its grasp that I enjoyed. Those days of damnation and self-loathing had left their mark and set the precedent for dealing with guilt, the age-old distortion of love. I drank to assuage the disintegration I could do nothing about, to deal with the distance that replaced recognition in Colleen's beautiful eyes, to ease the concession that God had again asserted omnipotence without a shred of beneficence. I was haunted by the fear that my denied homosexuality had reversed the role for my Galatea; that I was, in fact, a perverse Pygmalion.

The day of Colleen's commitment to Western State Hospital, I consumed seven double martinis and never slurred a syllable. The friend who accompanied me through the hearing kept count when he took me for a drink later to unwind. When he asked if there was anything else he could do, I wanted to say, "Lie naked with me. Make me feel valid." I went home and drank some more instead.

That her fears were hallucinatory, Colleen was rational enough to accept only in that initial episode. With each subsequent break, her condition worsened so that ultimately she not only refused medication and rejected her doctors but denied that she was ill at all.

The first sanity hearing failed to commit Colleen because she knew what day it was. The presiding psychiatrist, ignoring the hell Colleen's hallucinations had created for the children and me, focused on the single fact that she could say it was Tuesday and refused to commit her. Thus began an incredible chain of events that resulted in a debacle by the psychiatric/state community that was so bizarre it rivaled Colleen's own psychotic performance. There is, I'm convinced, a basic insanity in a system that allows insensitive and ineffective professionals to reap vast profits at the expense of patients contained in thorazine limbos for the rest of their lives.

For two-and-a-half years the spectre of paranoid schizophrenia moved among us, willful, arrogant, unsubstantial. Nothing worked. No one could do anything. Our only peace came from Colleen's confinement, and that was peace abated. She would not cooperate, and the doctors could not make her. Even if she would, even if they could, what was available to her? Theirs was a science so imprecise it approximated the title only in practitioners' profits. The only agents not impotent before schizophrenia were concrete, steel and debilitating drugs.

Midwinter was worst. Inevitably, the post-holiday redundancy of death and decline precipitated a crisis which left her more dormant than the last. The children were bewildered. Their mother did not attend, indeed scarcely responded, to them. Their father alone bent to their night cries, saw to their day needs.

My own father had succumbed to lung cancer before Tracy was born. It was my mother who flew at moment's notice to care for her grandsons whenever Colleen went into crisis, reaffirming what family means.

The McNaughtons questioned long distance what I was doing to their daughter, urging her to come home where she was loved and could get well. Colleen's symptoms were invariably in remission during those trips we did make to San Francisco, so her parents could never understand what the worst was like. When divorce became the only defense for my own sanity, they flew north finally. Sobered by her condition, they remained unconvinced about me. "This business is breaking her father's heart," Colleen's mother cautioned me. No one who loved Colleen emerged with heart intact.

The woman I had sworn never to leave was served with papers on the locked ward of the state mental institution. There is no easy way to record that fact. None but those who have been there can appreciate the necessity. I say that neither to excuse myself nor apologize. Given the same circumstances, the same need would dictate the same choice again.

Assuming responsibility for her, Colleen's brother signed her out of Western State and flew her to San Francisco where, of course, she resumed an intermittent existence of hospitalizations and, ultimately, indefinite halfway housing.

The divorce became final in 1971 with full custody of Drake and Tracy residing in me.

"I think I know what your problem is, Ronald," Colleen told me once while she was still with us.

"My problem?"

She nodded, her lovely hair unwashed, haphazardly pinned. "I think you're basically homosexual."

"What makes you think that?" I said, admitting nothing.

"I just think you are," she smiled, pouring hot water for a cup of what she'd begun to call "tay."

Her psychiatrist, in whom I'd confided the details of my past in the hope of helping Colleen, discounted the accusation. "That's common for an ill spouse to call the well one homosexual. Don't worry about it."

But I did, of course. Had I precipitated this unfathomable condition by not meeting Colleen's needs? Had she been aware of the purpose with which I avoided looking at other men? Was passion's dynamic absent from my fingertips when I touched her, an esteem she could not do without, a pretense she noted and blamed on herself? Maybe ... the byword of horrendous guilt, the blade that had furrowed and cross-furrowed my conscience all my life.

Colleen came back twice to visit when she was not in crisis. On both occasions her parents assured me she was doing well. At the end of the first visit, she wanted to stay but left when I said no; at the end of the second, she refused to leave and didn't. I'd gotten the clear sense that this time was different; she was settling in ... and the old symptoms taking over. Her refusal was flat. She would not go.

Twice before I'd had to have her removed under commitment proceedings. Those records facilitated removal now. I sent the boys to a neighbor, a surrogate grandmother who sat them in my absence, and waited, tension at knots within me. When the knock came Colleen was seated in the rocker by the living room window. In the distance Tahoma caught the light from the gathered clouds and brooded. Colleen looked up, as I opened the door, and saw the uniformed officers. Both hands settled in her lap, and for a moment she was totally vulnerable. "Is this really necessary, Ronald?" she asked, digressing into the rational.

One of the officers accompanied her while she packed. It was my thirty-fifth birthday.

"I'm sorry, Colleen," I said as she buttoned on her coat between the officers.

"Yes," she said, pausing to look at me. A brief smile quickened her lips. Her eyes scanned the room and the mountain, knowing this was final, and she sighed heavily.

I watched her descend the steps to the waiting car, and I sighed heavily as well. I would turn no more to the landscape of that molten soul.

CHAPTER 19

OBSCENITIES I: ROLE MODEL

I didn't connect the obscene call with Don Folkholm until months after the second call in August, and I don't know why. I could be wrong, of course, about it having been him the first time, but I had the distinct sense even then that I knew the voice. It seems so obvious in retrospect, but who's ever prepared for that blunt SUCK MY COCK! imperative when you say hello to a perfectly ordinary ring? In a desperate sort of way, an obscene call achieves some intimacy, I guess. And that one was certainly desperate, like a guy who'd explode if he didn't get off. Still, the obscene call couldn't touch the August one for impact, especially considering how dispassionately the second one began.

"Mr. Schmidt? This is Don Folkholm ... from the junior high?"

"Don! What a surprise! ... How's your summer going?"

"It's okay, I guess. I've been pumping chocolate freeze so long it's beginning to look like slow turd in a sugar cone, but at least I'm making some bucks for high school ... clothes, gas money, junk like that. I don't want to have to work during school if I can help it."

"Good thinking. Give yourself space to adjust over there. Do you know what your class schedule looks like yet?"

Don did not answer. For a moment I thought we'd been disconnected. Then he said, "I guess you're wondering why I called, right?"

"Well, I confess, not a lot of students call in mid-August, but it's good to hear from you. What's up?"

"Mr. Schmidt, I think I'm in love with you."

No curriculum guide suggests responses to that kind of declarative. Nothing in teacher-training classes, certainly of the sixties ... even of the eighties, equips the teacher to handle it. It's the stuff of OJT; the wing-it-fella-you're-on-your-own-common-sense-they-don't-teach-in-books sort of thing.

When I could speak, I stammered, "Don ... Wow ... I ... I'm ... I guess we need to talk."

A soft laugh hissed in the receiver.

"You know," I said, struggling for composure, "it's not uncommon for students to get crushes on their teachers."

"You didn't know, then ..."

"Know?" I repeated.

I closed my eyes. My thoughts raced across his three years at the junior high like a dying man's life in review. Nothing in that frenetic collage of classes and kids snagged on Don Folkholm ... except that he'd always been there, engaging ... quick to smile. Apart from that, he had not seemed remarkable by contrast with the 480 other students of his vintage, and I remembered nothing remarkable in my treatment of him.

"I thought maybe you felt the same," I heard him say.

I'd begun to sweat although not even the morning was remarkable against the norm of Puget Sound summers.

"Look," I said, "I think we'd better talk, in person, I mean. Can you meet me at the junior high in ..." I glanced at the chef clock licking its lips beneath the minute hand over the stove. "It's 10:25. In an hour? ... Oh, shit, you have to work at the Dairy Queen. ... Jesus, excuse me!"

I heard hissing again. Christ, was he enjoying this? "I took the day off just in case. I can meet you."

"Fine, I'll pick you up at 11:30 then."

I lived thirty minutes from school. With the other thirty I called the sitter, changed clothes, tried to collect my thoughts. Had I unwittingly led on this sensitive kid? How?

Out on the front lawn, Drake and Tracy rolled joy from their lungs and their bodies down the balding slope, unaware that a threat had targeted our lives, a threat that could damage my ability to provide for them as schizophrenia had damaged their mother's mind. The truth didn't even have to come out. Rumors were enough. Whom else, I wondered, had Don told? "I thought maybe you felt the same..." Had he misinterpreted a valuing pat on the shoulder? Yes, I was head-on confronted with my re-emerging homosexuality, but furtively so. Colleen and I had divorced in 1971, just a year earlier, and I had full custody of our sons. I was playing it very straight, traveling all the way to Seattle to indulge my long-repressed needs. What could possibly have led Don to suspect that I was in love with him or even suspect that I knew he was in love with me? And, Jesus, what had he meant by, "I took the day off just in case?" What did he know about me? What did he want? I hated that I was even thinking this way.

In the garage I leaned my forehead against the vibrating steering wheel as the Rambler wagon warmed up, and suddenly I was embarrassed. Don Folkholm was no predator demanding blackmail. He was the latter end of a boy at the beginning end of a man, risking a truth I'd never dared and wanting to trust me with it. And I had panicked. If I had never treated Don Folkholm differently from my other students, this was no time to start. I would do for Don what I would do for any other student ... my best as I perceived it. But what was that? In coming out to me, he was already ahead of me ...

I drove out along the Puyallup River road where Indians netted the ire of white fishermen and knew as I neared my 11:30 destination that Don Folkholm would have to settle for my second best, and I didn't like it. I could not, rather would not, admit to him that I was a homosexual, though in my heart it was that I knew that he needed, not for the sake of being sexual with me certainly, but for the emotional and physical well-being that would secure his dignity. Don Folkholm needed a role model, but then so did my sons, and I hadn't the honesty for either. Drake and Tracy were entitled to one parent, at least, who was constant and could raise them in security.

My best, then, lay somewhere between, in compromise. While I tried always to act responsibly, obviously I was not open and obviously not truthful, two counts of intrinsic contradiction. Role models cannot act a part; they must be the part. Lies won't cut it. The part is their essence, or it is nothing. It can be flawed, but it cannot be false. What Don Folkholm had offered me was the chance to be real, for him and for my sons, and I middle-roaded the offer. There's no such condition as half-honest, but I sure gave it my best. I acted the part of the straight liberal, sensitive to minority needs. I exuded compassion but kept my cover. My children were nearly grown before I told them who I am, and that was deprivation; that was neglect.

As for Don Folkholm, by the time I arrived at school that morning, I had devised a concoction of evasions and ought-to's that lacked the indiscretion of lies, yet gave me a basis for dismantling his feelings for me. How to direct those feelings toward a suitable object ... what suitable even meant, for God's sake ... were questions with answers beyond my ken at the time.

His expression, as I pulled into the bus zone, belied his telephone calm. How long, I wondered, had he rehearsed what he would say? The whick of sprinklers on the athletic field was the sole insinuation of plans for the silent campus. Summers ripen adolescents without warning so that what had not been distinct about Don's maleness in June had become a clear prominence in August. He was very trim, snugged his white pants fetchingly and taught contour to a navy tee shirt with a Seattle decal. Our eyes met as he leaned to open the door. He was aware of his irrepressible masculinity.

"Thanks for coming," he said as he climbed in.

This was really happening.

"If neither of us has a time line, I thought we'd drive out to Point Defiance ... Talk at the beach?"

"Sure," he shrugged. He looked scrubbed, his short blond hair neatly parted, his blue gaze keen against his tanned skin.

The slap of waves along Puget Sound measured the cut of fishing crafts and sailing vessels on the gray surface. Vashon Island's ferry scheduled us to a reality outside the unreality of the relationship we considered side by side on a log. I listened to grown pain with grown shame at my own insensitivity and at my own fear.

"I took every class you taught at the junior high, ran every errand you needed run." He gave that soft laugh again and looked directly at me. "I just figured you knew."

Stories of high school teachers who married their students were surprisingly easy to document, although, dating was a frowned-upon ethic. A senior high co-ed had slapped her math teacher with a paternity suit recently, sparking hot debate in faculty lounges throughout Washington. To me, as to most, the student-teacher relationship posed an impediment to romantic involvement ... Even had I allowed myself to savor Don's emerging physical attributes, I could not have acted on the inclination. Even when I have taught senior high, that sense of impediment has remained intact, though I am no more immune to the deceptively persuasive appeal of these youth in transit from childhood than other teachers. Around them day after day, one must remind oneself of that passage ... They are children ...

Yet Don, as we talked, proved my equal in same-sex experience. Active with a classmate since age twelve, he had recently answered an ad in a Seattle underground newspaper.

"I got sick after we did it the first time," Don said shaking his head. "I threw up all over the guy's rug. He was real concerned, wanted to know if he'd hurt me. I pointed to the medal hanging around my neck and said, 'See this? I'm Catholic, and what we just did was a mortal sin.'"

If the image of the Immaculate Conception slapping against his chest between grunts seemed sacrilege, it had also been his protective talisman against dying in that graceless state ... "Holy Mary, Mother of God, pray for us sinners now and at the hour of our death ..." That's why he hadn't taken it off.

What they did, Don said, was everything, and I had no reason to doubt him. I had asked the question, ostensibly, with his health in mind, but his answer clarified for me how self-serving was my need to know. The vicarious impact altered the tone of my own voice.

My cause for concern was genuine, though. For the young, consequences seem not to exist. I looked at this youth who had earned As and Bs three years running in my English, journalism and social studies classes ... because he loved me ... wanted to be near me, yet hated what he'd done with someone more honest, and said, "Don, I need to ask, did you and this fellow use protection? Are you concerned about VD?"

"No, we didn't ... and yes, I'm concerned," he said, "but I'm afraid my doctor would tell my folks if I went in."

"The chaplain at St. Joseph's is a friend of mine. He might be able to get you tested at the family clinic. I'll call him, if you like. There's a phone at the Boathouse."

Don nodded. The Vashon Island ferry headed toward us.

"I guess my next question has to be, what do you want to do about your deepening involvement with men? Some therapists believe that a homosexual stands a 50/50 chance of going straight through intensive therapy, if he wants to change badly enough. But, Don, others think that homosexuals should be counseled into self-acceptance. In fact, the psychiatric profession is removing homosexuality from its list of disorders, saying it's a condition natural to ten percent of the population. That's something to think about."

Don turned, his blue eyes flashing. "Are you kidding? Do you think I want to live like this?"

I watched his face silently. I did not tell him why or how I knew what I'd told him about psychiatric theory. For a moment I struggled with the impulse to say, "Don't waste your time trying to change. It doesn't work. I've been there. Oh, you think it works long enough to compound your mistakes and louse up more lives, but it doesn't, and anyone who tells you otherwise lies. Get on with who you are."

But I wasn't there myself ... Instead, I said, "Then I'll talk to my friend about that, too. Perhaps he can set up some counseling ... You must be hungry ... Let's get some lunch at the Boathouse Grill, and I'll make the call."

The chaplain was a compassionate man who had us in the clinic at 2:00, but the physician was an abrupt and judgmental man who had Don out at 2:05, untested. It took all my powers of persuasion to get him back inside and the chaplain's intercession to get him processed.

The psychologist agreed to tuck Don in at the end of his 5:30 session, which left us with four hours to pass, Don still traumatized by his first psychological fag-bashing. We talked about the narrowness even of educated people at times and how education itself guarantees neither wisdom nor understanding. In an effort to distract his tension, I suggested that we see the just-released Nicholas and Alexandra. The film would fit compactly into our time frame and provide the needed shift in focus ... I thought.

I had set aside my teacher's instinct to preview what I screen for students, not for a moment suspecting that that tale of ill-fated monarchs might prove inappropriate to Don's circumstances. The darkness of the theater could not contain my dismay at the homosexual/transvestite scenario luring Rasputin to his death. Don's elbow nudged mine as I slumped in my seat. "Don't sweat it," he whispered and followed with his agreeable laugh.

I apologized all the way to St. Joseph's Annex, which housed the mental health unit, where, with Don's approval, the psychologist recommended that I sit in on part of that initial session. I was, after all, the object of Don's homosexual affection. The therapist advised me in a subsequent phone call not to discourage Don's need to see and confide in me. My concern that such contact would lead him on, the therapist discounted, citing the positive support of a strong male figure whom Don could trust as the overriding consideration. Obviously, I had not shared with the psychologist the extent of my strength or my own reality.

During the fall semester, Don signed on as my journalism TA, often staying after class to talk or just be quiet near me. The custodian cocked his head at the pair of us, desk to desk, deep in dialogue, with the rest of the school shut tight.

But Don's patience with therapy thinned quickly. His parents, of course, had been informed and without knowing the reason consented to the cost. But whatever he confronted in those fifty-minute hours convinced him quickly that either he could not or would not change, and he set about ordering his life for the difference. My God, how far ahead of me he was.

His need to visit me paled with the passage of months also. I could see it coming—a reluctance any longer to confide, perhaps a recision of trust. I didn't know why, and he seemed unwilling to explain. Gradually, he stopped altogether.

When Drake and Tracy and I returned to California, it seemed Don Folkholm had become yet one more Washington wound. So I was surprised when he pursued contact with a warm letter months later. Correspondence coaxed the evolution of a friendship enhanced by eventual visits on long-distance trips. In a restaurant on Fisherman's Wharf in Santa Cruz, in fact, ten years after his August declaration of love, I finally came out to him as a gay man, apologizing for not having been there for him in the context he needed when he needed it. The undulant Pacific surged against the barnacled pilings, and we could feel the sway. He laughed softly and said he understood. I am still humbled by that.

Distances can be forgiving ... common bonds become more precious. We are close friends sharing each other's ups and downs, even relationships and break-ups ... equals finally. Curiously, Don is the conservative, the product of selected closets and open caution that began with that VD test, a family clinic physician and a teacher who sidestepped his honesty.

Once I quit sidestepping, I couldn't run fast enough into gay causes so that I sometimes find Don the stern parent as I have sung variously the praises of the baths, the Castro and coming out. The last Don to come to California had a vaguely corporate image and reserve in consonance with it. He watched me across Orphan Andy salads in the Castro as if I were moonstruck, and I knew that he would return to his lover in Seattle and shake his head at my part of his trip.

We hug warmly after these occasional visits here or there. At times I can tell by the spaces between confidences that he worries that I've gone too far. But he, of course, is part of the reason. He's with me every day that I enter a classroom with the present ten percent. I study those twenty-five to thirty faces and remember his voice on my phone: "Mr. Schmidt, I think I'm in love with you ..." I intend to be fully present.

CHAPTER 20

THE DISINHERITED

It was an arsonist who did it, ... a crazed man who hated God and set out to show Him a thing or two. Well, he did, ... the arsonist, that is. The charred stubs of St. Mary's burned-out nave gouged the belly of San José's sky like mocking fingers—stark evidence that vengeance is not always the Lord's.

Displaced from the softly prismed ritual that had daily renewed their lives, clusters of women, like Anna in the temple of Jerusalem, stood at curbside, their dour-skinned faces gray with the imprint of mourning, their thin-voiced Aves echoing against the locked façade. My mother and Aunt Millicent stood arm-in-arm among them that day, fear at work in their features. Each bead of each rosary slipping through uneven fingers marked a memory consecrated in that gutted sanctuary—a marriage, baptism, first communion, confirmation, funeral—the Christian traditions of Western Civilization narrowed to a local focus in the life of a parish. Gone now.

Even the spike-heeled prostitutes turned from the throbbing Camaros and vans to view through stained-glass eyes St. Mary's remains. The flush of the driven in his cheeks, a blond youth throttled past, his marrow-starved eyes scouring the corner of Third and William for other bare-thighed contracts more attentive to renewing him.

The recent plague of streetwalkers, pimps and johns angered the bewildered residents. The only red light ever to burn in this neighborhood had flickered in St. Mary's sanctuary confirming the gilded presence of the triune God. "Jesus is angry," wept a woman beside my mother. "That's why He's taken our church," and her eyes burned at the saucy strut of girls resuming their walk past the convent to the corner.

The nuns within that convent opened their arms to the dispossessed parishioners until the presence of those not under vow began to intrude on their religious habit. After all, they reasoned, mass could be celebrated in the hall just three flights above the school. My mother was seventy-two then, Aunt Millicent eighty-three and on a cane. These were modern nuns; they enjoyed reasoning. In fact, they reasoned so well that they overqualified themselves for teaching the very young. It was lay teachers and even a lay principal who stood now where white-wimpled, black-hooded Sisters of Notre Dame de Namur had once ensured the coming of little children to Christ. This freed the nuns to work in high school and in social service beyond this neighborhood where, in the same summer, an eighteen-year-old prostitute was strangled to death, another shot in the head just three blocks from the brides of Christ, and a spike-heeled shoe and drawstring purse were found in the midnight street—mute evidence of yet another would-be magadalen's lot.

Beyond this neighborhood, also, the lot of the ravaged church was being decided. St. Mary's would not be rebuilt, and the undamaged rectory and school would be demolished.

It was the archbishop who did it, an educated man, newly come out of the Midwest, determined to prove that the feudal system of the medieval Church was compatible with tax-exempt democracy. Well, he did, ... the archbishop, that is. The charred stubs of St. Mary's burned-out nave, declared the courts, lay solely in His Excellency's absentee hands ... stark evidence ... of something or other.

To the fore came the aging granddaughter of one of the German immigrant founders of the church. Did the archbishop know, she asked, that St. Mary's had been debt-free until the nuns withdrew from teaching its children? That $700,000 worth of insurance lay ready to counter just such a disaster as the fire? That the parish had actually purchased part of St. Mary's property from a previous archbishop? That the architectural curiosity (also St. Mary's) in which he celebrated mass atop San Francisco's Cathedral Hill had risen literally from the ashes of its own predecessor with pledges willingly encumbered by a faithful anxious to do its share—not the least of which was San José and, indeed, communicants of this very parish now in extremis? Yes, he knew ... for he was an intelligent man.

The parishioners sued the archbishop. My mother and Aunt Millicent had become rebels.

The gray-headed Jesuit pastor began to bald. He cautioned the elderly Annas against following dissident factions, reminded them of the authority of the archbishop and that the archbishop possessed all the powers of the priesthood—was, indeed, the full priest. He further instructed them that any communications from them to the archbishop should be addressed to "Your Excellency."

Aunt Millicent muttered in the tone reserved for discourse with herself, "Well, I've never questioned that before, but ..." My mother nudged her, whereupon Aunt Millicent scooted forward, brazening a question. "Tell me, Father. This archbishop. He does work for Jesus Christ, does he?"

The pastor swallowed. "Of course," he said.

Aunt Millicent nodded. "I'll tell you then," she said, explicit as only she could be, "I'm eighty-three years of age ..." Her cheeks colored and her voice mounted as it became apparent that everyone was intent upon her. "... and in all of that time I've addressed this bird's Employer by His first name—never Your Excellency ..." She paused and, doubling up her scrubbed fist, whacked the bench in front of her as she added, "so I'm damned if I'll use a title for some pompous mid-western fart who works for Him!"

The pastor's eyebrows arched as the ladies clapped. Aunt Millicent looked around, hand cupped to mouth, chuckling at her own daring. Where, the pastor asked, was their reverence? They must be guided by those who know best. The archbishop knew best. One had only to look at his urbane, Roman-collared attorney to be reminded of how much he knew. In open court that priestly official cited his law credentials from Harvard and Yale while the Annas listened, clutching their beads and holy pictures of St. Jude. Yes, the archbishop was an intelligent man.

The patron of hopeless cases writhed in uneven fingers as the court found for His Excellency and the archiepiscopal decree was pronounced: the age and diminishing number of St. Mary's parishioners did not warrant rebuilding the church, and the $700,000 insurance would be siphoned into the needs of other central San José parishes. Eighty-nine-year-old St. Mary's would never again house the sacred species. Worn-out wombs and arthritic genuflections have only a past. The tap of unstrung decades hit the floor in front of my mother, registering across the courtroom. Aunt Millicent turned to pat the beaded imprint from my mother's white knuckles.

Having done that which he had to do, quickly, and before motoring back to the archbishop, freshly installed in his thoroughly renovated chancery at St. Thomas the Apostle, the attorney for the full priest smiled at the disinherited members of the Mystical Body, one of whom wagged a warning at him, "You lied, Father, and I hope you're punished for it."

His sacerdotal smile deepened. "We must try to have a Christian attitude," he said and departed.

It was a lay person, Daniel Keyes, who wrote, "Intelligence and education that hasn't been tempered by human affection isn't worth a damn."

My mother and Aunt Millicent, living still in the family home, had become constants in the lives of my sons. Matriarchs of the Irish bloodline, they were there to give attention and to be paid attention to, nonvariables to the children of divorce, true roots sunk in South Fifth Street. But their own roots, Catholic to the core, had been badly shaken.

The wrecker's ball had staved-in one wall of St. Mary's School, two blocks west, by the time the boys and I rolled into the sparsely graveled driveway that Friday night. The echo of crumbling bricks lingered about the tall ceilings that ever before kept home safe, and those two fragile ladies shook with its abuse. They fawned nonetheless on the family's youngest scions as Drake and Tracy lugged in gear, including Waffle and a carton of unweaned pups. I hugged them both and felt the tremors that letting go had loosed in them. It was so throughout the parish. Waffle's wet tongue squandered affection on their nylons, her brazen teats lurching. My thoughts for the archbishop were not kind. What sort of shepherd tends his flock so ill? For the weekend at least, my mother and Aunt Millicent were distracted. Grandsons and grandnephews come easily to the art.

On Sunday, while Waffle nursed and Drake showered, Tracy and I paid our respects to the ecclesiastical ruins. Cloaked like a vulture on splintered timbers, a photographer pondered where to begin, his massive eye, drunk with indecision, finally flashing into focus: the vault of the crucifixion altar where Magdalen, Mary, John and the cross had vaporized against the hull.

"Watch out for boards with nails," I cautioned my sneaker-shod son.

He nodded, kicking bits of plaster and slats to one side. "Grandma's pretty upset ... about all this, I mean."

"Grandma and Grandpa were married here."

"How about Aunt Millie?"

"Do you mean, is she upset?"

"Huh-uh, I know she's upset. I mean, was she ever married here?"

I shook my head. "Aunt Millie never married, period. She only hoped to be." Odd the things we take for granted children know.

My son nodded.

Glass cylinders, chronicles of votive wax, caught the sun dully, one with a good ten hours to go on a twenty-four-hour intention ... and I wondered, would God credit an interrupted petition?

"What's that?" asked my son, pointing the toe of his sneaker toward a fallen Station of the Cross. "Jesus is laid in the tomb" was embedded in the floor, XIV shattered at the top.

"Sculptured scenes like that used to hang the length of both aisles, evenly spaced. They marked the special moments connected with Jesus' crucifixion."

I had not raised my sons in the Church. I'd had both baptized on the outside chance there really was a Limbo and the unthinkable occurred in either's infancy. I still suffered the abrasions of my "lost saints."

"People used to walk from station to station, praying before each one. A few even crawled on their knees. On certain days, the Church claimed, you could release a soul from Purgatory every time you did that ... made the Stations of the Cross. It had to do with indulgences ... plenary indulgences."

"Was it true?"

I shrugged. "I used to believe it was, and that was what mattered."

"You don't anymore?"

"No, ... I don't anymore."

He did not ask, "How come?" as was his habit. He was not ready to go further. Too many terms, perhaps, had to be hurdled. But neither was I ready to go that distance with him. I bent down to examine the thorn-crowned Christ, limp in the arms of the few who'd stood by, being interred in the Arimathean's tomb. I looked up from that wasted face to the surrounding ruins, and I knew that what had happened to St. Mary's was happening to me—the layers of my own façade disintegrating as I got at the essence within. The Christ in the arms of those mourners had answered "What must I do to enter the kingdom of heaven?" with, "Keep the commandments." Ten simple, direct codes—as unembellished as His own pale-ribbed corpse. But then, who's content to keep things simple? Theologians went to work on the Decalogue, building an edifice buttressed with such intricacy that the faithful could not be faithful to themselves, much less to God. Before long, all anyone could see was the edifice ... with plaster Christs evenly spaced.

I stood up again and watched my son mount the rafters collapsed in the center aisle. Sacred Heart had marked the religious milestones of our grammar school years, but St. Mary's owned all the rest. My sister's bridal train had sighed with its own weight as Kathleen moved serenely where Tracy now climbed. I'd followed my grandmother's casket to the sanctuary gates as a child and paced the same distance for my father as a man. And in between ... My eyes searched in vain for the carved closets where spilled seed and perverse lust had been purged from my soul. "Oh, my boy, you're much too young to be doing these things," whispered a priest when I was twelve. "Did you know," threatened another at fourteen, "that Agnew is full of people who sit around trying to squeeze one last drop from their penises?" At sixteen a confessor counseled, "Don't worry about attractions to other men. Once you get married, they'll take care of themselves." Lawyers and analysts, I think, owe much to the priest.

In the call of the Church to rise above our natures is, I suspect, the seed of our undoing. In the effort to be more than we are, haven't we rather become less? In denying ourselves, we never realize how fulfilling those selves might have been. Somewhere, amid the patina of sacred vessels, sumptuous raiment and the echoing vaults of columned cathedrals, a hierarchy lured to ecclesiastical privilege and princely titles has taught us distrust for ourselves and distaste for the callous-soled Carpenter they say they serve.

My mother and Aunt Millicent stung with the archbishop's betrayal. A tradition of reverence and trust succumbed to hard cash. Few prelates find value in requited virtue.

Yet the tradition of trust and of love between my sons and me was scarcely more sound. Would they feel betrayed when they learned that I'd tried so hard to role model for them that I'd never really been myself? That they didn't really even know me? I'd never trusted them with the chance. Everyone, especially the Church, said I shouldn't. What I was, after all, got confessed and kept under wraps, never loved and certainly not respected. Dare I trust them, my own sons, with myself?

I'd only begun to trust me with myself. Yet I knew it would have to be risked. Life without its essence cannot be lived, only played out. A role, regardless of the actor, remains a role. There can be no triumph in carrying through a charade except as performance. Would my sons, once I'd trusted them with the essence, prefer the role? I could not know without selling them short. If they withdrew from me, at least it would be me from whom they were withdrawing. That had to be preferable to loving someone I was not, to being false with them. "Thou shalt not bear false witness against thy neighbor" means nothing lest you discard false witness first toward thyself.

The trappings of the Church had come down around my head long before the nave of St. Mary's caved in, but the Church had been the mainstay of my mother's and my aunt's long lives, and they were bewildered. John XXIII's trek in the Shoes of the Fisherman brought shame to Vatican cherubs and consternation to communicants of the Latin rite. Having inaugurated change, he conveniently died, but the changes did not stop. Neither did they affect matters of substance: the celebrant consecrated bread and wine in the vernacular, facing the congregation; the costly organs that had swelled with Latin credos and litanies gathered finger-plucked ditties of grinning charismatics into their great throats, faint echoes of pale melodies.

Now, on South Third Street, even the house of that earlier devotion was gone, and an archbishop, who took no pains to know them, cut the Annas adrift.

How is the deconsecration of a church effected? Once blessed as a temple of God, how is it made secular again? And even if that is liturgically possible, how can the consecration effected by human lives be erased—that constant tide of devotion and doubt, affirmation and regret—that mark the ebb and flow of human faith?

"This," complained the photographer come down from his perch and discovering a tabernacle door in a pile of boards, "is typical of the insensitive way this whole thing has been done." He held up the scarred door to the Holy of Holies, glowing with sunlit angels. "They wouldn't let anyone come in and take these things; they just bulldozed them."

My son, lugging a marble column amputated from the base of an altar, came toward me.

Are ruins still consecrated? Does it matter? The decision had been made with feudal detachment and economic dispatch. Religion has thrown open the doors to the money changers, and His Excellency determined that restoration of St. Mary's was not cost-effective. It would not have mattered to the Carpenter, of course, in Whose name the whole exercise was conducted. Can you see Him inside waiting for worshippers anyway? That was never His style. He'd have been out on Third and William, I'll wager, investing time in the hookers and johns as the nuns in that corner convent worshipped what they wanted Him to be behind windows wrapped in wrought iron, as secure once again in their routine as the full priest in his new chancery out the Avenues in the City. And He would visit the houses of Annas deprived of their visits to Him. I'll bet anything.

CHAPTER 21

THE BASTARD

(or HELL IS FOR CHILDREN)

Drake glared as he sprinted toward the idling Dart. Pumping one arm into the sleeve of a sky-blue sweatshirt, he balanced the texts for his morning classes with the other. His sack lunch hung from his teeth. We were late again and he the last out, slamming the door on Waffle and leaving the screen ajar. Those Celtic features through which his mother moved in him twisted with the horn's last blast, and he tore the sack from his teeth mouthing the one word in all the world he should not have called me.

Beside me Tracy side-glanced and cleared his throat. My left hand wrenched the hand brake, lighting the dash panel, and I flung open the door. "Come on, Dad ..." but I was on the asphalt and striding toward my sixteen-year-old first-born, demanding, "What did you call me? What did you say?"

Drake stopped, retreating a few steps. "Nothing," he scowled, lips tight.

"Nothing?" I persisted, advancing. "Don't give me that! I saw you! Go ahead, say it. I'm tired of you muttering slurs under your breath. Say it so I can hear it."

He was six-three now, towering above me, but I had authority on my side. I grabbed the center of his shirt, clenching his Day on the Green decal in my fingers, and yanked. His still-damp, dark blond hair dripped on the cowl of his sweatshirt.

"What did you call me?"

He winced as my fist jammed his sternum. The lines of his mouth contracted. His beautiful eyes flashed darkly. "Fag! I called you a fag!"

The flat of my hand struck hard. He lurched up and out of range so the backward thrust glanced off his broad shoulder instead. Textbooks slammed on the concrete patio. "Don't hit me! Don't you ever hit me again!" he warned.

"Hit you?" I raged. "I'll pulverize you, you bastard! How dare you call me that! Bastard!" And my hand struck again, shoving him off balance into the ivy embankment behind the barbecue pit. On the locked utility porch, our devoted Waffle barked, scratched and whined at our conflicted voices.

"Quit it!" Drake yelled, his youthful voice glutted with tears.

Tracy watched, wordless, from the limbo of windshield reflections, spewing exhaust giving him a surreal quality as observer of the conflict. Drake sponged his sweatshirt against his face and struggled to rise, his fair skin braised from my blow. The indictment in his eyes caught me off guard with the double-fisted memory of my own grandmother, Fiona Finn. Thirty years dead, she brandished that wooden spoon she'd used to stir mutton and frowned at me, the face of a Dane masquerading in the brogue and ancestral names of Gaels. "Bastard!" she spat, wrinkled, wrathful, the blue too brittle in her ancient, angry eyes. "Bastard!"

I stopped, ears ringing, unable to distinguish her resonance from mine in the intimacy of blood divided against itself.

The recoil of tissue and tendon from their bond heals with a scar. The relationship would never be the same. There is no way back to innocence. I know. My view ever since of the Irish Dane has been through embattled eyes.

Uncle Wiggly on shared gingham and old lap ... my introduction to the rabbit gentleman who crutched his rheumatic adventures through my grandmother's voice with Sammy Littletail and Nurse Jane Fuzzy Wuzzy. She rocked us, Kathleen and me, beside the living room window where the light was good and the world passed between college and cannery along South Fifth Street. She read to us often but talked to us little and never about herself. Mostly, she rocked, thinking quietly, fingering the Irish horn beads in her apron pocket, a thin band of gold looped beneath her own arthritic knuckle. She rarely laughed, seemed always old. She passed evenings on the edge of the overstuffed so Muggsy could squeeze between her back and the chair's, the two of them dozing. My father, when he saw that, would whack Muggsy's black-and-white rump and tell Grandma for Christ's sake to sit back so she wouldn't fall off, but by then she was too startled to doze again.

She made pasties, old country meat pies with flaky crusts that held the steam through the first bite, and sugared pies thick with cots from the tree that leaned on the chicken-yard fence ... but I must work hard to pick out those aspects of her. The one thing that strides effortlessly to mind when my mother mentions her mother is that the latter woman called me a bastard once.

That she was right, figuratively speaking, is of little importance. She was my grandmother. That I was not only a bastard, but a self-righteous, sanctimonious pain in the ass, is not the issue. She was my grandmother. That I had precipitated an uneasy truce into another supper-table furor, has no bearing. Fiona Finn was my grandmother. To this day, when I pass her corner lot at Calvary, without stopping, what I remember is that she called me a bastard. I must work to remember the rest.

Few things make one as understanding about an offense as being guilty of it oneself. Calling my own son a bastard was the shuttle that dumped me on the threshold of forgiveness. Once the frustration peaked, I accepted the anger as necessary and the name-calling as purgative. I was suddenly on track with Grandma without even trying. Still, how does one petition the dead for forgiveness?

And what of my own son while there still is time for us? Bastard was easy compared to what he had ahead of him to forgive. Innocence in a child is expected, but innocence in an adult is a defect. The letting go is a phase that evolution hasn't fully worked out, a flaw in the progression of Alpha to Omega, a Jekyll and Hyde mix when seasoning begins and definition moves the features toward a beauty more sound than innocence.

But how, in any such resurfacing of self, do we deal with faggot? Bastard, at least, is solid and angry, a paradox of legitimacy in its ring of implicit admiration. Bastard is the only expletive to concede the first-rate exercise of the upper hand to the other guy.

Not so faggot. Faggot is ugly, derisive, despicable; the dreg of deep-seated fear and suspicion. The difference shows in the way the tongue wields the words and the heart reshapes the features. Bastard bludgeons. Faggot mutilates wielder and victim like a two-pronged pickax with thrust and recoil. Drake had to yank the blade out of his own guts before he could sink the spike into mine.

Did he know I was a faggot? He suspected, and the summons of his sixteen years required that he distill the difference between himself and me. In calibrating the margins of his own emerging manhood, he was suddenly not sure that I was a man at all, yet we were one bone and one flesh through descendant genes. I was no stain he could simply scrub off.

Faggots, of course, have feelings. My rage at being called one by my own son had as much to do with my own level of self-acceptance as it had with Drake's pre-set or after-the-fact conditions for accepting me. Either way he was serving notice that his suspicion threatened him. My rage, I confess, contained an element of vindictive celebration. Naming the suspicion forced us closer to the truth which I knew had to be spelled out eventually. But I understood his vulnerability.

I was, after-all, no longer just his father; I had become his teacher as well, a factor that qualified his friendship with his peers, whom, of course, I also taught. That I set and adhered to high standards in the classroom all but precluded his friendship with certain of them.

Neither Drake nor Tracy had wanted to leave Tacoma, but I saw the return to California as a desperate effort, if not to regain control of my own life, at least to improve the diminishing quality of theirs. The small mountain community that hired me late in the August of the bicentennial summer measured masculinity in Coors empties tossed from pickups with gun racks and barking retrievers on top.

I did not fish, hunt, coach, like football, have a wife, or any longer play the seat-him-beside-what's-her-name game. When I formed a long-distance relationship with another man, Drake probed its correctness. "You sure spend a lot of time with Degnan when we're in San José." I had just hung up from telling Degnan we were home safe and ready to eat.

I looked at Drake across the dinner table and nodded. Tracy glanced up from his tuna casserole. He'd been thinking too. I'd begun staying with Degnan on those trips while the boys tapped their roots in the old family home. Between times, Degnan and I strengthened our developing bond with telephone lines.

"Remember how it was with you guys and Topper in Tacoma? You were best friends, right? Some nights you stayed over, some nights he stayed over, and nights when you didn't, you got on the phone the minute you walked through the door because you had things to say that couldn't wait till morning."

Drake and Tracy looked at each other. They truly had not wanted to leave.

"Well, that's sort of how it is with Degnan and me."

And that was true, of course, but not the whole truth. What I was afraid to trust them with, I held back. The cry of the newborn is an appeal: "Love me for who I am," and we answer it with, "Sh-h-h..." Although I'd made strides, I was obedient still to that initial negative.

I wanted it to be different for them. I wanted my sons to welcome the world and affirm who they are, but I couldn't show them how. From my earliest perception, life was a game of hide-and-seek with no one ever knowing who was really it, and I hadn't the courage or the confidence to dash out of hiding, tag home and yell, "Free!"

I was so fearful that I would fail them as a single parent. I had so many roles to model for them that I never in those early years even considered saying, "Look, boys, this is who I really am, and you can be whoever you are." But that's when I should have done it. It would have been easier then. *Should* does no justice to retrospect. I didn't.

Colleen said to me once before her illness, as I meted out to Drake what I deemed reasonable discipline, "Be careful that you don't break his spirit, Ronald." That reproof tripped my tongue and salted my conscience through every scolding after. I do not blame the boys' mother for all my inconsistencies, but linked to my own reticence, that accounts for a number of slipped gears.

Scotch had brought amnesty to the scruples of my bachelor days when I could afford the glamour of discontent and, in therapy, indulge the drama of my difference. Gin became the elixir of choice as a closeted gay, single parent and teacher. It was not affordable either ... we had nearly lost the house to Colleen's illness-related costs ... but a decent gin undersold inferior scotch, and my taste buds were adaptable. It was the effect desired that was constant and upon which I'd come to count. In time I would surrender even the semblance of quality for that effect.

Loneliness allied itself with guilt and fear. The law, after the divorce, defined the mother of my children as a trespasser if she entered our home uninvited. Reasonable rights had been expected and granted, but she began an onslaught of attention the likes of which she had not come close to paying the boys in the last year she'd been with us ... rising to call them from San Francisco to wish them good morning, writing letters full of questions that her illness had not allowed her to express when she was with them. Her methods fluctuated with the moods of that illness, including periods of no contact at all, so that the effort to get on with our own fractured lives ran into continuous emotional detours and I drank.

I grew to resent those who predicted remission of Colleen's symptoms to the extent that she might return to us, and worse, those who knew someone else who'd gone through the same sort of breakdown Colleen had but whose husband had been cheating on her. I came to envy men whose wives had simply died ... and I drank.

Time eventually moderated Colleen's contact into an almost pleasant association, then just as inexplicably as with the other aspects of her illness, she opted for total rejection, a condition as bewildering to the boys as her earlier extremes ... and still I drank.

With Colleen gone, my homosexuality moved from understudy to center stage again, but played still to an audience of one. I paid a P.K., a preacher's kid, to stay with the boys while I sneaked off to Seattle's First Avenue, the original Skid Road, and the cinematic delights of the Sultan Theater ... a steady round of gay porn. The ticket seller, ticket taker, magazine sales clerk, and general manager of the Sultan wore a thin gold wire in his right earlobe. If he noted that the glasses I was wearing had no lenses, he was kind enough not to let on.

I had altered a pair of pants specifically for this venture by cutting out the right-hand pocket for easy access but would find, upon reading Portnoy's Complaint some time later, that the idea did not originate with me. When I was either sufficiently relieved ... or overcome with guilt, I would leave the screening room but get snagged on the skin slicks in the lobby. It was among them that I ultimately discovered a Gay Guide to the Pacific Northwest and the fact of the baths. The advertisement for Atlas Baths left little doubt as to its purpose, and I experienced a rush of venereal joy that the inheritance of Greek and Roman civilization included the tradition of such wallowing. The Jesuits would have us believe it had been buried in the collapse of those empires.

A lay biology instructor at the University of Santa Clara had gone so far once as to say, "Just wait till you guys get married and see what parts of your bodies are not sexual." I was particularly mindful of his daring as I turned the pages of that little guide. All my senses went on alert, my pores opened, my entire cellular structure was erect. In spite of the frenetic gropings and climaxes already achieved, my throat parched with renovated lust. I could scarcely verbalize my need for directions to the ear-pierced clerk.

Marking his place in his volume of Thoreau, he set the book on the dildo counter and aimed a graceful finger toward the east, looping it with the timbre of his voice to designate signal lights and half-blocks.

I thanked him and buttoned my old Air Force raincoat as I strode, collar up, an urgency in my step, out onto Skid Road. The preacher's kid had Wednesday night services to attend, and I had said I would be home in time.

Damp streets are not unusual in Seattle, so they were not the cause of my nearly rear-ending two other cars. The thud in my chest, as my eyes locked on the brass numerals discreetly announcing the Atlas Baths on the odd-numbered side, called to mind the palpitation I'd experienced as a child, and I muttered a quick but ardent, "God, if there is a God, don't let it be like this... at least for the boys' sakes." A bit of reverse guilt.

Maneuvering into an after-hours loading zone, I dashed across the street, sweating in my airtight Air Force issue. The Atlas was accessible only by elevator, and for that there were two other passengers waiting—one, a mild-mannered fellow in Levis and sneakers carrying a tote bag; the other, a woman with a sense of where he and I were going and a fascination for the elevator door. She did not once look at either of us nor even at the button panel which she finger-felt for her second-level stop.

My lips parted in a slight gasp as I wiped perspiration from my face and realized I'd left my glass frames in the Dodge. The doors closed on my oversight. I had no poetry to capture the moment—no die is cast or caution thrown to the wind.

I gave my furtive glance to the woman's soft behind as she exited the car into the second-floor corridor and wondered, despite all my years as a husband, what it would be like to be gutted with desire for her as I was by the sheer anticipation of what the doors' next opening would bring. Swarming in and out of their cerebral barracks, my morals rioted at their second eviction of the evening. The sneaker-shod fellow smiled sweetly over the doors' next closing and whistled tunelessly, watching for the 3 to light up overhead. His manner was one of coming from, not going to, the field of satisfaction, and I marveled at his composure. He did not look at me either except to note that there still were people who wore trench coats, then moved into position to exit.

The hall was paneled in dark wood. Behind the window secured with brass bars, a supple-toned Adonis moved under well-spaced track lights, chatting with my elevator companion and signing him in. My breathing was irregular, and my voice, when I found it, would be thick with reconditioned need. I tried to avoid staring, but each subclavian suggestion and pectoral ripple of this modified god subverted my eyes into undeclared anarchy. Slipping a towel and keys under the bars, he buzzed the whistler through with best wishes for a good time, then turned on me his clean gaze and sunlamp-sharpened smile.

What first took me back upon advancing to the window was the Levi waistband riding the clerk's tanned hips, exalting the soft-furred navel with an undone button.

"Hi," he said, and I ached as much with his tone as for the fact of his pants. "Got your membership card handy?" That was the second thing to take me back, and this I suspected was serious.

"Membership card ...?"

He nodded, "You've gotta have one to get in," and his slender knuckled hands brushed a fresh stack of laundered towels flat for folding.

"Damn!" I exclaimed softly. A door's breadth from fulfillment of my most flagrant fantasies, and I was thwarted by a two-by-three card.

Adonis watched me, his eyes prism blue and leaded, the thumb of one hand slightly arched on the terry cloth.

"I can't just buy one?"

"Well, yeah, there's a quarterly, half-year, or annual fee but ..." But— the one word summary of Paradise Lost. It was my turn to nod.

"But?"

"The bars. Someone at the bars has to recommend you."

"Where are the bars? I'll go to ..."

The soft gilt of brass sharpened the distance between us, and I realized suddenly that my fingers were hooked in the lower brace of the security grill. The clerk's expression had grown wary.

"Well, if you don't even know where the bars are ..."

His eyes followed the quick retreat of my fingers. My eyes filled and I thought, "Oh, shit, don't tell me I'm going to cry."

"Look, I'm not from Seattle," I blurted. "I just found out about you from the fellow at the ... I can't even think of its name now ... the gay theater."

"The Sultan?"

Adonis began creasing the towels into crisp thirds. "The Sultan, right. On First Avenue. I was just there. He gave me directions. Won't he do?"

A pause indicated that the point might be arguable, and I held my breath. But then he said, "That's really our policy. You do have to be recommended."

"Could I just come in and take a look around?" That clearly established me as a trench-coat undergrad, and I saw that all avenues to Atlas would have to be reapproached.

He was not unsympathetic. He tore a sheet from a two-by-three pad and jotted an address. "Okay," he said, "there's another place a few blocks north of the Sultan. Dave's. You don't need a membership there. Why don't you give them a try until you get known at the bars. Then come back and see us." He passed the slip under the rungs and winked. "It's really a hot place on weekends, but it'll do for beginners tonight."

"Thanks," I whispered. I folded the slip carefully. My wallet was in the glove compartment of the Dodge to ensure against blackmail or scandal in the event of a raid.

The evening was very young, but, as I nodded at Adonis, the clock behind him read 7:10, and that was too late for Dave's and the more penetrating sins of the flesh. My needs must yield to the P.K.'s schedule. Double martinis and left-handed screwdrivers would ease me down from the evening's disappointment and assuage the retribution of morals in tenuous reprieve.

I was scared by the time I called AA, scared and sick. The tremor in my hands had become noticeable to random observers, and a pervasive weakness kept me at the brink of nausea most of the time. Drake and Tracy were eleven and eight respectively. Eight hundred and fifty miles separated us from our next of kin, but she flew up once again to care for her grandsons, and I signed myself into a three-week alcohol recovery program at Puget Sound General.

My principal was stunned, not by my request for a long-term substitute, but because he'd had not the slightest inkling that I drank inappropriately. Indeed, I never drank during the day unless occasionally on the weekends and holidays. I'd maintained control enough to delay intake to late afternoon or early evening—that nebulous merging of light with dark, which, for me, the longer I drank, arrived earlier and earlier in my anticipation of the hour.

My mother wore her worries in her face and in the white coif that had too early marked her with age. Since my father's death through the prolonged indignity of cancer, she had responded without hesitation or question to the need created by Colleen's hospitalizations. She simply came on the first available flight following our call. Our pain had taken its toll on her already, and it was far from through with her yet. Here I was, on top of everything else, declaring, "Look, Ma, I'm an alcoholic!"

She was not quite willing to admit that I was one of those people. They were, by and large, a scummy sort. Adjectives are often a more accurate description of the speaker's feelings than they are of the noun they set out to modify.

She didn't want me to be that ugly word and, somehow, not saying "alcoholic" softened the reality, kept it at bay.

But then, even my brother, Allen, and his wife had trouble with the concept. They didn't believe I was really an alcoholic any more than they believed, when finally I confided to them my deeper truth, that I was really gay. A good woman, they advised, would solve both problems. They saw me as an excessive personality, predictably unpredictable, except that I was bound to outgrow whatever phase I had presently gone overboard into.

I was past needing confirmation of either my alcoholism or my gayness, but having the guts to make the admission publicly was not part of my own conviction. It took me two or three rounds of introductions before I could hurdle from "My name is Ron" to "I'm an alcoholic." It would take another four years before I could substitute gay for alcoholic especially without equating sexual orientation with illness. I am not proud that I'm an alcoholic, but I am proud that I can admit it because that's essential to my recovery, part of what keeps me well. But when it comes to being gay, I can now say that I'm just proud because that's essence, a part of who I am. That was not the case then.

None of the lectures, none of the group encounters or AA meetings even hinted at alternate sexual orientation. Puget Sound General's program combined diet, relaxation therapy, and medical supervision with all of the above techniques, and I still came out ignoring the basic truth that had put me in there ... except for one brief conference with the Red Bear. He was a huge man with a cinnamon beard, my counselor by choice rather than assignment. To him alone in the confines of his office I struggled with the confession that I am gay. He had urged me to give him whatever was weighing me down because his shoulders, he said, were strong, and after I had let it go, he would let it go. It was an appealing concept. When I finished he did a moving thing. "Stand up, Ron," he said, and I did. He rose opposite me and took me into the warmth of his massive freckled arms. "Thank you," he said. "Thank you for being."

I was undone by his kindness.

Steinbeck wrote in East of Eden, "Nobody has the right to remove any single experience from another. Life and death are promised. We have a right to pain." I would go him one better and say that growth is the obligation to confront that pain, met. And that is what was wrong with the Red Bear's desire to shoulder what weighed on me. His intention was good, his method incorrect. My secret left his office in my guts, not on his back, as it had come in. It is not in the nature of things to be otherwise.

If there were gay AA groups then, I heard nothing of them, and I did not ask. I was returning as ill-equipped, alone, and isolated to my outside existence as I had come in ... dried out, yes; marginally hopeful; terrified by the obligation of three weeks' sobriety.

On that twenty-first day of the program, Drake and Tracy walked out of the elevator at the end of the corridor. My suitcase stood packed beside the nurses' station. I smiled as the boys walked hesitantly toward me. Tracy wore glasses in those days—little round horn rims—and he unconsciously nudged them up the bridge of his nose as he picked up his stride, then broke into a run. I opened my arms, a laugh unbridled on the brink of my throat, and caught him as he flung himself at me, arms and legs clinging as I spun for balance.

Drake continued to walk, self-consciously smiling, allowing my hug when he reached his brother and me. My mother watched from the elevator entrance, tearful, worried.

I knew immediately that I would not maintain sobriety. The very act of signing myself out pulled the plug on the support systems that had created the artifice of hope within the hospital. My basic needs had not only gone nowhere, they had not been dealt with. I could not really believe in that ambiguous power AA addressed as Father and to Whom they would have me surrender my control as we joined hands at the end of each meeting. Their precept that I must put myself first, my needs before Drake's and Tracy's, ran counter to all the indoctrination I'd received in service to that same Father ... and counter to the message of in-the-closet cover among them where only once I mentioned me.

Smiling, we put Grandma on a Sea-Tac return flight to San José ... but she was not fooled. In the few extra days she'd stayed on with us, she'd seen how brittle I was. The habit of alcohol was awash in the memory ducts of my blood and my experience. It equaled the need of my cribbed sexuality, had, in fact, become indistinguishable from it.

The system in which I role-played, affirmed homosexuality only as the butt of humor and ridicule. Fellow teachers joked about a seventh grader who ogled their genitals in the showers, and I let that child go unchallenged for fear of how they would interpret my defending him. AA's formula for putting oneself first was correct but not candid in the context I experienced at that time. Its necessity to recovery and wellness is prime and basic. But it means cutting through the shit and pretense that garbage up our lives catering to others' expectations, that arbitrary code of conduct that requires bleating obedience. It means taking the risk of insensitive laughter, ridicule, disparagement, and scorn, and stepping outside all that by the simple, anguishing act of faith that allows one to declare, "I am who I am."

But I was not there yet. I smiled through outpatient meetings; took the boys to Bingo nights crowded and clouded with the anxious and the desperate overdosing on caffeine and nicotine in their campaign to stay sober. For a lot of them it worked. I lasted three more weeks then dug out the carefully folded address of Dave's in Seattle.

The preacher's kid had just shut the door and headed down the alley. Drake poked his head into the kitchen the instant the ice cubes hit glass. "What are you doing?" he asked, alarmed at the blue-labeled Walker's on the sideboard.

"What does it look like?"

"Don't ..." His sneakers squeaked against the linoleum.

"Just leave me alone; it's all right."

"Not if you're going to drink again, it's not." He grabbed the glass from the counter and spilled the contents into the sink.

"Goddamnit, Drake! Leave me alone. If you pour it all out, I'll just have to buy more, don't you understand? And we can't afford that."

He watched me, expressionless. I could hear Tracy scrambling out of the bean bag on the living room floor. My voice was edged with desperation. "Look, it didn't work. I'm sorry. The hospital or AA. Neither of them worked."

"Call the Red Bear guy," Tracy pleaded from the doorway. I turned from them both, poured more gin and gulped it down.

"Dad ...?" Tracy was beginning to cry. I shook my head feeling the surge in my blood, the warmth expanding my chest. I refilled the glass and swallowed the undiluted gin so that when I turned to them it wouldn't matter.

Waffle kept us sane, giving love, asking nothing; alternately the object of deep affection and private rage from the three of us. She taught us much about ourselves.

Listed at the humane society as cockapoo, she retained that coif but grew to airedale stature and, when wet, exhibited that profile. Her coat doubled the length of the airedale's but kept the shading, tending to black on the back with caramel legs and muzzle. She had an expression that went straight to the heart. While I believed in touching and spontaneously hugged my sons, Waffle taught us what hugging was all about. And when they kissed her wet nose I succeeded, most times, in biting my tongue. She was torn when we argued, whining from some deep sense of its wrongness and its rending. Freshly bathed and brushed, she entered a room like Zsa Zsa Gabor in chiffon, and those great brown eyes embraced us through blowing fluff with never a trace of guile. Waffle was an object lesson in love. Waffle made sense of love with every wet lick and slinky movement, while I verbalized but contradicted its essence at every turn ... then drank some more to cover my inadequacy.

I did not have hangovers, but I could not remember the nights before. People outside the family could not tell that I drank unless they saw me in the act, and even then they were unaware that I drank too much. My dusks, I mentioned, moved further and further into my afternoons. I resented the boys' soccer matches and swim meets because supporting their effort interfered with the evening's anesthetization. After-six commitments I restricted to necessities unless alcohol was available there.

A drunk learns to manipulate, but so do his children. One thing can be said for me—if I hadn't arranged for a sitter, I was always home ... not always conscious ... but always home. What the boys knew I would forbid them to do or to view, they simply waited for. Once I clicked off, I was not easily wakened. Those times I did stir to find them past their bedtime engrossed in filmed violence or mature-audience seduction, all hell broke loose.

Grim tales about abused children always sickened me. The suspicion that I was myself abusive I read in my sons' expressions as I ranted over their misdeeds and omissions. The taut time prior to drinking and the stupor following were hardest on them. The flush of the first few drinks mellowed me, vented effusively paternal feelings, yielding at times to melancholy. Love and guilt converged making this my time to compensate before turning that same love back on them as an instrument of guilt. I used my loneliness and their mother-loss as goads for cooperation and self-serving sympathy. The "I can't do it alone syndrome" is valid as "We can do it together," but I coupled it with "I may have to send you to your Uncle Allen or Aunt Kathleen. We can't go on this way." And, when late at night I would waken to the jittery, staticky blur of the television, I would find my unfinished drink, invariably within reach when I settled, removed.

Fiona Finn was right ... even if she was my grandmother. I was still a bastard. And Drake was right. Faggot is an epithet that grants no dignity despite the blood spilled in the earning. There are those who have given their lives to bring upper-case legitimacy to that six-letter F word, but I had given nothing at all. As long as I stood, ears stuffed, in the shadows of men like Harvey Milk who implored, "Come out, come out, wherever you are!" I was a faggot without title to the upper-case spelling.

Neither of my sons openly accused me of abuse. Drake came closest four years after our return to California. At age fifteen rock made the only acceptable sound-prints on his musical scale, and KISS posters wall-to-walled Tracy's room. Fundamentalists noised the charge that rock stars had leagued themselves with the devil and that their praise of the powers of darkness could be heard by playing certain discs backwards. Tempo and discord alone argued diabolical intent in my book by the end of any teaching day, but the latter charge seemed patently silly. How did one even play a record backwards? Bad enough that the school halls before, after, and between classes reverberated with Journey, Black Sabbath, and the Grateful Dead. The last thing I wanted in the waning hours of the day was more unabated crescendo. But there was Drake, head bobbing, foot tapping, as relaxed as if Babes in Toyland wooed the tensions of logarithms and Spanish translation from his tender mind and lengthening limbs. A half-gallon of low-fat milk split the bottom of the Bonnie Hubbard sack as I hefted it onto the counter with my grade book and papers. Drake had not heard me come in, say hello, honk for help with the groceries. A female voice throbbed, "because HELL! ... HELL IS FOR CHILDREN!" until the windows shook and the pathos shriveled in its clay pot beside them.

Sticks-and-stones fundamentalists surged into the bastions of my weakened resistance. While I gave no quarter any longer to doctrinaire creeds, this seemed a natural blasphemy. Even the blunt of mind must recoil at the perverse connection of children with hell.

"What kind of song is that anyway?" I shouted. Drake jumped, turning to look at me.

"What kind of person would write lyrics like that? Turn that damned thing off!"

Drake's head lolled against the couch cushions. He looked at me with the tried patience of a philosopher-king thirty-five years ahead of his time. "Have you ever listened to the words?" he asked.

"Listened! How could I not?"

"Hearing is one thing; listening is another."

"Don't equivocate with me!"

"Why are you yelling?"

"I'm not yelling, goddamnit! You can't hear me over that aberration you call music if I don't raise my voice."

"That aberration ... your word ... is about child abuse."

He stopped me dead. The fundamentalists scurried for cover.

"Run that by me one more time?"

Drake leaned over to lower the volume on the stereo, then, imitating my most distinct tone, said, "The song 'Hell Is For Children' is about child abuse. That's what Pat Benatar's singing. Not that kids belong in hell, but that they are in hell when ..." He shrugged. "You should listen to it."

She was there again, in the back of my brain, brandishing that wooden spoon. I tugged the knot from my tie and forced myself onto the edge of the couch. "This I've got to hear," I said, avoiding his eyes. "Play it again, ... would you?"

Drake obliged. Tracy even made a copy of the lyrics so I could study them minus the decibels competing for Benatar's voice, and they had the grace to leave me alone with the confrontations.

"They cry in the dark so you can't see their tears. They hide in the line so you can't see their fears. Forgive and forget all the while.

Love and pain can be one and the same in the eyes of a wounded child..."

I had the grace to be embarrassed but not to own the song's application to us. I was already manipulating my "I've failed you's" into the front lines of self-defense.

A real bastard.

I'm overdue at that corner lot at Calvary.

CHAPTER 22

SECOND ANDY

Andy is dead again. First time he never grew. In Sacred Heart he stayed yardstick size while even fourth graders bean-stalked him into neck strain. Squat and yellow, he'd have been the seventh grade's in-house hobbit had we known about Tolkien then. Andy didn't even talk unless he had to. He just watched with the brownest eyes I'd ever seen ... like he was contemplating, all the time contemplating. His crew-cut corn-silked out of his skull like sheared spines of dark gold. Kids make mascots out of Andys. Maybe the difference makes them nervous. They have to do something about them. One glance at him advertised like San José's old Fox movie marquee: ANDY'S SICK! "Stunted growth" tied up our tongues, defined sympathy for us and taught us more about fear. Little kids didn't die. Edna St. Vincent Millay said so: "Childhood is not from birth to a certain age ... Childhood is the kingdom where nobody dies. Nobody that matters, that is."

Andy mattered. But he died. And he was even a kid. When Fr. Onerazani said we should be glad, that Andy was so good God wanted him with Him right now, you could feel the virtue drain from our hearts. Anyhow, Andy just wasn't there one day. The spot on the porch where he used to stand and watch, we stepped around. We knew.

His raw-boned brother taught us about condolence ... and that was interesting because Pritchard (he answered only to his last name), Pritchard was the one nuns always forced to say, "Sorry."

A public school survivor, Pritchard's folks put him in Sacred Heart, my father surmised, "to slap the piss and vinegar out of him." I guess it worked. Sr. Nicene Creed came off the wall at him his very first day when he called Eddie Fosta out for laughing at his highwaters. It seemed like Pritchard got all Andy's growth hormones on top of his own. Not only were his cords too short, they snugged up everywhere—especially over his privates.

Leaning purposefully against the door jamb as the class single-filed to recess, Sr. Nicene Creed muttered a hooded warning about fighting as Pritchard passed ... and Pritchard back-talked.

I learned for all time the meaning of "the shot heard round the world" in that split second when Pritchard's head rocked ahead of the sound. A backward glance at Sodom and Gomorrah couldn't have locked us more solidly in place. Nicene Creed's wrath rained on Pritchard. Clearly, God was on her side. Of all the things she shouted, we remembered only Pritchard's carefully guarded first name: MARION! It cracked off her lips before, behind and between each assault: MARION! ... MARION! ... MARION!... Even Eddie Fosta looked sorry.

And even sustained shock wears out. Pritchard's set jaw eventually quivered. His eyes burned against the tears Sister wanted, and she discharged till they fell. That was on my mind as I shook Pritchard's hand awkwardly at Rancadore's Mortuary and said, "Sorry about your brother, Pritchard."

Pritchard knuckled back his grief as, one by one, his classmates blessed themselves at Andy's little casket. Gardenias layered the closeness like smudge in an early orchard. Andy looked out of place ... as if he didn't mind lying there at all. You sort of got the feeling that if you'd raised him to a sitting position, his eyes would pop open and he would say, "Ma... maa... Pa...paaa."

After the rosary, the grownups turned their backs on Andy and talked. Outside, I watched as Pritchard kicked the juniper planter with the toe of his scuffed shoe. Just watched. While he knew it and savored his sorrow. This thing Andy had done set Pritchard even more distant from us, crumbled his kingdom... Pritchard pretended it didn't matter. He tried to fit his fists in his corduroy pockets, but they wouldn't go, so he hung the thumbs from the corners. His voice broke toward a dropped octave and strung itself taut. "Shitty, this," he confided, indicating the chapel with a nod. I kind of caught my breath. I can't help wondering whether Pritchard grew into a mean s.o.b. the way Sr. Nicene Creed thought public-schoolers had to, or whether he'd made it to Sacred Heart in time. I know one thing: what he had going on inside singed the rims of his eyes and hollowed his nostrils wider than most. More ways than one, Pritchard made up for Andy.

Second Andy did his growing two months ahead of me and on the other coast. We were both thirty-seven on this coast, however, when our needs converged one August at the Bachelor Quarters up the peninsula from San José. Second Andy blended the temperaments of the Pritchard brothers so that, despite his own differences, one could read success in the habit of quality he demanded for his own person: Wilkes Bashford three-piecers, BMW commutes, a tri-level gambled against an east San José slope for a slant at the panorama. Parlaying the rules of the game into understated comfort, Second Andy traded off passion for the security of financially reciprocated affection. Second Andy was lonely. His partner Brad honored his bed but not his body—couldn't handle going down on him—buffering the isolation that aloneness can dupe one into taking for the real thing. If Pritchard's anger chafed his outside edges, sadness softened Second Andy's.

An out-of-state, in-the-closet summer repatriate that August, I took my chances on anonymous sex one humid afternoon in a BQ cubicle. Second Andy rubber-necked at my open door, then turned out of cruise stride, eyes brooding over the black thatch that ambushed his upper lip.

"May I come in?"

His confidence in common denominators suffered the loss of hangered labels and weightless weaves, elsewhere in that labyrinth, behind a door whose key glistened on snug elastic above his ankle. No bathhouse demigod, Second Andy had no supplicants in pursuit. His brown eyes waited.

Scooting sideways, I patted the made space. Thin gold threaded the contours of his neck as he turned in the muted light, closing the door. Terrycloth, tucked at his waist, parted up his thigh as he eased beside me onto the narrow pallet, resting his hand on my farther flank. My fingers traced the ivory swell of his bicep. I stroked the quiet call of his flesh.

Testing a kiss, we explored the evidence of aroused phalli with impetuous breath, contracting the signature of unrestricted touch to the abandon of mutual anonymity. We needed to rut. Shamelessly. Honestly. And we did. Bare heels slamming the wall boards. Frantic with the obsession repression imposes. Venting the impulse of natures compelled to express their splendor. Ignition rapt in the voyage of contact, male against male, rudders governed by the anarchy of skin and dogma of desire. Rutting... Rutting... Rutting... God, yes, splendor! And unqualified release. God?... Yes, the name most coupled with coming. Orgasm hauls the soul into the vestibule of beatific vision. Divinity dwells in the moment, sanctifies the act and renews us. We are born again in the candor of acknowledged need, more honest, more complete than we were before.

Haste claimed no margin on our narrow pallet. Lust, let go, left us tender, our sense of each other strong. Second Andy penned his number-with-the-view on his card and I, for the first time, dropped my encounter alias. We risked histories in summary, discovered needs to further assuage. "I want you in me," pronounced the clear scripture of bonding, "I want you to come in me," the rite beyond getting off ... an edited act pierced with the reality that in our fused bodies lay more than the accident of separate entities in rut; that, sexually connected, we were also expanded, ennobled. Reason, conditioned by the arrogance of episcopal edicts, we trusted to the madness of flesh; to core spurts; to essence thrust across the threshold of tongues; to the potential of person in squirted pearl—eaten, consumed, absorbed into the throb of each other's life force. That communion left each of us, always, more than we ever had been.

Steamy in that nourished aftermath, we finger-traced the after-play of thanksgiving with kisses drunk in given confidence. I knew before he told me about the difference we didn't share. His was the dialect of the too-precise, compensatory correctness. Cleft palate had designed the arches of his childhood years before ever the aim of arousal cautioned his sexual disparity.

For Second Andy the standard squalor of whiteheads, blackheads and hard-ons had been more heavily endowed with waiting than most. In the normal course, adolescence teaches one to endure. But beyond that, for Second Andy, what God's mercy had withheld, age delivered in the solemn aspect of a three-faceted exodus: surgically alterable features, facial hair to mask the trace and the independence to relocate. Second Andy cut out on the wasteland of his youth, but the indelible imprint of his waiting rode his adult carriage with subtle, ineffable sadness, etching his relationships, as I was to personally discover, with uncertain parameters.

His pain in my kiss, my tongue probed the remnant of our drawn seed in the effort to further ensoul. I defined for him the dimensions of my own confinement with its attendant ache for validation—and the stranger who had paused at my cubicle left my arms with the benchmark of affection. Second Andy had become my first gay friend. But he is dead now. Andy Pritchard had belonged to all of us and to none of us at the same time. But Second Andy belonged to me ... an innocence recovered from a kingdom's rubble. Second Andy is dead ... and that matters.

I drive 101 and glance east where the windows behind which he measured his worth still flash with the sun ... and I cannot fathom that they do it without him. The vigor of memory makes his death obscene. The glide of his pores resides still in my fingertips, marking recall a vivified pain.

Behind that flashing glass, we made love without being in love; clandestine, yet with all the valley in a dazzling drift of buildings and bay beneath us. In that qualified intimacy, we nursed the need at each other's core, sucked the sap that is the quality of flesh and character of soul—the stuff of life imbued upon merger. Second Andy lives in me. I have ingested his seed, digested his need. I am forever changed, and this change fondles his absence. I miss him even while I have him.

Some say that in that sucked seed lay the seed of Second Andy's death and the lingering threat of my own undoing. But prophets of fear are not privy to meaning's eloquence. Beauty owns no shame. God, Himself, could not fault our search for Him in the holy revel of exchanged seed. Hazard breeds in the hauteur with which society refuses sanction to homosexual relationships. Death is not the real issue; depersonalization is. Numbers pale beside belonging. The onus for gay promiscuity lies in the doctrine of denial among those who honor their gift of faith as the seat of reason for all. Rote quote of Romans, this and Corinthians, that falls from their lips like chips from the tablets of stone circumventing the Gospel of Love with the Gospel of Paul, the fanatic whose stroke-induced conversion shifted his penchant for violence from external to internal persecution. He is still stoning Stephens. Sunday after Sunday, apostles of the apostle mount pulpits across the nation to truss up the messianic message with Old Testament negatives, restoring fear to love and caution to fulfillment. What blasphemy to endorse the epistles of Paul with, "This, my brothers and sisters, is the word of the Lord." Fear, underwritten by Paul, has staged the quality of our loving and the character of our relationships. The closet is no place to thrive.

Second Andy's relationship with Brad was as selectively open as it was financially committed. Even had we been in love, there lay no option for us beyond the modified affection of occasional encounter. The distance of that context carves stark features on habit. Time, unkind in such lapses, makes brittle the edges of change.

I hesitated the first time Second Andy paused in our lovemaking to offer me amyl. I hurt the next. My single experiment with his first offer dispatched my brain in a reel that reduced orgasm to coincidence. Amyl did not court my senses; it forfeited them. My body's capacity for its own high backed away from such summits, cheated. I knew then that I was not necessary to Second Andy's desired effect. No one was. I never used it again, but Second Andy rolled away from each brink to plug his effect in each nostril. I mourned this inhaled dimension of his sadness. Wine and amyl contrived an orgasm that knocked Second Andy into a soft snore, his understated comfort underscored. Passion passed him by.

Comfort validated him, ministered to the respect he craved. Over lunch at the Stanford Barn in the fall of '78, he announced his intent to fly east for the 25th reunion of his high school class. How the varsity football squad had carried the last quarter-century particularly intrigued him. My surprise at this athletic allusion amused him.

"The only muscles I developed in high school were in my throat and the back of my neck," he clarified, "under the bleachers and after turn-out. By the end of senior season, every halfback, fullback and tight end had unlaced his pants for me with only a gasp and a grunt for a thank-you."

He poked the crust of his quiche, turning the fork reflectively. His brown eyes leveled on mine. "I'd like those campus hot-shots to know what the hair-lip faggot has done with himself."

He smiled. Hurts like that held on to him.

"I sometimes wonder," he mused once over a sunlit Drambuie, "what might have been had you and I met before ..." His silence shrugged across the portals of candle flames. We hadn't. And we couldn't. My parenting alone precluded that earlier possibility. Besides, we were not in love. He could settle for that. I was pretty sure I could not.

Second Andy indulged himself with others; he never pretended otherwise. Yet, some snag in his ethical fabric forbade me a like option. My pleasure in his person exceeded the sexual. I valued him and expected that what I thought we shared beyond bed could extend the relationship and, in that, I miscalculated.

Resentment redefined the boundaries of our intimacy when my need for bonding pressed its search into a vigorous six-month relationship with Chris, a fellow teacher. Double-tongue characterized the sincerity of our telephone contact during that interlude. Second Andy admitted that to me when my affair's demise readmitted me to occasions in his foothill sanctuary.

"Frankly, I was jealous of Chris," he said. His bristled upper lip marked time with his phrasing. His eyelids lowered self-consciously as I watched him, then lifted almost expectantly. "I know it doesn't make sense, but I was." His fingers turned the stemmed crystal shedding a prism across the linen. We had not made love yet, nor would we. Wine and his poppers had brought us full circle, so I settled for a quick rut. I like to think I hoped for more, but I settled. Second Andy was snoring when I left.

Degnan in my life had the sound of the real thing, and Second Andy sensed that. The last unreturned call I placed to the east foothills, Brad answered, summing up for me what I'd been stepping around.

"I told Andy, 'You're going to lose this man's friendship unless you respond.'"

That was clear enough even for me.

He did meet Degnan, as it turned out, though not by design. Second Andy and Brad still-lifed an, "Oh, God, it's another Friday!" at the Main Street Bar on Stockton Strip one evening as Degnan and I exited the dining room. Too early for the revelers, the pair festooned the bar with their silence, bartender at a respectful distance. I recognized Brad. Maybe it was his "late for the Watergarden" look.. Perched on an opposite stool, Second Andy watched ... eyes brooding. He had grown a beard. I had shaved one off. "My God, what a change! So this is Degnan." Hands clasped in a habit no longer comfortable. No one lacked the grace to suggest a get-together ... though I wished he would and mean it.

He was ill then. I should have known by the way he watched. Andy Pritchard had done the same from the porch at Sacred Heart. But I didn't pick up on it.

That last intersection of our lives magnified how disparate our directions had grown. Second Andy had once examined a need to march in San Francisco's Gay Freedom Day Parade in an effort to give something back to the community. Not only had I marched, I had plunged into multiple facets of the Gay Rights movement, including writing for Our Paper/Your Paper, the local gay and lesbian publication. I hope I'm wrong, but I suspect Second Andy's only steps down Market Street any last Sunday in June pressed no more than a sideline search for a shady curb. Ironically, it was through my activism that I discovered that he was dead.

I sent gay arts invitations to all my contacts in the community during my term as chair of the Arts Council of Gay and Lesbian San José. Most responded. Second Andy was among those who did not.

Midweek between San José's and San Francisco's Gay Pride celebrations in June of '85, I slit the seal on an envelope containing Second Andy's eight-month-old memorial card and a note from Brad explaining my unanswered arts invitations. Shortly after our Main Street meeting, Second Andy had been diagnosed with AIDS. By the last week of August, his warm ash had been scooped into an urn, his brooding transfigured into a bronze glow in the niche of a columbarium.

"I thought you'd like to know," Brad concluded.

I remained at my desk a long time, the notes between my hands hard as chiseled ruins from childhood's kingdom. Anger shoved both fists against sorrow in the space between mind and heart, accusation torn on the pain of useless reprimand. "You bastard, Second Andy! Didn't you know how you mattered?"

CHAPTER 23

SEED

I had decided to go whole grain. My sons and I were alone by then, and consciousness about their health and well-being had begun to impede my weekly reach for Fruit Loops and Frosted Flakes until, one afternoon in Safeway's cereal aisle, I threw down the gauntlet. I had yielded for the last time to those colorful, grinning despots that animated Saturday mornings with a hype that dictated Thursday's shopping list ... and the level of my sons' nutrition.

Tracy's expectant features synchromeshed directly from disbelief to assault mode as I accelerated the cart, with him in it, past the wanton stacks of refined, reinforced and reconstituted sugar fixes. His little legs, dangling from the child carrier, bolted forward so that I virtually doubled up from the force of his Red Wing belly whomps. He hadn't intended to kick his father in the gut with his boots; I honestly believe that. It was instinctive tantrum strategy, instantaneous withdrawal reflex, without malice aforethought. His little fist even stifled his outrage somewhere between tonsils and tongue-tip as the connection between his kick and my contortion registered.

Drake, however, clung to the Fruit Loop shelf, hitching up his highwaters and calling, "But, Dad ... But, Dad ..." at my distancing back.

Health food stores run to mature tastes. Clean. Serene. Sacked bulk and hand-lettered signs. No mass-produced "AS ADVERTISED"s to abrade consumer consciousness. Proprietors operate less for profit than because it's the right thing to do and assume your presence to be the responsible choice of a discerning human being. I loved it. It was as if, suddenly, I moved in an aura of my liberal arts degree, the mark of Abel stamped on my forehead. I was appreciated. I could entrust my sensitivity to these astute beings and feel valued. I loved it.

Drake and Tracy wouldn't even come in. Slumped in the rear of the Dodge, they alternately punched the M.D. toilet tissue bagged between them and competed for Waffle, whose wet tongue and plumed wag urged solace upon them.

A narrow, griseous woman with an expression vaguely exhumed moved behind the cash register, ringing Clover Blossom honey and yogurt starter for a girl in Ben Franklin glasses with Walden Two peeking from her backpack.

Slipping a pencil into the hair pinned above her ears, the clerk turned her thank you into my welcome with no duplication of effort. "Yes, sir?" she smiled wanly, her half-eyes secured by a cord looped behind her slender nape. The contact sent my preconception packing. It had been the light, I decided, that had cast her in pallor. Her features, in fact, were animated ... vigorous even. I sensed, suddenly, that here was a James Hilton centenarian who would lock the store and wander its darkened hallway to a door that, each evening, readmitted her to Shangri-la.

"How may I help you?" she pressed.

"I ... I'm looking for ingredients to put together a genuinely nutritious cereal," I said, "and, frankly, I don't know where to begin."

The wattage glowed in her gaze. With an opalescent gesture she beckoned and I followed, assured by her stride that hers was the truth of oracular insight. She stopped under a skylight in the store's exact center before a counter tiered with bulked grains, dried fruits, chipped bananas and shaved coconut. She turned, features transfixed, spreading her prismed hand like the Mediatrix of All Nutrition. "All this will I give you..." I half expected her to tempt. Instead, she said, "Any combination you see here will work, as long as it has the life in it."

My silence defined my dilemma. Had I missed something? Was I simply obtuse? Or was this health food nuttery? Was there, after all, something over the edge about these people? "Whatever has the life in it?" I ventured.

Her loose bouffant bounced. Her eyes pulsed full power. "In other words, if you planted it, it would grow," she instructed.

Came the dawn! It was the stroke of perception, the descent of the Paraclete ... I believed!

It had to make sense, after all. Any grain, any seed that masked in its mute and innocuous shape the capacity to sprout, had a power with an indisputable energy source. The simplicity of the concept astounded me. Incredulous, I marveled that I had never reached the conclusion myself, awed that the world was not banked at the doorjamb for this hoard of health. "The more simple," my Jesuit profs used to say, "the more perfect." God, in fact, was utter simplicity. It was mankind made God complex. Even so, I saw that what I now possessed had nothing to do with such complexity. I did not believe. I *understood*. Simplicity and power had become manifest in the cyclical principle, and it was wondrous to behold. It made perfect sense.

My conversion coincided with Anita Bryant's orange juice crusade against homosexuals from her Dade County pulpit. The astigmatism that so jaundiced Bryant's Bible Belt war against same-sex sexuality came clear as I stood before the shelves of sacked seed. Bryant's disgust that gay men "eat the male sperm" missed the exquisite simplicity of that queer redundancy and, ironically, focused more sharply the issue. At issue, beyond the heterosexual aesthetic that naked bodies in cavort be one male and one female, was the destiny of the dissilient sperm ... the male seed. That the pursuit of pleasure has created a contraceptive empire of detoured seed among heterosexuals and that oral/anal intercourse between opposite-sex partners as effectively rerouted the syrupy spurt from its "primary purpose" were facts not the least disruptive to the former beauty queen's tender conscience. One male ate another's sperm. Anita could not contain her horror. She talked in tongues that called to arms the congregation of American rednecks who like their Misses sweet.

Florida's Jeanne d'Arc had conviction, even courage ... certainly ardor. They quavered in her voice. She lacked insight, understanding and, most of all, compassion. I disagree with Christ. Thomas the Apostle deserves primacy among the twelve. It is blind faith that nails us to the cross. Bryant's capacity to conceptualize could never compass the sublime character, the essential sanctity of male-male loving. But I saw it, and I would never be the same.

Seed's function is twofold: to reproduce and to nourish. If reproduction is primary, nourishment is by far more common. Pleasure attends both. If every seed harvested from the Dakotas to the Gulf took root, Americans would need machetes to move. Millions of tons of grain reaped annually from the heartland fulfill their purpose, not in the vaginal troughs of tilled fields, but in the digestive tracts of the earth's best-fed people. We are, we are told, what we eat.

Seven-grain breads trim our platters of slabbed ham, hash browns and sunny-side up, fertilized eggs. Coast to coast and border to border, families breakfast, lunch and dine on seed of some sort that would, were it planted, grow ... at least before processing. While caviar can't be had in quantities sufficient for expensive palates, cattlemen boast the efficacy of mountain oysters to their squeamish city counterparts.

Seed consumption is an essential fact that doesn't lend itself to question.

Fish eggs and bull testicles are not in the same league, of course, with the consumers whose teeth grind them for their attributes. They lack the denominator of common species, are lower levels in the hierarchy. The goad in the Maid of Miami's chain mail seat was that male homosexuals eat the seed of their own species. Faith shielded her from the fact of the act among rutting heterosexuals. Bryant's commission concentrated on the quality of cannibalism in this rite among queers.

I recognize reasoning broached from the brink of balance. It is the risk of those who have not seen, yet have believed. The needs of my own flesh would summon me finally from the fissure of blind belief, but I did my time in that purgatory.

In the caved confessional of desire-driven youth, I plagued an aging Jesuit with questions of metaphysical nuance that Ignatian theology had not equipped him to deal with: "Father, if the sperm joins with the egg to produce a life, then, when I masturbate, have I committed half a murder?"

The white head weighed my need for guilt in the covert silence. There were at least eight parishes in San José, four of them Jesuit, and he had to draw mine. "No," he rasped finally. "Don't worry about things like that."

But I did worry. A sense of magnitude was upon me. At the core of my adolescent faith, the Holy Thursday miracle distinguished God from imbalance and bound me in its mystery. I could not get enough of guilt in my gratitude. If anyone could be worthy of the transubstantive generosity of Christ, surely it was not I. "Take and eat, for this is my body. Take and drink, for this is my blood." Unleavened bread and wine consecrated, their species altered, become the body, blood, soul and divinity of a barefoot Rabbi whose seed of hope became the harvest of conflict. It is an article of faith. Dogma indisputable. Even this distance into agnosticism, the concept of transubstantiation wraps me in retroactive awe. I've never stopped wanting it to be so.

"If I could believe," a nun once quoted an atheist, "that God was the true substance of the Catholic communion wafer, I would crawl down the aisle on my hands and knees and prostrate myself before their golden tabernacle."

Mexican people do that while Anglos frown on such self-abasing display. What gives Hispanics their capacity for awe?

It is a transcendent concept, a mystery plumbed always inadequately. Appetites appeased in a Sunday brunch, Catholics pile into the parish sanctuary for their soul food—Christ seed consecrated in hands that thump the pulpit denouncing homosexuals for making love.

I dreamed once during therapy of myself naked and hard in the throes of orgasm. I stood against a landscape vast as El Greco's Toledo, wafer-thin hosts ejaculating from my stiff phallus, consecrated Christs surging into that verdance, bounding into the copulative throat of Toledo.

I awoke to spasms, to seed spent on my stomach as if the hand of God had done the manipulating, the nectar of spirit and flesh gone wanting but for the renewal left in its ebb. It was not wasted. But it had no one to nourish. To the concept of continuance Mother Church lends the force of dogma—birth and resurrection—body, blood, soul and divinity in each swallowed host. Even so do Christmas and Easter reside in orgasm's incarnate residue, that plenipotentiary spurt that is the transport of body, blood, soul and humanity.

Habit makes the mystical mundane. Three meals a day in the fast-foods context alters the character of ingestion/digestion, the ritual taken for granted. It is a lost awe.

The power to sprout is itself astounding, but to grow into a vibrance that yields yet other seed is a tangency hidden in the commonplace, a fingertip miracle routine with repetition. The sunflower seed garnishing my salad is a sprinkle of power complex beyond imagining. Sown, it would rise to cast me in its shadow and, turning its ample face in pursuit of the sun, empower in the process hundreds more of its kind. It is a splendid simplicity the energy of which grinding molars and throat reflex release into the chamber of person, nourishing. It is an impassioned perception that returns me with reverence to the genitals of my lover and the nourishment of his seed at the coaxing of my tongue... all the power of his person in a single squirt from his core. Here is mystique. Here the miracle of power sourced in a vessel tooled for transcendence ... pleasure and the potential of person converged in chambers and ducts that await desire's edict. Orgasm's sperm. Ejaculation's seed. Spurted. Savored. Consumed. Not a person, but the power to imbue one. Nectared traits communed and absorbed, amending and appending.

But someone ... something has tampered with the process, interfered with the rite. In this age of packaged products pulled despoiled from market shelves, a virulence has invaded the silos of our seed. We live in a present that mandates a modified sacrament, that looks to the future to resume nature's rite of sacred species in systems restored. And that will happen. The act is intrinsically and mystically sound.

The Bryant brood in the '80's hatch has refined its venom. Chapter and verse punctures gape with ignorance as fundamentalists coil in the President's lap, their dry-leaf rustle become an Oval Office rattle: Drain the neighborhoods and workplace of gay seed silos. They strike even at each other from the floodlit warmth of political podia, and still the blind believe. Such faith has no virtue. Give me a Thomas anytime. He who must see and touch incubates awe. "My Lord and my God!" is that man's gasp.

Drake and Tracy, meanwhile, stay slumped in the back seat of my determination. Consciousness about their well-being motivates me even now, moves my pencil, in fact, across these manuscript pages. Prevailing evidence indicates that we pass this way but once, and my decision to make this passage count affects them. Happiness lies neither in length of days nor in the absence of pain. On the brink of fifty I have that yet to teach them. Oh, I have told them. These pages, I hope, will show them. The real energy for living feeds on honesty, draws nourishment from a sense of worth. Self-acceptance is the seed that has the life in it. It can neither be sown nor pursue the sun ... in the closet.

CHAPTER 24

CANTICLE

Her eyes stopped on me. I don't know why. She didn't pick Kathleen because Kathleen was a little girl. But Allen was there, and he was twelve. It should have been Allen she picked, but it wasn't. I knew I was her target as soon as the red-lipped woman slipped the knot of her sailor's arms and began threading the crowd along First Street. The sharp stink of firecrackers scattered revelers off the curb in front of Hale's display window where at least the mannequin retained decorum. Insanity was rife. Confetti and forty-eight-starred flags thickened the air at adult level, then filtered in shadows and oscillating pastel down to mine. My mother and father seemed oblivious to my wringing hands as I maneuvered behind them, out of range, I hoped, of those descending lips.

When the perfume chased off the sharp stink, I knew I'd been had. "Oh, no's!" rattled in my skull but no one paid attention. The woman's mouth pressed its full moist warmth against mine. "Happy Armistice, kiddo!" she exclaimed and mussed my hair with her red nails.

My parents laughed. Kathleen giggled, "Ronald's got lipstick on." Allen regarded me with narrowed eyes. Gladly had I yielded him the honor he envied ... even when, returned to her firm-flanked seaman, the woman rewove herself in the M-1 nest of his arms, one soft breast tucked each in those hands trained to trigger and stock. It was when she leaned her head against his chest and parted her lips for his insistent tongue that the chord of my canticle was struck. His red-lipped probe defined need like bronze rung in spires, resounding in naves. Then and there I owned that kiss. I went hollow with its ache. I was not of an age to call that desire, but it was. I was of an age to suspect what I felt for its pleasure, particularly its intensity, and to know that I must keep my own counsel about it. Mother Church wages early the campaign against feeling.

Twenty years past Armistice I idled my domed Morris Minor at a San Francisco curbside for another firm-flanked seaman whose quick eyes picked up my need and, breaking stride, leaned to the door I opened.

His thigh, taut with fabric, stretched effortlessly beneath the edict of my touch as he angled his duffel bag in back, waiting for my fingers on his firm flank to complete their cursory search of his black-flapped groin before settling into the seat. He was that considerate.

The descent of his blond head in my lap shone like divinely defined tendrils gilding consent. It was a rite of vessels venerated, mouth to phallus, moving from lust to the fine print of need with soul the mentor. A directive deeper than instinct guided the tender ravage of tongues to the implosion of loins and ultimate orgasm. It was in us. We had always known what to do. Leaves in the September sycamores rustled like ecclesiastical silk locked beyond our risked privacy, behind windows fogged with indulgence. Need transfixed us in that two-door tabernacle angled in Pacific Heights' shadows. An old resonance of that earlier seaman stirred the urging of my fingers at the tendons of this sailor's neck, and the lyrics of legend sanctified our testament. Here was the Song of Solomon versed in my lap: "Let him kiss me with the kisses of his mouth: for thy love is better than wine ..." Lines that had honed desire and would sweeten memory. "... By night on my bed I sought him whom my soul loveth: I sought him ..." Knuckles chiseled with urgency, cheeks hollowed with a hunger that drove the clean-shaven jaw to rise and fall on my phallus. "... I will rise now and go about the city in the streets, and in the broad ways I will seek him whom my soul loveth ..." Him whom my soul loveth. These ardent lips. This insistent tongue. Could this ciborium of my dispatched seed be him whom my soul loveth or was he, were these, only symptoms of my search? "I sought him, but found him not ..."

He spat my seed into the vertical space between moonlit cars, only a precursor.

Passion uncommitted relieves but doesn't fulfill. Loneliness threads the stroke of after-play. He left me with an Act of Contrition ... and his shoes. In the dark he had changed into civvies and sandals. His issue shoes troubled the floorboards all the way to San José, where the light in my family's yard caught their shine, swift kicks to the conscience ... and reminders of very good tongue.

I could not find my discalced sailor, but the search for him whom my soul loveth pressed the detour of another two decades ... the streets, parks, bookstores, theaters, restrooms where stereotype waged all the probabilities. "... But I found him not ..."

"Saw ye him whom my soul loveth?" Always his semblance. Ever a surrogate. Only a precursor. In the Watergarden's infrared corridors I sought him, contour covered in terry-cloth, whetting the Michelangelo in my touch. Sublet passion multiplied desire in my carnal search for the absoluteness of soul. Emission ebbed not with appeasement but with promise in the next flux, easing at last the four-decade chafe of my scruple-ridden mind. Penis after penis lodged in my throat while my own pulsed on tongues wet with the seed of my seeking. I became a whore to become a man, discovered the depth of Magdalen in the surface of numbers. Quantity holds the potential for splendor but remains a runner-up in an environment that refuses to nurture. How many arms must embrace, how many legs entwine to refine need? "Saw ye him whom my soul loveth?" Beneath the numbers stirred a constant, a caring that precluded anonymity. Consensual pleasure has hope as its nub.

Degnan quickened that hope, moved like dawn into my eighth day. I read his gentleness in the value of his touch. My pores knew first. I loved him quickly. Degnan ... "I held him, and would not let him go ..."

Naked when we met, we alluded first to common denominators and found the sum of ourselves divisible by two. I had loved the taper of his limbs in thin-flamed El Grecos, admired his stretch in Rodin's supple Age of Bronze. Degnan looks that he may see, hears when he listens. His is the wisdom for endurance, a sense of the long run that rides my impulse and tempers my compulsion. He remembers that he loves me even when I am not lovable. In Degnan I found the tendresse that gave away Du Maurier's scapegoat to the Comte de Gue's beautiful Bela. His fortune in the shards of a cookie once read, "You take a reverent attitude toward life and are most capable in the guidance of others." Every word is true.

Beyond rigidity, coupling tempered to caress, to care's incalescent canticle: "Let him kiss me with the kisses of his mouth for thy love is better than wine ..." and I understood that if God could damn me for such a draft, then I would neither have nor want His heaven.

The chord of my canticle is a weight sweet as the Beloved's head on the breast of Christ when he whispered, "Lord, who is it?" I have drunk at Degnan's lips, been nourished at the font of his being. I know the truth of St. John's intimate gesture and the pain of Christ's failure to be clear. Anita Bryant reviled homosexuals for eating the "male sperm," but all of life is nourished by seed whose power has been redirected from the soil in which it would reproduce. Its yield is nonetheless life.

It requires little to imagine the head of the "disciple whom Jesus loved" lean up, mouth ajar, to receive the tongue of his Savior in those moments of impending loss and ease the despair of what awaited phrasing: "Why have you abandoned me?"

Judas was a scapegoat. Mother Church is the traitor. "That ye love one another ..." passed from the lips of Christ into platitude carved up by sectarian hierarchies who instruct the faithful in Christ's intent. Pharisee and Sadducee are more than words on biblical parchment. They are mindsets. Today's priestly aristocracy simply go by different titles.

The Bible with which I grew up was imprimatured by Francis Cardinal Spellman and edited by the Douay-Confraternity of Christian Doctrine. Spellman was vicar of the see of New York and of the United States Armed Forces during World War II, facts that lent particular credence to his signature on that "divinely inspired text." Alternating between khaki and crimson, black-and-white newsreels kept the Cardinal's short form in the public eye and consciousness. God was clearly on our side.

The Word of God that bears the Cardinal's imprimatur runs 680 pages longer than Degnan's King James. Granted, it has larger print. But, more importantly, Mother Church included meticulous instruction on what God had in mind in His quaint parables. It goes to considerable length, for example, to impose a New Testament schema on the Old Testament Canticle of Canticles, making it an allegory of love between Christ and His Church, between Christ and the individual soul. Considering that Solomon ascended David's throne in 972 B.C., this energy seems academic, but more, it focuses on the spiritual dearth of committee intellect.

The spousal relationship of nuns to Christ has long been noted in the Church, even, in some orders, to the wearing of gold bands on the wedding finger. But what to do with men?

A spousal connection would be contra naturam, after all, so the necessity of projecting this relationship into a purely spiritual, nebulous plane, has left Christian males ill-defined, suspicious and suspect ... especially with that nasty New Testament business about "the disciple whom Jesus loved."

Prelates circumvent the issue and the embarrassment by declaring the soul sexless, but is it? My soul is the depth from which my loving generates. Is that love devoid of the fact that I am a man? I think not. My love is more honest than that. I reject the ecclesiastical blind spot that maims the virility of male love and would shackle, still, emotional castrati to the arches of unquestioning conscience ... alone with their uniqueness.

There is a privacy about each person's pain that makes empathy a noble but incomplete gesture. So intimately does pain fix the route of our progress that our stride is slower for want of it, affected irremediably by its absence. We progress only in the presence, immanence or remembrance of pain because, perhaps, nothing else equals its quality to endure. And, as with death, none of us takes pain's measure with quite the same stride. We overcome, succumb or simply survive at our own pace. The pace of overcoming, stride aside, is constant, but its reward is rapture. I will settle for nothing less.

The world is intensely sexual. Joy is the orgasmic interim, the diastolic interlude that marks pain's ebb in the act of being. Orgasm abounds in nature, throbs in beauty's essence. Even denied, orgasm is glimpsed God. Those who find no renewal in orgasm opt among unfortunate choices: perceived safety of ecclesiastical imperative, mental instability, or the rigor mortis of no risk. Pain is infinitely preferable. Joy not only renews; with it we surge on the lambent tides of potential, chancing to crest in sunlit spume.

Nailed to a crossbeam between the windows of San Francisco's Twin Peaks bar hangs an epigram that is the bane and the glory of every patron within assessing the intersection of Castro and Market without: NO CROSS • NO CROWN. Both challenge and indictment, it is a terse reminder that life is not fair ... but worth it. No accident nailed it to the crossbeam of a gay bar. Not a single eye coaxed from the thrall of shadowed jaw or the sweet swell of junctioned thighs need linger over its intent. Its four syllables move like fingers at the back of the neck, easing the strain of being oneself at whatever stage that happens to be ... or goading like prongs of conscience because the challenge went unmet. Pride and guilt. Joy and shame. Determination and anger. Eased. Provoked. NO CROSS • NO CROWN. Simple and incisive. Profound. In the yoke of each other's company, we derive grace from and for the fact that coming out never ends.

At Castro and Market, gay intersects with the globe, and the effort is constant. Pride parades and candlelight vigils weave the community into mainstream with prism-gamuted banners and costumed-seethe, haunting, hallowing our hollowed-out need: the right to be in a world that sets the beat even for drummers.

Out of step is a dangerous place to be.

Near midnight on July 7, 1984, in Bangor, Maine, Charlie Howard, a blond, effeminate, pretty, gentle, twenty-three-year-old gay man who carried a purse, swished when he walked, and lived by the motto, "I am what I am," was "chased, pummeled, kicked" and thrown from a bridge into the ten-foot-deep Kenduskeag Stream canal by three youths fifteen, sixteen and seventeen years old. They ignored Charlie's plea, "No! I can't swim!" so that those four syllables became the last that pretty, gentle Charlie ever spoke. His murderers pleaded guilty to manslaughter so that by age twenty-one, each could stalk the steps of some other Charlie.

Traditional churches will not bless the crown Charlie's cross bought him. His martyrdom is the more sacred for that ... and make no mistake ... it was martyrdom ... and it was betrayal. The youths who murdered Charlie Howard acted with the complicity of power ... police who shake their heads as they grin over "boys will be boys" antics with unintended outcomes ... families embarrassed that "one of those" is one of theirs ... the Church that condemns the pretty Charlie Howards among us as spawn of Lucifer, children of Satan ... and threatening damnation ... short of abjuring one's own inherent ... inborn ... natural being.

Innocents are raised up to believe in the protection of power ... family ... police ... church. When those powers turn in disdain from their purpose, it is betrayal ... flat-out betrayal. I believe in the devil, but his name is neither Lucifer nor Satan. It is Ignorance and Fear, the two-headed fiend nursed at the dugs of Mother Church to ensure her power.

Degnan and I hold each other through moments of that kind of mourning. I kiss him with the kisses of my mouth, draw strength from the draft of his love. I tilt my head to the insistence of his tongue, yield my fingers to awe of him whom my soul loveth. Together we probe the chords of our expanded canticle ... pretty Charlie ... and nameless others become chants in the litany of our difference, dimensions in our crescendo. "Set me as a seal upon thine heart ..."

Degnan ... I lower my head to the nest of his neck. I hold him and will not let him go.

CHAPTER 25

OBSCENITIES II: THE PERFECT IMPERATIVE

I remember the fore edge of Diego Cantata's English anthology as the tardy bell summoned fourth period to begin. Not that the bell mattered much to the mix of tenth through twelfth graders on that July forenoon. Summer session ran half days; it was all anyone dared. The door we'd propped open in the hope the outside 82° might moderate the inside temperature, and kids wiped sleep from their eyes anticipating the real world at twelve o'clock—buzzing over Santa Cruz summit, surfboards biting the salt breeze, or serving up orders at Wendy's with that new Technics stereo in mind. It wasn't the noise that bothered me. Had finances not dictated it, I'd already have the morning invested in my manuscript, after all. It was that book under Diego Cantata's elbow, aimed in my direction, with its felt-penned imperative: HELP !

Diego didn't notice me notice. He chatted in his mellifluously tinctured second language with the punk-haired girl on his right, his considerable girth tented in trench coat even in beach weather, his fingers idly lifting and dropping the text's hard cover. Bold strokes. Solid. Retraced for intensity: HELP !

As I bisected the discussion circle, the hush set in. By the time I paused at Diego's desk, his voice had no competition and the punk-haired girl bit the smile from her lower lip as her glance shifted to me. Diego stopped like alerted prey.

"Uh ... Hello, Mr. Schmidt."

Laughter rippled around the room.

"Hello, Diego," I said and reached for his English anthology. "May I?" I asked.

Diego lifted his elbow. "Sure," he shrugged. His chestnut eyes watched quizzically as I picked up the book, then widened in his butterscotch features as he remembered the fore edge. "Ah, I can explain that, Mr. Schmidt." His grin exposed strong, straight teeth.

"I'm sure you can, Diego. Let's see if anyone else can."

I held the text fore edge out and rotated for all to observe. "Spontaneous reaction, people. What can you tell us about this?"

For a moment no one said anything.

"It's a word," someone finally ventured.

I nodded. "That's a start. There's more, much more."

"Diego's in trouble."

Laughter.

"That depends on his explanation. What else?"

"It's gonna cost him thirteen ninety-five. 'Least that's what they charged me when I lost mine first week'a regular session."

"Think communication," I suggested.

"That's communication. How's Diego gonna explain to his folks he needs fourteen bucks for vandalizing school property?"

More laughter.

"It's what he wrote that's significant and how it relates to last night's reading assignment, in particular."

"To 'The Cask of Amontillado'?"

"So that was the assignment."

"I know!" Diego said, his hand flagging. "It's what I would've been screaming if I was Fortunato, chained to that wall and getting bricked in. God, that Montresor guy was crazy."

"Ah-h-h ..." I said.

"Ah-h-h ..." two or three imitated.

"Diego gets an A," said a voice from behind.

"Well, Fortunato doesn't scream HELP ! but he sort of does in a different way," said the girl with the punked hair.

"How, Davonne?" I said, returning to my seat in the circle. "Can you find that for us?"

Beaded strands from her triple-pierced ear shimmered as she riffled pages and followed her designer nail down the text. "He says, '*For the love of God, Montresor!*' and it's like all italicized. That's like saying HELP !"

"Only it takes a lot longer," said Chet, three seats to my left. "Anyway this is a story and you gotta use sentences. HELP ! ain't no sentence."

"Isn't no sentence," Davonne corrected.

I held up Diego's book. "You're saying this is not a sentence?"

"'Course not. It's just a word."

I held the silence.

"It must be a sentence."

"I don't see how."

"I know," Diego said. "It's one of them whatchacallit sentences..."

"It can't be a sentence cuz it gots no subject," Chet insisted.

"Has no subject," I winced.

"That's what I said."

"But it does have a subject," I persisted.

Diego waved frantically. "Imperative!" he blurted. "That's what it is, an imperative."

"Ah-h-h ..." I said.

"Ah-h-h ..." the imitators imitated.

"It's a command or request," Davonne offered.

"That's what imperative means," Diego countered.

"Well, you didn't say that."

"Fight! Fight!"

"You're both correct," I intervened. "Diego has given us the Latin label and Davonne, the English derivatives."

"So? ... I still don't see where the subject is," Chet said.

I pointed again to the broad stroked HELP ! "What part of speech is this?"

"An action verb."

"Exactly, and who is performing the action?"

"Whoever hears ... Oh, it's the you thingy," Davonne said, slapping her forehead.

"Understood you!" Diego blurted.

"Right again. You, understood, is the subject of this sentence."

"Good job, Diego," said another student admiring the fore edge eloquence.

"Whyja write it?" asked another.

"Yeah, rehearse your thirteen ninety-five explanation on us."

Diego tugged the halves of his trench coat and grinned. He looked up at me and said, "Well, see, ... now don't take this wrong, Mr. Schmidt, but sometimes I feel just like Fortunato in school; you know what I mean? Like I'm getting walled in and nobody listens or gives a ... nobody cares."

Davonne smiled, the gold beads swaying in the alcove of her neck and dyed hair. Her Eurasian eyes watched Diego, and the room quietened.

"Well, okay, you listen, but this class isn't like most others. I don't know what Fortunato did to Montresor; in fact, I honestly doubt if he did anything. Like I said, I think Montresor was crazy, but I hated him because I knew what Fortunato felt like."

It was the kind of moment teachers wish they could bronze.

Then, a boy who had listened quietly till now said, "I think Fortunato got what was comin' to him. 'Fact, I think we oughta wall up the rest of the faggots too and just get rid of 'em."

Several students guffawed. A few grew silent and watched me. Diego leaned his forehead against his hand and muttered, "Oh, my God!"

"Kyle," I said, "maybe you were absent when I said that epithets are not allowed in this classroom."

"I don't know what that means, epi ... whatever."

"Put downs," Davonne explained, "like killer words. You said 'faggots'; that's an epithet."

"We want to hear what you have to say, Kyle, but the way you phrase it needs to respect race, religion, color, creed, and sexual orientation."

Kyle shifted. "See, I didn't even finish the story. Soon as I discovered they was fag ... fairies, I told my dad, and he said I don't have to read no story about fairies."

"What gave you the idea 'The Cask of Amontillado' is about fairies, for God's sake?" Diego demanded.

"Wait ... Wait ... Wait ... Let's back up just a bit," I said. "Fairies is as much an epithet as faggots. Can we use accurate terms here?"

"Sorry," Diego replied. "Homosexuals. What gave you the idea the story was about homosexuals?"

Pale streaks on either side of his mouth lengthened Kyle's narrow face. He flipped through his anthology and pointed to the second column under Poe's bold title. "Says so right here: 'He accosted me with excessive warmth ... He had on a tight-fitting parti-striped dress ... I was so pleased to see him that I thought I should never have done wringing his hand.' Now I think of it, sounds like they're both queer."

Moderate laughter. Mid-circumference two fellows nudged each other and watched me.

"You're skipping parts," Davonne challenged. "Anyway, it says right in the sentence before where you started that it was carnival season. Don't you know what carnival is?"

Kyle smiled tightly. Davonne's beaded strands quivered.

"It's Mardi Gras," she explained, "like we have in New Orleans."

"Don't matter," Kyle said. "Men dressin' like women's against the Bible, and the Bible says homosexuals' an abomination. Go to San Francisco sometime. They're all over the place. My dad says you can't be sure you're goin' with a woman till ... well, till you get her home. Any guy tried that with me, he'd have to get a face job before he could pull it on somebody else."

More hands rose, indignation competing with laughter.

"Let me just clarify the cross-dressing concern Kyle has. Cross-dressing is called transvestism, and it doesn't necessarily have any connection with homosexuality. Many transvestites, in fact, are heterosexuals.

"One thing more. Kyle has used the Bible as the authority for his views. Now, no one is required to answer what I'm going to ask next, but if you choose to, it could be very meaningful for the sake of this discussion. How many of your families regularly attend church?"

About half the class raised hands, some reluctantly.

"Okay, now of those who attend church, how many have women family members who wear hats or veils to services?"

One hand sneaked tentatively up. "My grandmother," Haley Bix said.

I nodded. "Next question is more personal: how many of you are from homes where divorce and remarriage has occurred?"

Over half the hands went up this time ... including Kyle's. "Twice," he said.

"According to St. Paul, women must cover their heads when they pray, and as for marriage ..."

Diego nodded. "Jesus said, 'What God has joined together, let no man put asunder.'"

The class was still. Finally Kyle said, "What's that got to do with the queer story?"

"Do you mean 'The Cask of Amontillado'? The story in which you think Fortunato is a homosexual?"

"That's the one all right."

"I thought you thought the Bible had something to do with it, Kyle. You brought it up."

"You're twistin' my words."

Diego shook his head. "No, he's not. You did bring it up. If it's supposed to work against cross-dressing, then it ought to work against divorce and remarriage; that's a lot more serious."

Kyle stared at Diego for several seconds. "Some que... 'scuse me, homosexual propositioned my dad once ... in a bar. My dad punched that sucker's lights out."

"Why?" asked Davonne.

"Why?" Kyle repeated, incredulous.

"Yeah, was he insecure?"

Kyle shifted as several students laughed.

"Davonne does have a point. When you come right down to it, isn't a proposition a compliment of sorts?" I asked.

A number of heads nodded. Diego leaned toward Kyle and said, "If you don't want to, you don't have to. Just say no thanks and walk away. Why beat somebody up for appreciating you?"

A blond girl with intense features had brooded through the dialogue. Suddenly she threw her pencil into the center of the circle and it stuck in the carpet. Everyone looked at her.

"Jeanie?" I said, "Are you okay?"

"I just can't handle this topic. I don't care what anyone says, Kyle's right. People like that are disgusting, and I don't think we should be discussing them."

More hands went up.

"Chet?" I said.

"I don't agree ... with gays or with Jeanie. I believe it's wrong cuz my pastor says it is, and my folks say it is, and the Bible says it is, but I think we should be able to discuss it. I mean, I never thought about what you said about women havin' to cover their heads to pray. That's stupid, and practically everybody I know's divorced and remarried at least once. I just never thought about it till now. I don't want nothin' to do with no gays personally, but like Diego says, if the Bible's 'sposed to apply in one case ..."

"Why don't you want anything to do with gays, Chet? Do you know any?" asked Haley Bix.

Chet grinned. "No ... Do you?"

Laughter.

"Hold it a second," I said. "Jeanie, you said you couldn't handle this.

Do you want to be excused to the library till we finish? That offer is good for anyone else who finds the discussion offensive."

Jeanie shook her head silently, her jaw working vigorously on gum.

"Okay, but I appreciate your sharing your feelings with us. In fact, a lot of people are sharing important things. And you know, Chet, I don't think you were being malicious, but your response to Haley's question is the kind of technique prejudice uses to frighten people into silence. 'No ... Do you?' sets the scene for guilt by association. If you know someone, and especially if you defend someone who's gay or lesbian, then gosh, maybe ..."

"I don't mind answering," Haley said emphatically. "I do know someone gay, and I really care about him. And if anyone thinks I'm gay because of that," she shrugged ...

"Lesbian," I suggested.

"What?"

"If anyone thinks you're lesbian," I clarified.

"Right," Haley nodded. "Anyway, my neighbor is nineteen, and he's the sweetest guy you'd want to meet ..."

"What's his number, honey?" asked one of the elbow-nudgers.

Haley bristled. "He had to move away because of jerks like you, you know? It really pisses me off. He's always doing something for someone else. You just sit there and make stupid remarks. I used to be able to tell him when things got too heavy for me, and he knew how to listen without telling me back. He'd let me talk and ask a question now and then that let me figure it out for myself. It's just not fair there's no place for him in my neighborhood, but guys like you live in every other house."

"He just sounds too precious," the elbow-nudger said, but even his pal looked embarrassed.

"Did his whole family move?" asked Davonne.

"Are you kidding? His folks couldn't handle having the neighbors know. They didn't even ask him to come home to visit."

"That's what I'd do," Kyle said. "If a kid of mine tol' me he's gay, I'd tell 'im, 'There's the door and don't come back.'"

"Oh, sure," Haley said, "and if the law suddenly changed and said it was a crime or a sin for you to want girls, would you change?"

"Nope," said Kyle, "I'd kill myself before I let some slime faggot go down on me."

The room fell totally silent. Outside a school bus pulled into the loading zone.

"Anyway, like I said, I don't see what this has to do with English," Kyle finished.

"One of the goals of a literature lesson," I said, "is to relate universal themes to our own circumstances. Kyle, you suggested that Fortunato was a homosexual, and we took a look at that. Whether he was or not is not as important as what we can conclude about the human condition, the predicament that people continue to create for one another, in the hope that we can learn from that conclusion. Look, for example, at this tragic character's name. Why do you suppose Poe chose Fortunato for the name of a man who was going to be walled alive into a crypt?"

"A what?"

"A crypt ... a tomb. What does the name Fortunato come from? What word do we derive from it?"

"Fortune, I guess, what else?" said Chet.

"Of course. Fortune. And what does fortune mean?"

"Wealth. Riches."

"In some cases. Besides that?"

"I know," Diego said, "it means like fate or destiny."

"Ah-h-h ..." I said with no imitators this time. "Is Fortunato like Diego in any way?"

Diego watched me. There was a ripple of laughter distancing us from Kyle's hate.

"His book!" Davonne said, beads dancing against her jaw. A number of eyes lit up. I raised the anthology again, fore edge out and moved it for all to see: HELP !

"Diego feels trapped like Fortunato did," Davonne explained. *"For the love of God, Montresor!*, all in italics is a classy way of crying for help."

"That's despair," Diego said.

"And what does Montresor reply? In fact, what is the implication of his reply?" I coaxed.

Chet raised his hand. "He says, 'Yes, for the love of God.' That's like Kyle saying you can't do something or be a certain way cuz the Bible says so... and people who believe in the Bible making the decisions for everybody else."

"That sucks!" Haley said.

The mood was locked. Some obscenities are too eloquent to challenge.

"Let me tell you one of the saddest imperatives I've ever heard," I said as more busses rumbled to a stop outside. "It was on KGO news on October 29, 1984, just nine months ago. Police had been called to an apartment complex where loud religious music and cries: 'Let me out ! ... Let me out !' disturbed the neighbors. Complaints included a strange burning odor. The police were greeted by a woman and her boyfriend who shouted over the loud hymns, 'We're burning Lucifer in the oven.' The officers discovered the charred body of the woman's four-year-old daughter in the oven. The victim's five-year-old sister was standing in the kitchen watching, according to the news report, unharmed."

No one stirred.

"The saddest sound in all the world: 'Let me out !'" I raised Diego's anthology and ran my finger along its fore edge: "HELP ! ... *For the love of God, Montresor!* ... Let me out," I whispered.

"Did that really happen? What you said about the four-year-old in the oven, I mean?" Diego asked.

"It really happened."

"I don't see how anybody could do that," Jeanie said.

"Check your history," I reminded. "Forty-five years ago other ovens were specially built to purify a race. The fumes of twelve million corpses polluted the breath of Europe as the Nazi chain of command carried out its orders. Jews and Gypsies, Jehovah's Witnesses and political dissidents ... yes, and homosexuals. It's a horror too great for the mind to take in. It takes a single child in her mother's oven to finally make you cry ... 'Let me out !'"

The bell rang as I bisected the circle one more time and handed Diego his text. "I'll pay the damages if they charge you," I said. "I owe you that much."

"Thanks, anyway," he grinned, "but this is one anthology I plan to keep."

CHAPTER 26

MOLOKAI PILGRIMAGE

I have a certain terror of saints and other heroes. By their lives they show me what I should be and should do, and, while I embrace with all my heart their devotion, their dedication, their daring, I contend with my fear. I am not all that I would be.

It was so at age seven; it was so at age forty-seven. I attained the age of reason in a second-grade desk among the dark panels of Sacred Heart, and that was effortless. But simultaneously, said the nuns, I must claim Adam's legacy held in trust my first six years of life. I could now sin. The acuity to distinguish right from wrong meant I could hazard my immortal soul, and so I rehearsed velvet-draped "Bless me, Fathers" and invented items for this new controlling agenda in my life.

To offset this class-scale loss of innocence, the good Sisters of Notre Dame de Namur paraded before me and my generally less-impressed peers, role models of heroic proportions ... most often canonized, certainly beatified, or, at very least, one whose cause was being pushed for consideration.

The world was smaller then, although the war just ending would change all that. Flight was still mostly propellered and life took longer. Other countries seemed farther away, the way planets do now. The zeal of a Xavier for the heathen Indies was a sacred craze that only faith could properly interpret. Catholics who really loved God longed to be boiled in oil or crucified upside down to earn the crown of martyrdom, but all that happened at an incomprehensible distance. The other side of the world could not be conceived of by second graders except as sentence parts. Father Damien brought it all closer. The bizarre little Belgian discovered in 1873 how he might work a tedious, ugly, painful martyrdom on one of the islands in the hula girl chain. Molokai was the infernal Eden, the bin of human discards, the place of abandoned hope. Molokai was how the discreet spelled leprosy ... and the destination of any hapless enough to contract that Old Testament curse.

As Francis of Assisi had found God in a leper's embrace, so Father Damien sought salvation in a thousand-member congregation whose living decay refracted as many proofs of the soul's integrity, if not its immortality. Yet, we have no smooth-complexioned reproductions of Damien before which to kneel or light-flickering candles. When his febrile lips moved with his own Nunc Dimittis, at the end of sixteen arduous years, Hansen's Bacillus Leprae had too severely eroded his features. Disfigurement does not inspire piety. Mother Church, despite the effort of nuns to push her steatopygous rump in such causes, seemed unwilling to let go the notion that disease is a judgment. Damien's crown remained unbuffed by the lace sleeves of those who assign sanctity.

But not in my heart. Father Damien sank a challenge straight through my awe at the lips of the white-wimpled nuns. My mind's eye considered his cleansing of sores, his abiding the stench of parishioners packed into St. Philomena's Church, his endless thrust of the spade because Holy Viaticum was the reigning sacrament. One description lingers, like his fingers in the flame, of the moment he seared his flesh and felt no pain ... and of how, after that, he addressed his congregation as "We lepers" instead of "Brethren."

I pinched my parts for weeks. While I felt called to emulate the valiant priest, I had no compunction about avoiding the particulars of his peculiar martyrdom. It had been an ugly dying. I wouldn't mind going to God intact. I could wait for decay until the coffin closed.

I am no less credulous about Damien at forty-seven than I was when my heart canonized him in second grade. It is that veneration of four decades' standing that has detoured Degnan and me from the pursuit of pleasure in what is, for us, more aptly the hula boy chain, and I reflect on that with each sure-footed clop of my mount down the steep face of Molokai.

"Allow me this one day's pilgrimage out of our ten in Hawaii," I had pleaded with Degnan, "and you can plan the whole rest of the vacation."

Plead is too strong; I had rather to convince. Degnan tries to protect me from what he calls being too intense. In that effort also, of course, is his own guarantee against that intensity.

Besides our front and rear guides, Rare Adventures, Ltd. (a name that, if anything, belies the intense) has booked five other persons into our caravan: a slender youth behind wire-framed glasses who very much keeps his own counsel, and two pairs of women. Both of one pair are middle-aged and heavyset to the latter extent that their courage in mounting the mules scattered our earlier attention. The other pair are oddly combined: a narrow, dark woman with ashram eyes companions an over-the-hill Barbie Doll who lashes the beast between her legs, with tongue and with rein, the entire descent. We marvel at the long-suffering of her long-eared Job. A buck at any brink would bring us all surcease as the twin colonies of Kalaupapa and Kalawao yawn beneath us into the Pacific.

I could not have predicted at age seven that fear of an even deadlier sort than haunted this shore would bind me still closer to Damien, whose 5,865-day martyrdom took its measure one by one in this place where kings and prelates were loath to lead or follow. That he believed enough to risk himself is the sacred craze delivered to our shores. His lesson that overcoming is done by steady, persistent confrontation has threaded the forty years of my metamorphosis and left me damp on sands that still want shaping ... and I wonder: Was he ever frightened?

I am.

Degnan and I are four years into our relationship and have sought counseling to teach our egos the skill of co-starring and the technique of moving downstage gracefully. We stood around on the Diamond Street steps of the counselor's Castro office one morning, watching his out-of-breath, short-legged trot. He'd just come from Ward 5-B at San Francisco General where another client was having to let go a lover whose immune system had broken down. The well client had held his lover as if the cup of his arms could levee the life force ebbing from their midst, and his face raised to the counselor's with the awful knowledge they could not.

Problems of ego pale in that light. And yet the reason we were there goes straight to the heart of both problems: how do two members of the same sex build a life together in a society that refuses to acknowledge, much less bless, such a bond? The commitment required to nourish each other in a relationship others call sick and perverted and queer is an energy that most had rather diffuse ... reinforcing the promiscuity that social norm has all but forced upon us ... until the '80s and AIDS.

That's not to say promiscuity wasn't pleasant. We made the most of what was allowed us and bathhouses were. Neither court nor cathedral would condone our unions, but they looked the other way to get us out of the bushes. The bars and the baths spawned most of our monogamy ... especially the baths. We value sex more than straights. Our approach to person is more direct. Skin is premium as a key to the core, not the prison of the soul. That's more honest. Churches can't handle that, and what churches can't handle they condemn ... as they did the Hawaiians ... as they do us.

Syphilis and leprosy were unknown among the Polynesians until the advent of the haole, or white man, in these islands. Yet missionaries blamed the devastating spread of these diseases among the kanaka, or natives, on their ancient ease and openness about their sexuality. Leprosy, the haoles even decided, must be a fourth stage of syphilis since its incidence was so high among the "licentious kanaka." This exquisite arrogance in place, missionaries set about civilizing the Hawaiians ... which meant that the kanaka could annul their differences or be stamped out... as the diamond-studded fists of modern fundamentalists warn the gay community ... in Jesus' name.

The trade wind confirms us at sea level as our mule mounts lope on into Kalaupapa. I study the lush terrain. It is hard to place in this salt-sprayed Eden a cast like that in Ben-Hur when Judah Ben-Hur strode into the valley of lepers searching for his mother and sister. No pitiful creatures pull veils across bandaged features as they endure the light or falter into the shadows of musty caves. Celluloid images dissipate in this Elba of despair where the chrism of experience has done the anointing. I am quickened by the knowledge that within my own school district are fundamentalists who would legislate me out of their children's classrooms and ticket me to such a Molokai because they cannot stomach my loving Degnan.

I watch the wind muss the soft rim of Degnan's tonsure where he rides ahead of me, note the tendons at the nape of his neck and the tautness descending the taper of his back as he rides, controlled, and I cannot fathom the hatred that, in Jesus' name, would have us conform. I wonder that love can be so dichotomous.

A pair of dogs gambol toward us from a shaded grove where a white van idles. IKE'S SCENIC TOURS letters the side panels. Four other tourists, flown in by helicopter, wait in its warm shade. Ike Keao steps down from the driver's seat to greet us. Our guides move among us catching reins to tether as we dismount. Barbie seems reluctant to surrender Job.

Ike's skin is darker than that of most Hawaiians we have seen, mottled with black spots. A native of Oahu, he is sixty-two and his hair is gray. His voice rasps as he loads us into the van. His hand spreads along the back of the front seat as he backs the loaded vehicle across chuckholes. The fragments that are his fingers confront us with the fact of this place, and we become casual in practiced ways. This is no tour. It is a pilgrimage.

I bounce in the back between Degnan and the woman with ashram eyes, penciling impressions in my notebook.

"You're a writer?" Ike asks my reflection in his mirror as he shifts into first.

"... and a teacher," I tell him. "Do you mind my taking notes?"

"Take all the notes you want, Mr. Writer," he raises an index finger minus a joint, "but no pictures of patients without their permission."

I nod in compliance as we accelerate onto blacktop.

Ike talks continuously as we motor through streets that could fit Anytown, U.S.A. except that surfscapes sub for tract trees outside every casement. An old woman unloads groceries from a '65 Buick in her driveway. At the corner, a man putters in his garden. It is a still place. Ike Keao tells us it is a dying place, but not because of leprosy. The colony's oldest patient died three months earlier at ninety-nine. Kalaupapa's remaining one hundred three patients range in age from forty-two to eighty-six, and in every case their leprosy is arrested. Since 1946 sulfone drugs have made control of the disease possible everywhere, but a reality here. In fact, new cases can now be controlled within seventy-two hours, and patients remain in the general population, a threat to no one. Debilitation, disfigurement and death are no longer the lot of lepers nor those diagnosed with Hansen's Disease, as it is now called, at least in nations with advanced medical standards.

The landscape at either side of the road thickens to jungle density as Ike clips along into the outskirts. He tells us that in third-world countries, leprosy is actually on the rise with infected mothers passing the disease to suckling infants. Fifty babies were born to Kalaupapa patients in Ike's time, and not one of them contracted the disease. But the newborns passed from the womb not into their mothers' arms but into the arms of relatives on other islands where they would be raised to an age that would guarantee their immunity before having any contact with their parents. Ike Keao's son was sixteen before he could visit his mother and father.

Immunity. What's in a word? The absence of it is ravaging the gay community.

"What will become of Kalaupapa when there are no more patients?" I ask.

"When we're all dead?" Ike says. "You can say it, Mr. Writer. We could leave here now, but we choose to stay. This place that once spelled doom for us, today is beautiful. We will die here. Then Kalaupapa becomes national park. It's already arranged."

The road tunneling through tropical flora pierces the edge of a clearing, and the van bursts into full sun. Ike steers into a turnout and angles to a halt before a white-steepled church.

"St. Philomena's?" I ask.

Ike nods. Leaning on the steering wheel, he points upward through the windshield. "Visitors came looking for Father Damien in the advanced stages of his leprosy. That's where they found him, repairing the roof." His gray head nods. "We needed more like him ... "

"Everybody out. The tour continues inside."

I am seven again, and reason has nothing to do with anything. I study the structure, waiting my turn to get out. This is a shrine. A faith that did not question made it so, and it remains holy despite ignorance gone vincible. That is consecration. To the right, untended, sleep those for whom sulfone came too late.

Ike heads our meager procession up the couple of steps, into the aged nave. It smells worn. We are bidden to front pews to minimize strain on his damaged vocal cords. Ike has an Elijah look—a visage that has begun to repeat itself among members of the gay community who have gazed on the source of current fear and gone wild with calm. He waits for silence. Barbie is hushed by her own echo and his eyes.

For a year longer than I am old, Ike Keao tells us, he has lived at Kalaupapa. At fourteen, the age of my eighth-grade students, Oahu health officials forced him aboard a launch with thirty-three other lepers for transport to this isle of the damned. The year was 1936, and fundamentalists then as in our time spoke as literalists about the damned. As with

AIDS in the gay community, those who conditioned the Hawaiians for syphilis and leprosy relieved themselves of responsibility through evangelistic scapegoating.

In his book Holy Man, Gavan Daws writes:

"Whether or not they could bring themselves - as representatives of the West, of course, not as individuals - to accept responsibility for having introduced syphilis and leprosy to the islands in the first place, they insisted that the root of the Hawaiians' disastrous condition was indigenous. This root they identified as the endless and endlessly renewed sexuality of the culture. The Hawaiian view of life was permeated by the generative principle. Sex was the expression, the ultimate incarnation, of the beauty and power of the forces of existence, something to be celebrated privately, publicly, ritually. This perception was essentially what had reduced Damien himself in his days at Kohala to 'black thoughts' of 'insupportable melancholy.' So with the convinced haole Protestants of Honolulu. Even where disease was not directly concerned, they discovered among the Hawaiians the presence of another deadly infection: sex."

Haoles, non-Hawaiians, had much to learn from the sexual mystique of the kanaka, native Hawaiian, but guilt-driven fundamentalism plays into the hands of power and wealth. To the godly go the spoils. It is easier to take from those who need saving. From those who refuse saving, it's a duty.

Damien himself was victim to this scriptural superiority, believing the sensuous bronze-skinned natives to be licentious and leprosy the usual, though not exclusive, result of promiscuity. But he, at least, did not judge them. His pious counterparts knew less of loving. "Thy neighbor as thyself" is a key presumption that emasculates fundamentalist Christianity.

That paradox is epitomized in Daws' description of King Kalakaua's coronation ceremony in 1883 at which "his royal hula dancers publicly extolled the vastness of his inherent mana: his procreative powers and his sexual potency. The English-language Hawaiian Gazette was deeply shocked: 'No cleanly wantonness this, but a deliberate attempt to exalt and glorify that which every pure mind must hold as the type of what is to be kept out of sight, and out of mind as the representative of all that is animal and gross, the very apotheosis of grossness.'"

One does not love "the very apotheosis of grossness," of course. One buttons it into obscurity and pretends not to have one. Such a dogma admits no basis for the loving of one's neighbor.

Victoria ruled on the British throne in 1883, making chaste the entire empire, imposing pubic penitence throughout the sphere of her influence. Never mind that modern museums abound with ritual phallic symbols from global tribes. The very nakedness of those captive to such practice attested to their animal grossness. The accoutrements of conquerors hang with the drape of authority. Right has been dubiously defined since Cain bludgeoned his brother.

What was true of that 1883 editorial remained true of the humorless clergy of the 1940s and of the fundamentalists in the 1980s ... denying the physical format of God's own image in us. Confessors cautioned my adolescence against even the number of seconds spent bathing my genitals lest, inadvertently, I hurdle into the venereal quagmire. Insane distinctions were drawn to delineate the effects of prehistory brooding in our unconscious that surged mercifully into wet dreams but could afterwards entrap us through indulged reflection. Conscious manipulation of the genitals plunged the soul into peril unless the manipulator were a Church-approved spouse whose primary intent was conception. Confessors maneuvered my conscience through my youth like a demolition ball. I am mouth-ajar awed at the devotion of prelates who, all their lives, refine the distinctions of Jesus' injunction to love one another.

Chilling to think of the generations upon generations of kanaka who lived in these islands, sexually fulfilled, because they had not received the benefits of haole civilization ... most important of which were the waters of baptism to cleanse them of guilt they didn't know they had.

Ike Keao knew. Missionaries mixed the mortar of salvation but entrepreneurs financed its spread and politicians made it secure. It was a profitable partnership that eased the transfer of power into the hands of those who knew best. Those who knew best sentenced the fourteen-year-old to Kalaupapa for the good of the godly. Ike's view beyond the shed lace of waves as the lepers' launch neared the landing was the prophecy of eroded features in those waiting like shore birds to greet the reinforcements of their ever-dwindling numbers.

Ike did not want to leave the deck, but the reluctant were thrown into the shallows by a crew hardened to its task. Wet sand sucked at his feet as if repulsed by what he would become if he continued. He would never again arrive, only watch and wait to appease the appetite of this awful Molokai.

The smaller of the two heavyset women lowers her head. Barbie's ponytail quivers.

Some, Ike tells us, seeing what they would become, waded ashore, made nooses of wet garments and short work of the mortal phase of their damnation.

Ike's blunt knuckles indicate the cemetery beyond the right wall. Father Damien, with his own hands ... because no one else had the strength, buried two thousand lepers in his sixteen-year purgatory. Mother Church requires three first-class miracles to ensure deeds to heavenly mansions ... and papal infallibility. Damien merely pushed back the margins of despair among a people for whom drunkenness and rape had become the why-not quality of their dying. He weighted the scales of their restored dignity with his own loving.

Ike's arrival on Molokai coincided with Damien's departure, although the latter had been dead forty-five years. In posthumous obedience to in-life superiors who wanted a saint to swell their order's ranks, Damien's remains were exhumed from the foot of the stone cross beside St. Philomena's and shipped to Belgium for a state funeral and entombment as the Sacred Heart's Fathers set the wheels in motion for beatification. In 1995, one hundred six years after his death, Damien de Veuster was beatified by John Paul II. In 2009, the leper priest was canonized by Benedict XVI.

Why one hundred twenty years? Father Damien died a leper. Leprosy had been thought the fourth stage of syphilis—the morally repugnant due of a morally repugnant person. And Father Damien had his detractor, a fundamentalist preacher named Reverend Doctor Charles McEwen Hyde, who claimed in a letter subsequently published that Damien had earned his leprosy.

Robert Louis Stevenson, whose recently published the Strange Case of Dr. Jekyll and Mr. Hyde gripped readers, dipped his pen in fresh ink to protect the dead priest against the monstrous attack of this new Hyde. Even had Damien the flaws of a man, Stevenson pointed out in a piercing defense from which the Reverend Doctor never fully recovered his prestige, those flaws could not detract from the priest's heroic sanctity.

According to Daws, Joseph Dutton, who worked side by side with

Damien during the last three years of the latter's life, "saw defects of character, but said that such faults were consumed like straws in the fire of Damien's charity." Damien, in fact, told Dutton that he had never had sexual relations... and that virtually on his deathbed.

Promiscuity enjoys bad press—ensures a readership and packs an audience. Jeweled fingers flash its abhorrence across Sunday morning television screens as fundamentalists thump Christ's message with Paul's qualifications: "Love me ... or go to hell."

The Eden insight that graced Hawaiian sexuality has a flawed equivalence among gay males. We have no tradition of its innocence. While the kanaka had to be taught to feel shame, we had to teach ourselves to reject shame. The geographical isolation that nourished the serenity of kanaka sensuality has only a dark and rectangular parallel in the dimension of gay sensuality. Closeted joy has the shape of guilt. It broods through pretense and deceives trust in those who ought to care.

Whether, indeed, promiscuity is indigenous to Hawaiians or to homosexuals is academic. What seems indisputable is that both value sexuality as indigenous to human nature—an "endlessly renewing, generative principle; the expression, the ultimate incarnation, of beauty and power of the forces of existence, something to be celebrated—privately, publicly, ritually."

That celebration has suffered the bondage of interpreted scripture on the tongues of pharisees whose guile transcends age. High priest, cardinal or Falwell, theirs is a legacy to which whittled glory holes are pathetic testimony. Something yearns in me for an accounting of such sanctimony.

I remember the soft-lit arches of one celebration and columns strong as thighs among which sinuous shapes gone pale at the groin moved, shadowed and furred. Men caught in each other's reflection of God. Sleek and filmed with steam. Awed with the search of desired touch. Flagrant with naked revel: nipple sucked; phallus kissed, coaxed, consumed; toned length to toned length, arms flexed in gentleness, coaxing to summits; lips fondling a weighted sac; nose inhaling culverted fur as a narrow length thickens the throat with pulsing; slender-thighed thrusting—urgent, urgent, urgent. Men ignited with each other's wonder, ministering consensually to passion conditioned at all levels of sense. Mouth to mouth, resuscitating lust. A thread of semen loops, sheer crystal, from the tip of my tongue to the tip of the phallus whose thighs ease their shudder between my palms ... and my breath breaks with the mouth nursing between my legs, the nibble of its mustache intense.

An even, an innocent exchange ... Qualified innocence. Paid admission. Members only. Openly hidden from whom we must not offend; who love God by hating our difference; who forbid us monogamy and condemn our promiscuity; who abort reason from the narrow canals of inflexible hearts.

I feel no guilt now for my celebration or the sanctity it has taught me about my body. Out of the gulf of celebration, Degnan and I have formed our own tributary ... grateful, humbled, yes, and determined.

I do not know how or why we have been spared the present fate of so many in the community, at least, until now. I believe, deeply, that the fault of that fate lies not in celebrated sexuality but in flawed fundamentalism whose scripture is fear, whose truth is duplicity, whose love is a commission to destroy. I am committed to counter that fault with steady, persistent confrontation, taking the measure of my own spirituality day by day in this place where kings and prelates are loath to lead or follow. I would be a fool not to be afraid.

Degnan taps my notebook and I look up. The rasp of my pencil has replaced Ike's monologue. The lead is worn nearly to the nub. We are alone. Degnan tilts his head toward the door where the woman with ashram eyes is watching her step down.

"I'll be right there," I tell him. "I just need to finish these notes and take a couple of pictures." He nods, touches my knee. I pencil rapidly, turning for blunt lead, listening to Degnan's sneakered recessional, revering the sound because it is his.

Damien did not fully understand his promiscuous kanaka, but it appears not to have entered his mind to reject them either. He did not stand at a safe distance and judge. He moved among them as only saints before him had done to buttress their living and make sense of their dying, always at risk.

I think of other Damiens I know, of men and women who move with equal determination into the void of present terror, breaking its grasp by refusing defeat; by standing their ground; by not slipping quietly back into the closet and pretending never to have emerged. And I am humbled.

I have stood hand-locked in AIDS-support groups where shared energy counters the trend of decimation. "He loves me ... He loves me not ..." throbs like a lotteried pulse up one arm and down the other ... up one arm and down the other in this '80s' daisy chain where scoring could be forever. Pierced with the stigmata of bigotry, we pool our strength, willing away the stark tendency from concupiscent features and lesions from supple limbs as we plot the pragmatics of fundraising and hospices and running errands and telling family and ensuring primacy to lovers in final arrangements and lobby the federal government to put its weight behind a cure. And I am humbled by those who risked before they knew no risk was involved, ... physically.

How many men with AIDS have I held in my arms and wondered: was it comfort I gave or comfort I sought? Labor pains and death throes are one agony working double shift. Only the fool thinks to avoid it. The distance between womb and tomb is one letter, and what we do with that distance is our call to sanctity, or heroism, at least. It is the pain of that distance that can be avoided or confronted, so it is not AIDS or leprosy that are the issue at all. The issue is the exercise of the right to be ... and therein the acquisition of human dignity. That is my Molokai, and I have that in common with every man, woman and child in the universe. My commitment as a teacher makes particular my concern with the child, the fourteen-year-old, whose singular launch needs safe docking in a port whose authorities prize conformity over integrity.

Attitude is the problem.

I glance up from my notes and examine this church whose plainness is duplicated a thousand times across the mainland, yet its peculiar difference holds and moves me. These floorboards, this stucco, this sunlit glass housed Damien's distance and are consecrated with his confronted pain.

I will walk momentarily among the epitaphs to the right of St. Philomena's and conjecture at the courage and despair of those who sleep beneath, able to fit neither name nor feature to recall. I know only the vague posture of their living. I am reminded that weekly I page through published epitaphs in the Bay Area Reporter, concerned that among names I don't even recognize might be a face that once nestled between my legs ... and that is a sublime terror to which I will not succumb. Degnan and I intend to survive. We will love with published caution until the celebration regains its full guarantee... but we will not stop celebrating. We owe that to those whose distance claimed them too soon and to all who carve dignity in the features of this present pain. We owe it to the young who stir with a difference they cannot define ... until someone mocks it. We owe it to each other and, of course, we owe it to ourselves.

Like leprosy, AIDS is responding to medication and will one day be cured. Attitude is less simple. When AIDS is history, attitudes will still need confronting. Coming out never ends.

It is still inside. Ike's Scenic Tour is an absorbent murmur against the tropical density. My knees are unused to kneeling now, but I slip to the floorboards and touch my lips to that musty surface. The wood that bore a childhood hero becomes the weight of a midlife mentor, its texture harsh with empathy. I shall measure the days in my distance, sainted Damien, and, one by one, confront their pain.

CHAPTER 27

MAUI AUDIT

At 8,000 feet, the road sign warns: TURN ON LIGHTS IN CLOUDS, a wise caution at 4:30 on a Maui morning with only a crescent and hard stars overhead. Degnan is driving. That's best. He hasn't had breakfast. Who eats on a 3:30 rise? I do, actually. My appetite is the only absolute left in my life.

Our Dollar-Rent-a-Car threads the rim of Haleakala—turf of the ancients, source of legend, Olympus of a saffron-skinned people whose voices sound the way fawns look.

We are not alone. Other lights occasion a curve, ahead or behind, in the circuitous climb. Degnan and I exchange dash-lit glances, acknowledging each other's anticipation about the druidic drama about to enfold. Through my mind run long-ago lyrics: "The world is waiting for the sunrise."

Leveling into a 10,000-foot-elevation parking lot evokes sci-fi contiguity, an extra-terrestrial déjà vu. Disconnecting the seat belts triggers Japanese chimes, a pretty, almost offensive technology for so celestial a proximity. Degnan removes the key from the ignition.

The sequence of slammed doors confirms us as conspirators with the disembodying dark flecked with coned lights pursuing the peak. Sleep-softened voices fall in around us, vaguely chanting. An inside-out surface of million-year-old core-pebbles crunches underfoot. I smile. Disembodiment is a false perception. Spirits converse without volume, move without tread.

My Puma snags an outcropping. Set lava is stubborn stuff. My balance gone, my Argus falls. Coned lights detour, determined. We have not brought one.

"Jesus Christ, Ron!" Degnan fleshes out my substance. His hand grabs my arm, all five fingers pronouncing his concern. Clumsiness has its reward.

"You all right?"

I nod.

"Ron, are you all right?"

"Fine ... Thanks."

"You dropped the camera?"

"'Fraid so."

Degnan steps off, his second "Jesus Christ!" muffled. He asked about me before the Argus.

Glassed against cold and for observation, a stone hut hugs the crater's crest. Space available exists inside, but we haven't come for that kind of snug. We stake our claim to butt space against the stone foundation as, second by second, the horizon grows less dark. Pilgrims wrap themselves in surplus blankets and settle lotus-legged, facing east.

"Degnan?"

"Ronald."

"Did you bring our blankets?"

"We left them in the car."

"I'll go get them."

"You might miss something. Just enjoy this."

"Aren't you cold?"

"Move closer."

A few yards away a fellow wraps his arms around the girl cradled in his legs. I nudge Degnan, nod in their direction.

"The altitude getting to you?"

"Who'd notice? It's dark."

"It's getting light. That was the point of coming, remember? To see it happen. Just listen."

"To the sunrise?"

"You're so strange. Why do I love you?"

The sound of the sun rising is giddy laughter; four teenagers coupled in blankets, getting stoned.

Our surroundings take on lunar definition. Twilight bathes the stark crater. Grasses gone to seed shiver on the fore-slope. I feel like God wondering what to do with the first day.

Orange bleeds into the horizon silhouetting naked power in a format of cloud. I tremble. Who, in his right mind, would pack a jacket for Hawaii? My legs drawn up against my haunches, I scoot still closer to

Degnan. Bracing the Argus C-3 on my knees, I examine angles.

"You get a sense of awakening?" Degnan asks.

"Mmm..."

"Why don't you snap the picture?"

"I'm trying to focus. There's nothing to focus on."

"You should get a good camera."

"This is a good camera ... It's ..."

"Thirty years ago it was. Cameras today focus for you."

"... just the pits to focus."

I should have packed him some trail mix.

My fingers are cold.

"Hey, Little Prince," I say. "We're on the other side of the asteroid ..."

"What does that mean?"

"You remember. The story of the little fellow who couldn't get his fill of sunsets and kept scooting his chair across his asteroid to see more?"

Degnan nods, pats my knee. "So strange."

Laughter reels from the stoners. "Okay, sun ... Everybody lean toward that side of the world."

I nudge Degnan, tilt my head toward the stoners. "That's Little Prince talk," I say. "Only he had his head on straight."

Degnan points into the void with a "Let there be ..." gesture. "That streak of cloud," he says, "it's like liquid lava." He is silent a moment, then adds, "This better be spectacular, or I'm writin' Mother Nature."

I snap a picture.

Headlights down the mountain slip in and out of curves like beads in a decade of joyful mysteries ... When will Mother Church let me go?

There is no wind. Cumuli stand like blessed statues at the pagan dawn.

I snap another picture and mutter, "Shit!" softly.

"What's wrong?"

"You don't want to know."

"Ronald!"

"I forgot to wind the film after the first shot."

"Jesus Christ!"

"I told you you didn't want to know. Trust me."

"Today's cameras ..."

I nod. "... advance automatically. My Argus takes great pictures."

The underside of the cumuli ignites, the Pacific a magenta drift in the cloud's calm interim.

"Gawd!" says a stoner.

The sleep-softened chant gathers pitch. Shafts of light stream through ducts in the aggregate of mists, shedding the night sheath. Phoebus rides, his supple radiance rushing ahead of him.

"Can you get that picture?"

"The camera's jammed."

"That's because you dropped it, Ron. You gotta pay attention."

I shrug. "Who needs pictures to remember this?"

"A few would be nice for the album."

"Shh ... Listen."

"To what?"

"To the sun rising."

Degnan traps a chuckle. "So strange."

The lucent clouds alter the crater's contour. The air is almost tepid. The vaulted horizon fades. Gods never look back. I press my elbow against Degnan's. His less-firm response carries a between-the-nudges innuendo. He's dazzled, but still pissed.

The sun's force dispels the anterior chill from our bodies. I can feel it on my exposed face, hands and along the length of my trousered legs. Lie on me, Phoebus. Charge me with your full-body, ephemeral caress.

The girl cradled in the fellow's legs raises her face to his. He leans. Degnan and I hold each other's eyes.

This time his elbow gentles mine. Stoner smoke pierces the mood.

The ranger station has about it a dailiness that disconnects our link with the preternatural. I see about me the Temple's moneychangers and regret the absence of one wild enough to topple counters and flail a whip. High-gloss renditions of the divine Pele and sort-of-divine Maui exchange owners for cash, extending myth beyond Greece and Rome. National park do-dads tempt even the tasteful in this outpost where natural souvenirs are illegally pocketed and fraught with Polynesian spells.

Turning from the display case, I discover a demi-god moving between us and the maps charting volcanic vistas in their sunny sweep from the windows. His classically chiseled features ride a unison of limbs that, at a striding height of 6'4" or 5", redefines grace. Levis slope into the seam of his rump, a second skin. My watching has alerted him. He and the woman with him watch my watching peripherally. She is aware that he is aware and not secure with that.

"Be a little obvious," says Degnan, examining charts with less-than-professed attention.

I hate charts but quit my study of Levi-skinned deity and attend their tedium. My loving secures Degnan against even the competition of demi-gods. My watching is simple: reverence auditing beauty. But I have yet to convince him of that.

It is hard to be convincing when one must be guarded. All my life I have guarded my longing, and now I must guard my having as well. I ache to hug Degnan ... hard. I want to abandon caution from moments that deserve passion and feel as valued as the fellow with the girl cradled in his legs, watching the same sunrise Degnan and I pressed elbows over ... but the environment isn't safe.

CHAPTER 28

MAUI MAHALO

Degnan and I are on time. The Maui Lua Luau begins at 5:00 with alohas scaled to middle-mainland expectation ... a concoction of Tiny Bubbles and Fantasy Island. Billed as free and unlimited, the mai tais epitomize half-truth and, according to Degnan, pack no more punch than my fruit beverage. What I am nursing, however, is a punch to my pride.

I don't intend to book conflicts everywhere I go, but more often than not, it turns out that way. I'll concede to a ready shoulder, but someone else whittles my chip. How, for example, could I foresee that the innocuously lovely lei would entangle me in gender rituals that presume my personal choice? Is the matter with Hawaiian mystique or mainlander machismo? And why, I find myself asking, must I be pawn to either?

Sipping papaya juice, I stalk the field of contention, eyeing the two lines, one of which must be traversed. In one, a coconut-cupped dancer with lovely hula hands loops strung shells around the corded necks of husband-fathers, kisses their fresh tans and quickens their stagnant arms for pictures. Ten feet east, a Polynesian body-builder drapes mother-wives in plumeria, letting his fingers lag at the bikini lines of their sunburned bosoms. Torso rippling with sunset, he snugs their bloomed pelvises against his saronged thigh and smiles for pictures. Degnan stands apart from my stalking, uneasy with what's in my craw.

"I guess I can handle a shell lei," I say, homing in at Degnan's side, "but I want my picture taken with him." Him's smile is as white as the laurel-laced plumeria garlanding his hair.

"Don't try to prove anything, Ronald. Remember, we're on vacation. It's time out for ten days."

"But, Degnan, ..."

"Ron, these people won't understand. Please don't do it." For emphasis, Degnan strides to the westerly queue to await his shells from Lovely Hula Hands. He is pissed. His gait leaves no doubt. And he is hurt.

Arms folded on his chest, his eyes avoid me, and the broad tonsure in his soft hair convenes in a determined wrinkle between their pale gaze. All year he has bitten his lip over the time my commitment to gay rights has denied our relationship. As I turned from setting the message recorder before leaving home for the airport, Degnan wrapped me in a bear hug. "No telephones, no articles, no issues for the next ten days. We are each other's agenda." I had not seen him so relaxed in months.

He is not relaxed now as I fall in behind him. He feels me there but does not turn. His grape-colored Izod pulls taut across his shoulders.

"I love you," I murmur.

His head inclines. With his sandal he flattens the grass. I lean forward so that the broad brim of my Guatemalan palm leaf hat taps his shoulder blade. Degnan twitches.

He was with me when I bought the hat at the Castro Street Fair. He chose a sash, in fact, burgundy and white, and rolled it thin for a hatband. I get compliments on my hat and even though I know I don't look like him, I feel like Truman Capote when I wear it.

My unbleached cotton buccaneer shirt hails from the same event. It's handmade too. Only the shorts are not, but they match. It is an ensemble, I suppose, which, while I wait my turn with Lovely Hula Hands, watching *Him*, makes me a tad obvious. I almost wish Tattoo would dash through the grassy compound shouting, "The plane! The plane!" distracting the crowd from this purpose and rescuing my esteem, but no such luck. I doff my hat, bend my head, and shells rattle over my ears. Lips brush my cheek and for just an instant Lovely Hula Hands and I share glances. She's not amused either.

A stir, like fecund wind, ushers the Mistress of Ceremonies into our midst. She is a handsome woman, Mistress, with her heritage fixed among sun-drenched ancients. She is ample-bodied but not fat, her makeup flawless, her nails manicured, hair meticulously styled and pinned with white hibiscus. Her red muumuu flows with her sense of motion, and that is always conscious. White orchids cascade over her breasts as she teases red-blooded males to a stage rigged for more photos with more coconut-cupped girls. Mistress is polished, schooled in how to make mainlanders swell with their own largess. She has made peace with the present. There is no money in heritage.

I haunt the periphery of this exhibition, watching these heirs of primitive eloquence play at their own defeat ... and rationalize my own submission to the management's choice of who would share my photo.

Mistress' hands fondle the trade wind. She herds us to a clearing where damp sand packs pigs against coals and hot stones, baking the evening's entrée. Shovels pass from hand to hand as guests are encouraged to unearth the canvas-covered course. I step into a turn, discovering quickly how scant are sandals against hot sand. I dig, the last thrust of the blade connecting with sheathed corpse. All the reasons I have ever considered in the case for vegetarianism converge.

Maui Lua employees take over. Bare-chested and saronged, they grin whitely as Mistress identifies the steamy folds of canvas as Captain Cook's sail. The white folk are delighted, but already she is moving us on. More mai tais, she urges; more rum. It is fair turnabout.

I look back at the pit where the pigs lie gutted, their baked flesh falling away beneath steaming snouts. Sweating men have lost their grins hoisting carcasses onto palm leaf litters.

Degnan taps my shoulder, points to Mistress who has seen our lingering and shoos us to the bottle-necked gates of the dining arena. Inside stretch long tables, angled for viewing, between a stage and lavishly arrayed buffet. Potted palms and torches circumscribe the feasting complex.

Degnan and I draw chairs to an otherwise settled table. Illinoisans flank my left and his right. His Land of Lincoln table mates are three teachers in whom figments of anxiety have begun to reroute their features. Women too competent for men, they have taught too well, become too secure. Eyes assessing, they apply principles learned in coping seminars to the fact that we are two males past forty from near San Francisco traveling together.

My Illinoisans are passive people seated across from a hard-bodied youth with the world at his fingertips ... and his parents on either side. Freshly delivered from duty aboard a nuclear sub, son expounds the wisdom gleaned from his four-year enlistment for his captive Illinoisans ... everything from the only bad thing about nuclear submarines to the kind of car he bought with all the money he saved. Mother adjusts elegantly framed bifocals and explains, "He's only been out since June 26, so this is his treat." Her hand strokes the back of his. "Oh," she adds, leaning forward, "that's his sister on the other side of his father."

Directly opposite Degnan and me, a pleasant Texas couple explain that this is their first trip to the islands. She is, in fact, utterly lovely, but watches me constantly. From the moment I tucked my Guatemalan palm leaf under my chair, I have felt her eyes. My grizzled look belies the six-year variance in Degnan's and my ages, of course. Thinking that she already has us figured out, is she trying to qualify me as his sugar-daddy to boot? Her eyes pulse broadmindedly. Degnan draws Texans and teachers into animated sharing about Maui must-sees.

Beside the Texans, newlyweds wear Do Not Disturb smiles for their hands-beneath-the-table privacy.

The sky has deepened. This closer contact lends frame of reference to the mood, reminds us what we came for. Mistress glides beneath the torches, mounts the stage, repeats a Maui Lua welcome. For us haoles she reviews the succulence spread among the dark leaves of the buffet table: roast pork, ribs of beef, raw salmon, plum-colored poi, coconut pudding ... whetting appetites. Live entertainment will follow the feasting; recorded music accompanies it.

Raising an index finger, Mistress mimes an "I almost forgot." She aims through gates to the far side of the stage, at the thatched-roof restrooms and explains their labels. "Menehune uses the door on the left," she says. Spreading her hand on her ample bosom, she pats among the orchids. "I'm menehune," she adds, "and kane ... that's man ... uses the door on the right." Raising her hand from her breasts, she lets it go limp, leans confidentially toward the audience and says, "Those others we don't have a place for."

Back-slappers laugh at this members-only slur. Applause is appreciative but not rousing. No one here knows any of "those others," of course, but some are now worried that the entertainment may be one of those dirty shows. Tiny Bubbles fills the air, however, straight from Lawrence Welk at 33 1/3 rpms and people begin rising for the buffet.

I can't tell whether I'm pale or flushed, only that I'm not getting enough air. I have passed out three times in my life and fight now against that crumbling consciousness. I want to stand, brandish my hat and shout, "Then you have no place for me!" But I stay seated. I cast about my mind for some excuse for such cruelty, but find none. I reason, scatteredly, that any protest I make would include Degnan in an action to which he clearly had not consented, yet silence means unconscionable complicity. I resolve that Mistress' joke will not go unchallenged.

Fatigue resists my rising, but a suffusing chill signals return of my control. The woman from Texas studies my expression as her husband guides her toward the food.

Degnan shakes his head as he watches Mistress descend from the stage. "Somebody ought to tell her ..." he says.

"You know it," I reply, "and you're looking at that somebody." Degnan nods.

Vegetarianism isn't close to an issue yet as I stab my way through the platters. I eat through sorrow, despair, joy and rage. They all take energy, and food is the constant that sustains me. I do not understand loss of appetite.

My thoughts race between vulgar retort and what I should say as I piece together what I will say. I am not noted for calm in crisis. My voice will quiver; my hands already do. I spot Mistress moving among the tables and time my return so our paths intersect. She turns her achieved radiance upon me.

"I have to say this," I begin, clutching my plate.

"What?" she asks, slipping her arm around my buccaneer cotton. She is ready to be complimented.

"How many people would you say are here?" I ask, looking around.

She scans the crowd. "About three hundred. Why?"

"Because, statistically, that means at least thirty people at this luau are gay."

Mistress is a cool lady. Her narrowed eyes widen. "Can you tell? Can you tell?" she demands. Her hand works my shoulder through the collarless fabric. She cocks an ear to my trembling voice and pointedly examines the poi shivering in my plate.

"Lady, I didn't pay twenty-eight dollars to come here and be insulted. Your toilet joke showed unforgivable taste, and I'm not letting you by with it."

Mistress molds a naughty school girl look. "Well, I was just having fun."

"And twenty-nine or so other guests are licking their wounds in silence so you could have fun. I thought the famous aloha spirit included everyone." I feel as if I'm shaking apart.

Mistress glances quickly from side to side. She has progressed to the reprimanded stage of her school girl look. "It was all in fun," she reiterates.

"Not for those of us who are gay!" I state emphatically and pivot, as smoothly as sandals and my trembling allow, toward my table. God, I wish I could be collected about confrontation and carry it off with a bit of savoir faire.

Degnan touches my leg as I sit down. The eyes of Texas are upon me, looming large with what they cannot say. I speak little during dinner. I am ravenous and, despite Mistress, the food is excellent. Tiny Bubbles bastes random conversation to the fabric of dusk, imposing a pattern.

When my hands have steadied, I rise to replenish Degnan's and my drinks. As I ladle, Mistress purrs at my side, "I'm sorry if I offended you. There's no difference ... no difference."

I look at her. "So why try to make one?" Resting the ladle against the bowl, I continue. "You know, I came here this evening to enjoy myself but wound up working a disturbing word problem instead.

"Word problem?"

"Yeah. I figured that if you stage a minimum of one luau every week with approximately the same number of people each time, and, as I suspect, you use that same joke against each audience, ... I figured that you hurt a minimum of 1,560 people a year. Hurt them deeply. That's calculated cruelty on a mass scale. I can't forgive that kind of fun."

A Polynesian child of twelve or thirteen loiters near the punch bowl, watching the ladle longingly, as I steady the drinks for my return. I hear Mistress ask, "Are you a girl or a boy?" I shake my head.

We do not return directly to our Kehei condo following the show. Degnan and I seem of one mind as I share with him my confrontation with Mistress. We cross the road between headlights and set off across the sand.

The stunning Hawaiian with whom I'd longed to have my picture taken had also been part of the show. His talent included standing and sitting on a flaming hibachi, an attribute for which I found it hard to clap. By the end of the show, I felt I'd witnessed once-proud creatures trained to the hoop and the scooter. I shook my head at this contrived remnant of ancient grace and demoted my rage to depression that Mistress had made me part of the act. She even said "Mahalo" as we left.

Underfoot the sand retains the day's strength. Trade wind rustles fern and coaxes palms to catch the moon in their fronds. The surf at this beach is a constant redundancy of lit waves. We strip at the edge of undergrowth and follow moonshadow into the water. Hawaiian salt water lacks the chill to really invigorate but musters enough sand to feel scrubbed, and that is what we need. Degnan's slenderness slips in and out of depth like an El Greco nude teasing the shallow light. He angles his head as I swim near.

"Don't get any ideas," he cautions.

"Degnan, just kiss me."

"You never know who might be watching," he says as his feet churn foam and he eases away. I know better than to pursue. Arms spread, I lie back in the buoyant tide, allowing my moonlit body to shimmer at the surface ...

It's hard to swallow.

CHAPTER 29

EXILE IN THE GOLDEN CLOSET

July 6, 1986. Liberty Weekend has ended. The hundred-year vigil of the Lady with the Lamp has been fêted at the Golden Door in a manner that defies memory and makes déclassé the Pearl Mestas and Charlotte Maillards of this world. Long live David Wolper, grand impresario!

The Actor and his Co-star, snug in their carefully choreographed old-fashioned values, have been tucked in with tributes from such luminaries as Old Blue Eyes: "What you, Mr. President, ... (nod) Nancy, have done for this country ..."

With narrow grace, in the interest of civil accord between their country and this, François Mitterrand and his first lady suffered the harbor winds of the July 3rd Governors Island inaugural before returning to the surrogate womb where fused the Laboulaye soul with the Bartholdi body to become America's Mother of Exiles. An umbilical sense of pedigree pervaded their presence.

John Paul II blessed America by videotape as his entourage of white-cassocked, crimson-cinctured prelates accompanied him through Colombia, exhorting the huddled masses to reject violence in their struggle with "crushing poverty." Screened in St. Patrick's Cathedral for Manhattan's chic R.C.s, the prerecorded pontiff extolled America's leading Lady as "the welcoming symbol for the tired, poor, uprooted people of the world ..."

In person, meanwhile, John Paul motored into squalid slums, his hand dispensing blessings through the bullet-proof panes of his papal tank, like manna to assuage a people's despair.

He kissed the Colombian earth. Eyes moist, he sowed hope in the people's impoverished breast: Mother Church, he assured them, seeks justice for all. The Vicar of Christ then boarded his jet and returned to the Vatican palace.

The Holy Father's descent on Bogotá couldn't compete with Liberty Weekend headlines here in the states, but the shadow of that jet, inscribed with the Keys to the Kingdom, passed like a cool hand on the brows of huddled Colombians.

But issues spoil a party.

Face freshened for her second hundred years of immigrants, the Renewed Colossus of the eroded century charmed the focus of this sharply reduced globe with her own preoccupied visage. We had the weekend off from the space race, terrorism, … even hunger. Willie Nelson's Farm Aid concert raised only $500,000 of the expected millions. Lady Liberty subbed as our sun in that triduum of self-approbation, fixed us in orbit, exacted recognition for her long vigil.

Like the grains of sand beneath their zories, celebrants jammed the shoreline of New York's darkened harbor, hushed before the laser beam that reversed its own command and caused a collective gasp. Liberty, unveiled, launched a Roman candle extravaganza that festooned not only the statue but the entire Manhattan skyline like a pyrotechnic garden of Nebuchadnezzar and embossed for all time, upon the dazzled psyches of enthralled viewers, the definition of awe.

More immediately, sanitation engineers in the City of New York tallied the drift of Big Mac empties into the wind caverns of Big Apple skyscrapers. Drained Pepsi and Classic Coke cans rattle the same. City scavengers had no doubt about the real thing as they geared for the morning after the three-day bash with the nine-digit guest list.

Lee Iacocca, high priest of the American Dream, had begun to pivot perspective back to the mundane on Sunday evening with recognition of the 700 French and American men and women who, every day for two years, had latched their belts to scaffolds and refurbished the 151-foot, copper-skinned Lady. Uncommon laborers, they took center stage for a bow. It was a munificent moment in a magnificent feast of patriotism … that left me out.

Liberty's dugs offer me no succor …

I watched your party by satellite, Mother of Exiles. The testimonials to Freedom and Equal Justice for All carved a grand hollowness straight through the core of my belonging. For too long now, your austere countenance has scanned the seas for the tempest-tossed. Behind your back, the highest court in the land denies me my dignity and treats me as wretched refuse.

Six days earlier, June 30, 1986, five justices of the United States Supreme Court rescinded my invitation to the historic gala in a decision that declared that the intimate acts with which my male partner and I fulfill each other, even in the privacy of our bedroom, lie outside the protection of Constitutional guarantee. That decision, based on the 1982 case of Michael Hardwick,* arrested in the bedroom of his Atlanta, Georgia, residence, confirms me as a criminal in twenty-four of the fifty states which still retain statutes against sodomy—that ugly Old Testament label derived from the city whose only "just" man offered his two virgin daughters to be gang-raped in exchange for the safety of two visitors (albeit angels) who were total strangers to him. (Genesis 19:7–8 for Chapter and Verse addicts.) Here feed the "ancient roots" Justice Byron R. White cites for prohibition of homosexual acts by the Founding Fathers and the thirteen original states. The scriptural source presents a moral cripple as a just man. Lot's example serves the present court as insidiously as glaucoma in its majority perception of human dignity.

With "ancient roots" in so bizarre a Judaeo-Christian value, why wonder that the high court dumps Equal Justice, like so much jetsam, at Liberty's harbor-bound feet?

Until 2003, states had individual license to mine their borders with penalties for sexual activity in a manner so arbitrary that it negates the premise of a free and unified people. The same acts with which my male partner and I legally make love in California could have imprisoned us for six years in Nevada, where identical acts between opposite genders pose no crime at all. Oral or anal, heterosexuals in the bordello belt do it with legal sanction. Even today, in Utah, however, statutes remain on the books penalizing homosexual behavior, justifying not protecting them from hate crimes.

Such moral hypocrisy would be laughable were it not so treacherous. While in ancient times no citizen of Rome could be crucified within Rome's jurisdiction, today in America every gay citizen must mark his map to circumvent the possibility.

The decision of these grand interpreters of Constitutional intent tacitly endorses violent discrimination against me everywhere. Fag-bashing may be illegal throughout the union, but when twenty-four of the fifty states consider the bashed a criminal, where's the real harm? No one decent got hurt.

The decision suggests that the deepest needs of my nature rise out of a flawed humanity and equates the exquisite acts that deepen my personal bonds with a furtive blow job in a dingy latrine. The justices, in fact, virtually shrug out an amendment to that equation: I might as well get it that way because not even my bedroom is safe. At all times the significance of "it" fits their "ancient rooted" system of values.

The decision coerces still more thousands of homosexuals into the artifice of marriage with the result that both partners and their children become the exponential victims of Judaeo-Christian terrorism. Hypocrisy is a national treasure to which justices White, Burger, O'Connor, Rehnquist and Powell have lent their collective arrogance.

If the face of arrogance has familiar features, it is with good reason. Arrogance is ignorance in the hands of power. It conspires to keep minorities in their place and thereby gild the myth that this nation under God is indivisible. But gilding the myth requires gelding the attribute—gutting its second syllable so it fits offensive minorities.

My immigrant father had neither minority status nor invisibility in mind when he made his own ascent into the long arm of Liberty seventy-two years ago. The Freedom and Justice he'd crossed the Atlantic to claim, he died thinking he'd secured for all his issue. His gay son laid bare the lie.

My German-born father did not know he had produced a faggot son with his constitutionally guaranteed act of intercourse. I was afraid to tell him. I sat at his deathbed two decades ago wishing we had something to talk about ... father to son. His chest, like a massive oak leaned into the earth, was decaying with cancer. He'd calloused his hands so I wouldn't have to, sinking wells in California's fertile valleys. Boraxo didn't make cleanser enough to scrub his knuckles clean. I used to watch his hands and wonder whether work was really honorable or he just made it seem that way. He took their strength for granted. He could cradle a lug wrench as if it were his grandson's downy head and make either act seem sacred. That's what threatened me about him. I never learned to reconcile his gentleness with his power. I feared his masculinity because I was trying to prove I had it. I resented his softness for what it might reveal about me. I was afraid it would betray me.

My naturalized father loved a Judaeo-Christian formula, not a son. Both of us were robbed. I'd invested thousands of dollars in years of psychotherapeutic probing to make myself straight and wound up not self-possessed but dispossessed—a prostitute to the American Dream.

It took me twenty years, one marriage, two children and a nearly fatal addiction to alcohol to finally say yes to myself. Twenty years. I might have been emerging from a Georgia prison for a single act of sodomy; the time frame was the same. Yet, at forty-three, I'd actually done double that stretch in the preconceptions and prejudices of persons who do not need to know me to hate me. I know about huddled masses.

I thought of that as Liberty Weekend closed. Costumed representatives of the Melting Pot's minorities filed onto the Sunday night stage in New Jersey's Giants Stadium, and I said to my lover as we watched, "Do you know what's missing from that parade?"

"What's missing?" Degnan asked without shifting his gaze from the screen.

"A drag queen," I replied.

"Tch!" he said, then looked at me and smiled. "All the world loves a clown?" he added.

It's true, of course. The way the straight press handles reader repugnance over same-sex genital activity is by photographing what provokes laughter or blue-haired tremors of disbelief. Run-of-the-mill gay rights marchers rarely claim visibility in a lens.

"You've gotta have balls to get rigged in an outfit like that," Degnan observed in one such march as a pair of Miss Kitty clones in meshed stockings and dance-hall heels teetered ahead of us ... and we laughed, embarrassed at their courage.

Clown derives from the Latin colonus meaning colonist, and that significance lends the drag queen a more precise perspective. Those of us who can be invisible too often take our air through cracks in the closet door waiting for hairy-chested beauties in off-the-shoulder satin to exhaust the minefields of Judaeo-Christian tradition, shoving its absurd perception of us up its own inflated nostrils. "Give me some queens, who are stout-hearted queens, who will fight for the right they adore ..." and a few dykes on bikes who can lay tread where it counts.

What you, Mr. President, and your beloved first lady, have done for this country is to create a climate in which a majority of Supreme Court justices can wrap the "ancient roots" of religious bigotry around the rights of gay and lesbian citizens in a church-and-state stranglehold. That is a tribute you richly deserve and, in your arrogance, pompously accept.

In his eloquent dissent, Justice Harry Blackmun, joined by justices Stevens, Brennan and Marshall, wrote, "Only the most willful blindness could obscure the fact that sexual intimacy is a sensitive, key relationship of human existence, central to family life, community welfare and the development of human personality ... In a nation as diverse as ours ... there may be many 'right' ways of conducting those relationships, and ... much of the richness of a relationship will come from the freedom an individual has to choose the form and nature of these intensely personal bonds."

That such reasoning was even arguable ought to alarm every citizen. That it became the outcry of a defeated challenge should stun the sensibilities of every American who values human dignity. One hundred years is too long to scan the horizon, Lady, without knowing what's going down behind your back. Come, Mother, ... visit the in-house exiles.

*On June 26, 2003, the Supreme Court, in Lawrence vs. the State of Texas, overturned its 1986 Bowers vs. Hardwick decision and abolished all sodomy laws in the United States. Same-gender marriage became legal in Massachusetts in 2003; in Connecticut, Vermont and the Coquille Indian Tribe in Oregon in 2009; in New Hampshire and Washington, D.C. in 2010; in New York on June 24, 2011; in the Suquamash Tribe in Washington on August 8 2011. Same-gender marriage was legal in California from June 16 to November 4, 2008 before Proposition 8 halted the ceremonies. The Supreme Court of California is expected to rule soon on whether Proposition 8 violates the constitutional right of same-gender couples to marriage. Progress is happening but slowly and painfully. The United States Supreme Court must ultimately accept this immense human and civil rights challenge.

CHAPTER 30

FAMILY TIES

My father had a hard time believing a marine could be queer, but Eddie was. I knew that the instant I opened the door and he was there on the porch in cutoffs and sleeveless sweatshirt, the early sun making his skin all tawny. I had never seen him before. Eddie was a scion of the Irish stock that had remained in New York, my grandfather's great-nephew, and we knew little about that side. An aunt of his had lived for years in the East Bay but, like the rest of that side, we knew little of her also. So Eddie was a complete stranger to me—handsome, well-built and, I was certain, wearing nothing under the wide cuffs of his ragged cutoffs. His glass-blue eyes held mine as he asked, "Is May here?"

My testicles shrank up. Everything about Eddie made me feel the way I knew I shouldn't, and I hadn't a clue how to handle it. I was doing the therapy thing in those days and pretending I wasn't, while Eddie obviously was and appeared not to give a damn who knew. People like that are scary.

"May?" I repeated. Young men did not come to the door asking for my mother by her first name. That he was somehow connected made him all the more threatening. His hair cut a dark blond swath away from his tanned features. My mother, I realized, was no longer the focus of his attention, and I tried to avoid his eyes. The shadowed culverts beneath each shoulder sheltered dark tufts like smoke that didn't dissipate.

"Would you be Ron?" he asked.

"Yes ..."

He pulled open the screen door and extended his hand. "I'm your cousin Eddie from New York. May should have received a letter that I'd be mustering out at Camp Pendleton and stopping by."

My mother hates to have anyone catch her still abed, even, as then, on a Saturday when she and my father took their ease later than usual. But she's a gracious lady who puts the best face on the unexpected. Eddie was sipping coffee opposite me at the kitchen table when she came out, tying her robe, apologizing for her hairnet and kissing him welcome. Eddie moved lithely, the solid taper of his thighs caught in pale fuzz as he rose and leaned into her hug. The issue of bloodline cut right through the fact that, otherwise, they were perfect strangers. My father was late to the table, the first symptoms of his cancer claiming its margin of his energy. Aunt Millicent stirred in the back bedroom, her enthusiasm for tracing the family tree alerted. Beneath the chatter, Eddie and I sensed, almost stalked, each other.

I excused myself, finally, to work. Saturday overtime helped me afford the fifty-minute sessions that Eddie had all but unraveled in half that time. His strong hand grasped mine as I rose to leave, and he noted that I noted the dark arches of his cutoffs as he straddled the chrome chair.

He was still there when I stopped by after work. Actually, I wasn't living at home any longer. I stayed over on nights when work kept me too late to drive on up to the Santa Cruz summit where I'd taken a mountain cabin. Eddie, who was a year older than I, had learned that—and the fact that I'd been recently through a broken engagement—during his getting-to-know-us visit with my family.

He invited me to go for pizza and, reluctantly, I accepted. By that time in my life, of course, I'd had numerous homosexual encounters, all furtive, fraught with guilt and part of what I was trying to exorcise from my psyche. Never had I sat down knowingly to socialize, much less share a meal, with one of them. I was convinced that everyone at the pizzeria had him pegged and, therefore, me by association. Most disconcerting of all was the volume at which he said that he hated wearing clothes, that he mowed his aunt's lawn in the East Bay in his leather bikini.

"I never wear underwear," he added unnecessarily, all the while studying my reaction.

My mind was a warp of rammed defenses. I volunteered nothing, struggled more with the mozzarella than it warranted and avoided topics that could turn the conversation personal. Yawning, he wished he could stay down another day but hadn't a place to sleep. I looked away from his blue gaze. My chilly cabin had one bed and no neighbors. I was torn between what I wanted to say and couldn't.

When I left him back at my folks and his car, he sat beside me in the darkness of the driveway and said maybe we could do something together from time to time, that he'd like to get to know me better, that he enjoyed my company. I felt his eyes as I stared ahead through the windshield and said, "Sure, that'd be fine."

The whole family knew about Eddie in short order; liked him, mind you, but ... knew about him.

I saw him probably a total of three times, the last at my father's funeral when I introduced him to my wife and felt the buffer of that security as I sat next to him. Everything else came word of mouth about Eddie, fractured by the faction-effect that afflicts families.

A goal of these latter years when finally I arrived at the acceptance Eddie had achieved twenty-five years ago, has been to contact and level with him about myself. But I kept putting it off. I still see Eddie in my mind as the vigorous and virile youth who quickened my pulse early one Saturday ... and I've kept thinking there's time, there's time.

A trickle of relatives followed him out from New York through the years. Oddly, all but two have died. His mother has buried all her children. Eddie, too. She called my mother the other day to say that Eddie had died the previous weekend ... of alcoholism. Eddie was fifty. He was being cremated, she said, and his friends would set adrift his ashes off Angel Island. A longtime friend of Eddie's, she added, had died just six months earlier, also of alcoholism. Time was when families hushed up that kind of thing. Strange how the disgrace of one era gains respectability in another.

"Do you think that's possible, the two of them dying of alcoholism ... so close together?" my mother asked when she telephoned with the news.

"It's possible," I said, knowing what she was asking. "It's possible."

And I felt a great sadness.

CHAPTER 31

OBSCENITIES III: BY-THE-BOOK RISK

A child in our district had died—fashioned a noose with her own hands and connected her neck to a tree in her yard. Indications suggested that she'd timed the effort to coincide with a relative's arrival. The finality of her miscalculation must have struck even her as awful before consciousness bowed to her miscue.

Shock caused her true friends to feel they must follow. Shock waves swept the district. Counseling and a close eye, hundreds of close eyes, went on watch. Confidential memos circulated on likely prospects, some of whom had already notched their psyches with aborted efforts. It was a bit macabre. Introspection. Who missed the cues ... even the miscue? And how? True friends. Family. Teachers. Guilt by association. Was it safe to get close, close enough to be responsible? On the other hand, what was close? Who was close? Does a suicide have close friends? Aren't suicides the loners about whom everyone afterwards says, "He was a kick in the ass to be around," or "She always kept to herself," or "He started running with the wrong crowd," or "She just didn't seem the type," or something?

What about notes? Did she leave any notes? Pass any prophetic scribbles to friends? It's the underground railroad of the classroom, note writing. Kids between classes exchange misspelled passions scrawled during Lee's surrender to Grant, folded during a discussion of non-collinear points.

"Shelly,
How come you didn't wate for me at brunsh? Are you made cuz Randy called me last nite? Alls he wahted to no is if you still waht to go with him since him and Alicia broke up. Write back.
Luv ya,
Gynger"
"Gynge,
I'm not mad at you. I hope you tolded Randy yes. I really love him alot. Alicia is such a bich.

W/B.
Your friend forever,
Shell"

Kids who drop out with "Good morning, class," can pass a full forty minutes in the underground. Kids who cannot double crease a simple business letter, angle four cornered planes into foolproof fits. They never come loose, those notes, in hand-to-hand transit across the room or even in sweaty palmed, between-class hope as hall monitors urge the tardy past appointed he-loves-me-she-loves-me-not rendezvous in the halls.

Self-esteem is a big topic in education with a not-too-committed following. The district's answer, for example, to the child who strung her esteem to the limb in the yard was to bring to each school site a county psychiatrist to in-service staff. That he hadn't the latest statistics on teen suicide or cogent suggestions for heading off kids at risk bothered some of us. What he did tell us that we hadn't known before was that he doesn't take night calls.

I complained the next day to my principal that the in-service had band-aided a gaping wound and that we were ignoring the real issues of our charges as we primed them to perform on the CAP or SAT or PSAT or Nelson or this competency or that proficiency so that the results would satisfy parents which would satisfy the school board. At the same time that California Superintendent of Schools Bill Honig exulted in March 1987 that the latest CAP scores proved the thrust in state education was correct, the media also reported that each year in the United States 500,000 teenagers attempt suicide and that 6,000 succeed. A sense of alienation, of not being accepted, of separation from peers and from family claims one teenager every ninety minutes, yet the obsession with test scores intensifies. That is most surely neglect.

I confronted that neglect with the principal, citing the esteem gone begging in our midst. Yes, some kids come to us with strong egos backed by solid homes, but significant numbers do not, particularly in the plain of untilled hormones, tried identities and sexual awareness that is the level of secondary students.

The golden calf of test scores has degraded teachers into technicians of whichever latest package promises the biggest results, pumping in data like programming computers. Feedback is the goal. Of course we are graduating illiterates. Of course teenagers are committing suicide.

We are ignoring what the child has inside and needs to develop, needs to let out, and that is the great heresy of American education, the cardinal rule sharded at the feet of our failure.

Educare, the Latin root of education, means to lead out. Early in my career I randomly encountered students expressing ideas exquisitely wrought in a fashion for which, despite my conscientious efforts, I could claim no credit. What read between my fingers was the product of some muse, the innate, at least immanent stir, of a soul that wanted only a climate to breed. Teachers, I discovered, are midwives to the most extraordinary process ... or should be. Yes, we provide skills, but real teaching is not putting in, it is allowing out, tending the environment, creating safety for the risk a child must take to value himself, to develop her self-esteem.

How can that value stay so untapped in a thirteen-year-old, that esteem be so starved in a nineteen-year-old that each wants to die? How can we teach only math or only English or only human body or only history in forty-five-minute segments and expect an integrated person at the end of the day or quarter, semester and year? How do we teach to a test and allow a child the joy of discovery? How do we take our separate subject matters and say, "Listen, this is what's important and you must learn it now," when the note in his hand reads, "Don't you like me anymore?"

What I said to the principal was that we must risk becoming involved in issues real to kids and make subject matter relevant to their needs. The English classroom lends itself perfectly to that process, a province through which all concerns interact ... and, besides, issues give purpose to skills. What worth has a nonrestrictive clause in isolated drill to a student worried about his need for frequent masturbation or same-sex attractions?

"I can guarantee you," I told the principal, "that at least ten percent of this student body suffers a lack of self-esteem and probable suicidal tendencies because they are gay or lesbian. Nothing is done for these kids. They have no one to confide in and no one to emulate. I can say this with certainty because I've been there. I am myself gay."

Instantly the oxygen thinned in the office. I pretended not to notice. "Are you willing to risk that kind of involvement?" I challenged.

The principal examined his brown leather arch, his fingers peaked beneath his nose. "What you are suggesting is what we have counselors for."

"Counselors push paper ... especially in this district. You know as well as I do that the superintendent has told them, 'You do not wear a white coat!' They schedule classes and administer competency tests. If there's time left over, they comfort some kid in tears."

He nodded. "Unfortunately, that's often true. Be that as it may, their job description covers what you're asking of me, and I'm here to tell you that neither you nor I have the qualifications or the credentials ..."

"I've lived those qualifications. I own those credentials."

"The State of California wants it on paper. I might also add that if what you have just shared with me about being gay were to become generally known, it would bring down the walls of this district. This is a very conservative community, and homosexuality is a highly controversial topic. It does not belong in the classroom ... Let me qualify that. If it were to be raised at all in a classroom, it would be in human body and then only as mandated by the state ... and by the district."

"Homosexuality is raised in every classroom where one kid calls another 'fag,' and it festers like pus-ridden contagion if the teacher's too insecure to stop it. That way it is a disease. It's called homophobia.

"As for the human body teacher, I suggested the topic of homosexual family members for her evening discussion series. She gasped and said she wouldn't touch it. She wouldn't even say the word homosexual; she just pointed to it on the survey sheet I was returning to her. According to her, every human body teacher in the district was hauled in for questioning five years ago when the instructor at the other junior high raised the topic."

The principal nodded. "Then you know the mood of this community."

"That mood doesn't alter the fact that in this student body of 800 kids, at least eighty suffer their difference because the school board and the administration fear controversy. Silence is a powerful teacher. It's an endorsement of fear and violence. Silence teaches the most virulent form of bigotry. It's child abuse, plain and simple."

"That's a strong charge."

"When a girl hangs herself and no one knows why, and, worse yet, no one wants to deal with why, strong charges are in order. I'm tired of the hypocrisy in education, sick of the people who point to our failure but refuse to let us get involved. I want to get involved. I need support at your level. Are you willing to risk that?"

The principal turned the toe of his shoe this way and that, then looked at me with an expression at once profound and amused. "I've always considered myself a moderate risk taker," he said, "but I'm no kamikaze." He chuckled.

The rims of my eyes burned. "Kamikazes took no risk," I pointed out. "Their fate was sealed from the moment they sat in their cockpits. I have every intention not only of pursuing but surviving this mission."

As I left the principal's office, I marveled that the walls of an entire school district could be threatened by the good intent of a single homosexual. The texture of biblical mortar clearly lacks cohesion. I tested the walls, muttering, "Gay," as I passed and grew bolder when nothing happened. "I'm gay," I said, but there wasn't so much as a tremor, and I wondered if all believers are deluded.

Immediately I set up appointments with my union reps. I'd lost one job already to my candor and was determined it would not happen again. As in that previous district, I was once more on temporary contract. I'd sacrificed tenure in the Sierras to return to the Bay Area, unaware of how deeply vulnerable that made me. I hadn't realized my options as a first-time temp but even if I had, in fact, I'd been too stunned to act. I'd never been out of work in my life much less let go because of who I am. My administrators knew I was gay. I told them the morning after Governor Deukmejian vetoed California's gay rights bill. It was my private protest. All three ... principal and both assistant principals ... were supportive. What mattered, they said, was the quality of my teaching. So certain were they that I would be back come fall, they asked me to co-advise the Honor Society.

In the interim summer, however, I wrote a note of my own, a letter to the editor of the San José Mercury News for its shoddy, biased report on San Francisco's Gay Pride Parade. Following its publication, the personnel director, who once bragged to students that her ideals were so high she could see the Golden Gate Bridge from the Empire State Building, expressed regret that the position they'd scheduled me for just wasn't materializing.

That it was my letter that axed me one of the administrators confirmed over coffee that fall. "I've never understood the need of gay people to say that they're gay," she said.

I looked at her, astonished. "Bea," I said, "you don't have to tell anyone you're black. But crass remarks are made about us all the time by people who assume no one they know is gay. It's a matter of pride to speak up. I owe that to the kids I teach ... all of them; to those who've already put their lives on the line ... especially the Harvey Milks. I owe it to those who *can't* pass, men defined by delicacy and women endowed with brawn. And, Bea, I owe it to myself."

California Teachers Association and California Federation of Teachers both supported my rights as a temporary teacher to rehire over any similarly qualified candidate with no district experience. Both clearly knew that I was gay and that my then-current district had begun greasing the same wheels used by my previous district to ease me out—lower enrollment, teachers returning from leave, inter-district transfers. Three positions had opened at the high school, in fact, while I taught summer session that year, and I requested an interview for one of those jobs. As I stood in the outer office getting mail from my box, the principal, unaware that I was there, called the D. O. with her door wide open. "Ron Schmidt wants an interview," she said, "and I think politically it's the correct thing to do."

I stopped that afternoon to see my no-kamikaze principal. "I hate to sound paranoid," I said, "but the word seems to be out that I'm not to be rehired because I'm gay."

He was guarded.

I related the incident with the politically correct high school administrator. Then I asked, "Did you tell the personnel director that I'm gay?"

The principal slapped his brown leather arch. "No, I did not!" he said vigorously.

"The personnel director does not know that I'm gay?" I persisted.

"Well, ... yes, she does ... I guess I did tell her ... but that was after I told the superintendent."

CTA's regional director listened attentively to my plight, picked up the phone and arranged for me to meet with the association's human-rights commissioner, an astute and compassionate black man who did understand why gay people need to say they are gay. Their support, added to the extremely effective on-site vigilance of my CFT representatives, secured my temporary position for a second year and supplied the thrust to move me into permanent status with my third-year contract. That, in a district that kept employees temporary as many as five to seven years. The district whose walls could so easily crumble had a confirmed homosexual on its permanent staff, and administrators from top to bottom knew it. So did many of the teachers. Within the context of education, I took whatever opportunities came up to dispel ignorance and demystify homosexuality. Always, I was lobbying to risk involvement with kids in the issues they face.

I took that lobby to a California State Assemblyman as well, a man who had been the graduating president of Santa Clara University's student body the year that I was a prospective freshman. I'd sat among high school seniors from around the Bay Area in the campus' historic Adobe Lodge and listened to the idealism that the articulate young law student would evolve into a political credo over the next thirty years.

I did not meet John Vasconcellos personally until I was myself a Santa Clara graduate sitting in a jail cell while my single call to a priest friend brought the young attorney to my aid. Lewd and lascivious conduct with another male in a parked car, secluded and consensual, was my offense.

It was the effectiveness of that counsel that helped me seal up my closet for the next two decades, avoiding the disgrace that would appreciably have altered my life. His presentation to the court that I was already in therapy, backed by the testimony of my therapist that I stood a 50/50 chance of a cure, persuaded the authorities that I need not be added to the operational costs of the Atascadero state facility for the sexually perverse.

Recovering from bypass surgery following a heart attack in 1984, Vasconcellos was quoted in the San José Mercury News on the conviction he'd come to espouse: "Openness is the best path to living." Throughout his career, accounts of his idealism had bolstered my own zeal. The timing, this time, coincided with my confrontation with my no-kamikaze principal. I went to see the assemblyman.

"I believe in the honesty you're asking for," I told him, having capsulized the years since our legal encounter. "Tell me who else in education believes as you do so I can network with those who will listen and understand and support the needs of the ten percent. I want to make safe the environment for gay and lesbian teachers to be role models for every student body's most derided minority. I want to take the doors off kids' closets so they can thrive instead of brooding about their cover and mulling whether it's worth it."

And Vasconcellos gave me names, letters of introduction even to three superintendents, a principal and an educational lobbyist. And each of them did listen. And each of them advised that these things take time. And I thought of the girl for whom time had become the final miscalculation between a rope and her neck and I knew that time is the one commodity none of us can afford.

The superintendent in one particularly affluent district had dealt with homosexual teachers three times in his career, each as the result of arrest. One teacher simply moved on; the second remained, with board approval, as long as student safety was guaranteed; the third "blew his brains out." The superintendent lamented the needlessness of such pain but reiterated that these things take time. It turned out he was himself gay.

Up the peninsula, a second superintendent detailed his unsuccessful efforts to bring speakers on homosexuality into health classes. Instructors of such courses tend to be coaches who feel threatened by the topic so provide neither the preplanning, nor the support, nor the backup necessary to the effort. He lamented that these things take time.

At that same time that I was making the rounds of open-minded administrators, a joke was also making the rounds at Bellarmine College Preparatory, my alma mater. "Have you heard about the latest Cabbage Patch Doll?" a teacher asked the secretaries between classes one morning. "This doll is gay, has AIDS and comes with a death certificate." My sister, Kathleen, who was a secretary there at the time, passed that along, adding, "Would you believe that teacher is a Jesuit priest!"

Is it for people like him that time must be taken?

My alumni magazine for July 1985 featured a cover photo of a handsome Bellarmine senior with the logo: "The Jesuit Ideal 'Becoming a Man for Others.'" The inside story details the hours of Christian service this youth had logged beyond those required for graduation. That the young man deserved the plaudits cannot be contested, but I wondered as I read whether the priest with the Cabbage Patch joke had ever been his teacher and how, then, he would select the others for whom he was becoming. I wondered whether his orthodontically perfect smile had been spent on the Cabbage Patch joke ... and I worried about taking time.

The photo of another youth was featured that summer in the Triangle Project newsletter. That story reported how the expressionless figure, hands in pockets, walking the streets, is one of over 600,000 homosexual youth under the age of eighteen in the state of California alone. Nearly 200,000, it is estimated, will develop chemical dependencies. Over 100,000 will attempt suicide. More than 10,000 are throwaway, runaways living on the streets of L.A.

From whom do they run? Who throws them out? The joke-tellers? The Christian who qualifies his love? The time-takers?

The time-takers are wrong.

The ten percent are in my classes as they are in every teacher's classes. Every time a faggot slur goes unchallenged, education fails these students, and that neglect is abuse. Every time we fail to mention the homosexual orientation of persons who have moved history, art, literature, science, we fail these children, and that neglect is abuse. Such failure denies homosexual youth the chance to identify with role models and to develop the esteem essential to well-being. Such neglect is clearly abuse. Acting on that conviction has placed me at loggerheads with administrators and, in one particularly bizarre incident, with parents.

It began with a note again, one I intercepted in class. The accidents I have altered to protect confidentiality; the essence is a combination of truths gleaned from twenty-two years of students, convened in one I shall call Tierney. Tierney was a boy whose facial bone structure stunningly foreshadowed the man he would become. His teeth had outdistanced his jaw at fifteen, but the latter held the promise of strength when it caught up. He was a spontaneous boy whose moods took on a tendency to the volatile. His work could be exquisitely sensitive and creative but was randomly done. The times he seemed totally focused, writing copiously, I was often dismayed that his effort was unrelated to the assignment.

It was not the first note I collected from him, but it was the note whose interception affected him most. He watched me as I read, his face paler against the auburn fall of his shoulder length hair. His angry script recounted his parents' discovery that he and the addressee were more than just friends. I glanced quickly at the top of the page again. Tierney was in love with another boy. His eyes convexed with worry as I penned, "Please stay a moment after class," on a 3x5 card and set it on his desk. His hair broke on his shoulders with his nod.

I circulated among the students, checking progress on rough and revised drafts of their essays, answering questions, offering reinforcement. My mind, however, incubated the need in the note—including the threat to run away and the declaration that Tierney did not want to live without Dirk. And I remembered Don Folkholm, the gay student I'd tried to help with half-truths early in my career, and I knew that I must respond to Tierney's need more honestly.

Fortunately, that class backed up against lunch so that when the bell rang there was time to conference. "Can we talk a few minutes, Tierney?" I asked.

He nodded, silent, possibly hostile, certainly prepared to be defensive. His eyes ran a quick check on mine. He sat down.

"You're not in trouble with me. I want you to know that, and you don't have to say anything to me. But I might be in more of a position to help than you realize. Parts of your note I am legally bound to act upon: the threat to run away, ... the suggestion that you don't want to live without this other person."

Tierney nodded, tears welling in his eyes.

"Am I reading the name correctly, Tier? Does it say Dirk?"

Another nod. "He doesn't go to this school."

"Your folks are really upset."

"I can't ever see him again as long as I live at home. They're all the time telling me, 'You're sick!' or 'You're crazy!' and 'You're goin' to hell!' They want me to leave."

"They're afraid," I said. "I suspect that they love you very much, but they're afraid. All their lives they've believed homosexuality to be wrong, and now here is their son involved with another boy. Their fear has gotten in the way of their love ... It happens ... but that doesn't make it easier for you."

Tierney shook his head, his sensuous mouth a wrinkle of pain.

"Lots of people share that belief, Tier, and they don't accept what I'm about to say. But I'd like you to listen. It's important that you know. Major studies have been done by people named Kinsey and Masters and Johnson ... the names won't mean anything to you now, but they're well respected in the medical world. Those studies revealed that most straight people have same-sex attractions, even relationships, at some point in their lives and that it doesn't mean that they are homosexual ... only that they have had a homosexual experience. By the same token, most gay people have a straight attraction, even relationship, at some point as well, but it doesn't mean that they're straight ... only that they've had a heterosexual experience. Adolescence is often the time when that happens. Sexual awareness is very intense. There's lots of experimentation.

"On the other hand, that research has also shown that ten percent of the population is gay or lesbian, Tier, and even the American Psychiatric Association acknowledges now that homosexuality is a normal and natural condition for that ten percent."

Tierney blinked, wiping his tears with the back of one hand.

"That's a lot of people, when you think about it, yet most people will tell you they don't know anyone who's gay. Newspapers and television play up stereotypes and focus on negative issues instead of facts that would break down fear and misunderstanding about homosexuality. Kids rarely get to see that homosexuals are regular people; that's why I'm telling you that I am gay, Tier."

The dark lashed eyes watched me, focused, still damp.

"Ninety percent of the kids in this school will say they don't know anyone gay, yet I'm a part of their daily lives. Everyone knows someone gay or lesbian. It's the fear of what you're going through that keeps the fact hidden. I'm here if you need to talk, especially when things get heavy ... like they are now for you and Dirk and your family. I know people in the gay community who can be very supportive, and I'd like you to invite your folks to come in so I can share those resources with them. Talking with families who've already been through this can make a whole lot of difference ... make it a whole lot easier for you to stay at home."

Tierney's hair shimmered like spilled copper. "They won't come in," he said. "They don't want to understand. You don't know what they're like. They wouldn't listen to you if they knew you were gay, and they won't go to no groups."

I shrugged. "It's worth a try."

I watched the anger at work in his features, then pulled open the drawer of my desk.

"Look," I said, handing him a card, "my main concern at the moment is about the other things you've written to Dirk ... about running away and about not wanting to live without him. This is a hotline card like the one I have on the wall ... Here, let me star a couple of these for you.

Ask your folks to come in and talk. If they won't and things get really stressed, call. I'm putting my own number at the bottom. You can call me anytime," I said handing him back the card, "but, Tier, don't run. I've attended meetings where runaway kids tell what it's like on the streets. They sell their bodies just to eat and come in out of the cold. They get into drugs, bad. They worry that some homophobic psychopath might be their next trick. Running away is no answer ... and, for God's sake, Tierney, neither is suicide."

He had calmed some, his damp lashes, grown steady, had begun to dry. He listened.

"It won't be long before you can legally exercise your own decisions. It won't matter that someone tells you you can't see Dirk; you can do it anyway. From now till then seems like forever, but it isn't. Forever is what happens when you act in desperation. *That* can't be fixed. Dealing with your folks' fear is an investment in what you and Dirk can eventually share. If you love somebody your minds are already together; your hearts are bound."

I glanced at the clock. "The bell's catching up with us," I said. "Promise me you won't run and that you won't ..."

Tierney shifted in the desk. "I won't do anything stupid," he said, "but it's all set for us to leave after school."

My heart sank. "At least come back after sixth period then so we can talk some more, look at alternatives, find you someplace safe to stay."

He didn't answer. The bell rang. Immediately there were kids at the door.

"Tierney?"

"All right."

"I'll see you at three then."

He nodded, got up, paused. "Thanks," he said.

But there was no Tierney at three. I had no alternative but to report my concerns for the boy's safety.

The assistant principal did everything by the book, the Good Book, and if it couldn't be done that way, he didn't do it at all. In his office I discovered Tierney and a woman, obviously his mother. The AP saw me pause outside, so did the taut-faced woman, but they did not ask me in.

I dallied about the attendance office until the assistant principal walked Tierney and his mother to her car, watched him watch the mother drive the son home and I thought what a strange word is home ... what an ache there is in its sound. Robert Frost's definition threaded my thoughts:

"Home is the place where, when you
have to go there
They have to take you in ...
Something you somehow haven't to deserve."

I marveled at the pain of blood become obligation.
"Do you have a minute?" I asked, holding the door for the AP.
He tried to look neutral as he nodded, and we headed back to his office. He was a large man, girth-wise, whose lack of stature made him cute-fat, and kids teased his tummy with patting hands as he smiled. His eyes were perfect ovals, and his face would have been perfectly cherubic but for the fact of his forty-odd years. I half expected his wings to unfold as he pressed leather with his back and looked at me guardedly across the expanse of his desk and narrow experience. I realized suddenly I'd caught him before he'd had time to consult his Savior about me.
That he knew about me was obvious; that he would say nothing about what we both knew about Tierney was also obvious. His lips did not meet as he listened to my concern for the boy and the strain he was under, to the efforts I'd made to deter running and dissuade self-destructive tendencies. I urged that my request for a parent conference be relayed in the hope I might help at least through resources at my disposal.
"Thank you for giving him that hotline list," the AP finally said. "I've been working with Tierney and his family a long time. I've been recommending counseling for the whole family. I think they're finally going to get it."
"Counseling through the district psychologist?" I asked.
"No, through our church. We go to the same church. They're Christians too."
I called Tierney's home that evening to ask how he was, explaining that I knew he had been very upset and inviting the parents to come in to talk, that perhaps I could help.
The father was civil. Tierney was doing pretty well. He thanked me

for my call, responded not at all to the conference request. I knew I was in trouble.

The call on my intercom phone during my first-period prep next morning got right to the point. "The principal wants you in his office at 9:20," said the secretary.

He was seated at a desk behind which he jotted notes on a yellow legal pad, venetian blinds angled for privacy. I was instructed to close the door and be seated.

Without looking at me, he asked, "Did you, yesterday, tell a student that you are a homosexual?" His blue script materialized on the page faster than he could write.

"I did," I said.

He looked up at me, his glasses intensifying his expression. "You did tell a student that you are a homosexual," he emphasized.

"I did," I repeated. "I'm not going to lie to you."

He resumed his writing.

"Please explain to me why you did that."

"I can't do that," I said. "The conversation was a confidence between the student and myself. I took my concerns that he might run away or harm himself to the assistant principal, as the law requires, but the content..."

The principal shook his head. "The question of confidentiality is no longer at issue here. The student has already broken that confidence. I have just left his mother at the elementary school where she asked that we meet to avoid having her son or his friends know that our discussion was taking place."

As I listened to the circuitous web being spun about me, I did not think to ask that a union representative be present. I was still insufficiently seasoned. Foolishly, I explained.

"I believe," the principal went on, "that you acted out of what you perceived to be the boy's best interests; in fact, everything else you did—trying to talk him out of running away, dissuade him from self-destruction, giving him the hotline list, going to the assistant principal, even calling the parents—those things were excellent. But telling the boy that you are a homosexual and suggesting that homosexuality is an acceptable lifestyle," his voice thickened, "those were serious errors in judgment and infractions of district policy."

"Obviously, I disagree."

"You disagree? Do you set board policy?"

"Board policy is denying Tierney the help he needs. Should I sit back and pretend homosexuality doesn't exist while this child toys with suicide and I know help is available? The board does not reside in my conscience."

"The law backs the consciences of the parents, Mr. Schmidt, and right now these parents are extremely upset. They have instructed me to instruct you to cease any discussion with their son on matters related to homosexuality. Further, you are not to tell him that this conversation has taken place or that they have brought this injunction against you."

"That's absurd!"

"That's the way they want it. How they deal with their son is their right."

"Their son has rights also."

"Where questions of morality are concerned in the case of a minor, the courts will support the parents, not you."

"Questions of morality?"

"This district does not support homosexual lifestyle, and you have no authority to discuss it with your classes or with individual students. Telling a student that you are homosexual details what you do in the bedroom."

"My telling any student that I am homosexual no more details what I do in the bedroom than you telling a student that you have a wife details your bedroom activities."

"I have no choice, Mr. Schmidt, but to take this matter to the district office level."

I spread my hands. "What happens to Tierney, meanwhile?"

"Any crisis situation should be referred to the assistant principal who's been working with the family."

"Are you telling me that you're leaving Tierney in my class?"

"At this point the parents have not instructed me to remove him."

"You're serious?"

The principal's eyes wished I would go away, permanently.

"I will hear from you then, regarding the D.O.'s reaction."

But I never did. The parents and the administration wanted it under wraps. The principal never raised the matter of reporting the incident again, and my union reps and attorney advised against raising it either ... but cautioned me to keep accurate records on all that had transpired. The likelihood was that the incident would be used against me later.*

If God and His anointed Christians were helping Tierney, it was hard to see how. Tierney's grades plummeted. He developed a brashness, began coming to school in collarless shirts that staged his hickeys in black-and-blue browns. An earring pierced his right lobe, glowing in the auburn cove beside his neck. He acted out, talked out, yet kept it curbed for me. He knew my concern, sensed it still ... in my how-are-yous and the space I gave his anger. But, obviously, that wasn't enough.

Again I requested a parent conference and again was denied. Again I offered names and numbers of gay and lesbian support groups for our own counseling and administrative staff to better cope with Tierney and again was refused. Even Parents, Families and Friends of Lesbians and Gays (PFLAG) could not be contacted. It was not a board-approved resource.

The AP admitted that the boy's parents had not followed through on counseling, even Christian derivatives thereof. Tierney was under consideration for transfer into Opportunity, the catch-all for kids who can't mainstream ... and one step away from the throwaways who haunt the street. I protested such placement for Tierney and personally handed the Christian AP information on Parents, Families and Friends of Lesbians and Gays (PFLAG). He took it reluctantly, said he was sure Tierney's parents would not accept it, that like him they viewed homosexuality as a sin just as lying and stealing are sins. As he thanked me, I had little doubt where he would file it.

Tierney's attendance rate had been sporadic; when he'd been gone five days, however, I returned to the assistant principal.

"He's run away, hasn't he?" I asked.

"Tierney?"

"Tierney."

He nodded. "Been gone a week. We think he's staying with friends, but they deny it."

"Did you share with his parents the PFLAG brochures I gave you?"

He turned toward his book shelf. "Actually, there's another organization we haven't tried yet. I was going to suggest that?"

"What kind of organization? Does it recognize homosexuality as acceptable orientation?"

He shook his head. "Helps them out of it."

My anger took hold. "Would you agree that none of your religiously based efforts have succeeded so far?"

He did not answer, merely watched.

"Isn't that correct?" I pressed.

He swiveled slightly in his chair, nothing any longer cherubic in his expression. "I suppose."

I leaned forward. "I believe you have a moral obligation to set aside your personal religious beliefs in the interests of this child. This is a public school, and agencies exist that can meet the needs of a boy you consider a sinner. The code of ethics demands that you be objective in providing options that will help a student develop his sense of worth. To refuse is neglect ... in fact, it's outright abuse. Tierney has made good on his threat to run away. Let me remind you that he also talked suicide. If he winds up strung to the end of some branch, this district is culpable; you are culpable."

Then he said it: "Why are you so interested in this boy?" And I wondered why it had taken so long to ask. It had glazed the pale surface of his innocence every time I raised the topic of Tierney. Tierney loomed between us now as he had been the afternoon he handed me a sheaf of poems and asked if I would read them. And of course I did, commenting on the sensitivity and old eloquence in one so young. He wrote of the changes he'd undergone but didn't understand and of the isolation of his evolution. In a couple he mentioned Dirk by name, and I was glad of poetry and his love of it, glad that language had a subset that still permitted him to work through his pain and nurse his esteem ... for us to communicate. "Moves me to tears," I wrote at the end, and he smiled when I handed them back. Esteem is such a fragile thing.

"I am so interested in this boy," I said, "because the person he is becoming doesn't fit the expectations of the people who have power over him, so they are wounding him with the sticks and stones of their limited love. 'Sick and sinful,' they call him, 'crazy and perverted.' But those are obscenities, and it bothers me when adults teach them to children, especially when the adults want the children to believe the obscenities about themselves. That's what I think is a sin. And any religion that promotes such ignorance is obscene. And any adult who acts on such ignorance is obscene.

"Does that answer your question?" I asked. "That's why I'm so interested in this boy."

As I left the Christian propped in his leather chair, I wondered where Tierney was and whether he still had the hot line list with my number at the bottom. I wondered whether he would trust me enough to call if things got really tight. I wondered whether I'd even given him reason to trust. I knew that if he called, I would respond in the most meaningful way that I could and that I would then risk a lawsuit by his parents and the district's move to dismiss me. And I wondered, with all the adult modeling that was available, why on earth should Tierney make a choice that was reasonable?

It was a time that tested my sobriety. I went home that afternoon, collapsed on the bed and called Degnan, who was midway through his two-year transfer to St. Louis.

"Talk to me," I said to his hello, "I'm feeling vulnerable."

"What's wrong, Pookie?"

I told him, concluding, "Sometimes it all seems so useless."

"That's dumb," he said when I'd finished.

"What ...!" A little explosion went off inside.

"I said, 'That's dumb.'"

I leaned up on an elbow, receiver to ear. "I call you for support, and all you can say ..."

"Ronald ... Ronald ... Ronald ...," Degnan interrupted.

"Listen ... I said, 'That's dumb,' not you. Letting yourself get defeated. You know the kind of shitheads you have to deal with. Why should today be different than the other times?"

"I guess I'd just like to see some progress now and then," I said, easing back against the pillows.

"Face it, you may never see any change in a bunch of assholes who are into denial, but is that who you're in this for? Who was that kid you told me about from your first year in teaching? The class dummy, remember?"

My eyes filled up. "Joe," I said. "That was Joe."

"Tell me about Joe."

"Well, you already know ..."

"Ronald, tell me about Joe."

I sighed, slipping my free hand behind my head. "He was the class dummy," I began, "a beautiful dark-eyed seventh grader who hid beneath a shock of equally dark hair falling over his forehead. Joe never raised his hand for anything except to pass out books or collect other kids' papers or carry the bats out at recess. All the other kids wanted Joe on their teams because of how the ball found his mitt when he jumped for a fly, but they all smiled secretly if Joe was called on in class. Everyone knew Joe was dumb.

"It was a parochial school and I, of all people, was teaching two sections of modern math. I had D'ed my way through math myself, but the nuns were confident God would see me through.

"I stood at the chalkboard one day for thirty minutes trying to explain the transversal of two coplanar lines and, in desperation, asked, 'Do you understand?'

"All thirty heads nodded, mouths slightly ajar. The fear that I might call on someone for feedback was dense. That's when I noticed a flicker across Joe's expression. His eyes quickened, and his hand moved toward his mouth. It was as if he wanted to raise his hand but didn't know how.

"I remember thinking to myself, 'Jesus Christ, do I dare?' Yet what was the risk for him? No one understood. If Joe didn't either, at least he'd have tried.

"'Joe?' I said.

"And Joe stood up, as the nuns required, hesitant but with an unfamiliar awareness at work in his features. He pointed at the board and in thirty seconds explained what I'd been trying to get across for thirty minutes.

"The silence was like an audible gasp. As if on cue, all heads riveted on the class dummy, and Joe shed that image right before our eyes.

"'Joe,' I said to him, 'You saw what no one else in this room saw, and you explained it so that everyone could understand. I really appreciate that.'

"I'll never forget the look on that boy's face as he sat down. He'd set himself free of the dummy dungeon with his little, awful risk. Joe convinced me there's no such thing as a dumb or stupid child, just kids who haven't been allowed out."

Both ends of the line were quiet. I could hear Degnan's breathing.

"Tierney's another Joe, Ron," he said. "The focus is different, but the issue's the same. Because of the focus you're catching flak, but you've still got a kid who needs you."

"I love you," I said.

"I know, and I can understand why."

We both laughed.

"Just one more thing..."

"What's that?"

"Call me Pookie again."

Degnan laughed. "Goodnight, Pookie," he said.

*By the end of his career as an administrator, Pincipal Don Schaefer, described in these pages, grew, through numerous conferences with parents concerned about their children being taught by a *homosexual* teacher, into a self-proclaimed advocated for LGBT youth ... and a staunch supporter of my rights as an openly gay teacher. The quality of my teaching had never been in question.

CHAPTER 32

CLASS ACT...IVIST

Tonee Mello had us mesmerized ... my ninth graders and me. I knew that would be the case, of course. I'd sat with him in front of an open Franklin Stove in the rustic lodge at Saratoga Springs several months earlier, just the two of us, talking late into the night. I'd been in love with this man since first meeting him at a Gay Fathers' potluck he and his then-partner, Alan Paul, hosted in their East San José ranch-style tract home in 1982. Together they parented Tonee's biological son, Jon, two adopted sons, and three foster boys from juvenile hall ... an inspiration in and of itself. In 1986, Tonee's family was among six others featured in the breakthrough documentary, NOT ALL FAMILIES ARE STRAIGHT.

Tonee was an anarchist at heart, and that night, with the firelight etching his strong features, his dark brown eyes shone with an intensity that matched his resonance as he talked about changing the world, short of revolution, in small, consistent steps and detailed what those steps were. It was, quite literally, as if I were in the presence of a white light ... the only sound aside from his voice, the crackling fire. Clearly, I was in love with him ... and clearly he was having that effect on my students.

It was Tonee's second visit to my classroom. I'd developed a guest speaker series on controversial issues. Speakers had included the mother of a murdered daughter who became an advocate against the death penalty after an agonizing decision to meet her daughter's killer on death row; a homeless Vietnam vet who recited poetry on Castro Street for donations; a gay couple who were advocates for same-gender marriage and parenting; representatives of Mothers Against Drunk Driving; a health educator who discussed safe sex using a clear plastic dildo to demonstrate condom use; among many others. Parent permission slips were required for students to participate.

Tonee's first visit had been to speak against war, his experience in

Vietnam, in particular. He said afterwards he would never do that again ... Vietnam's talons were still deep in his soul. Indeed, years after his honorable discharge, he'd suffered severe Post Traumatic Stress Syndrome that sent him into a tailspin. He'd taken off in a VW van for an extended period, driving across the country searching for balance. It was during that time that he became a grassroots organizer, helping to set up Food Not Bombs cells and Needle Exchange programs wherever he went, and it was that organizing he'd come to speak about in my seventh and ninth-grade classes on this occasion.

Tonee understood kids. He'd grown up in severely dysfunctional family situations. He and his half-sister had different mothers. When he was a kid himself, his mother pimped him in the front seat of the car in which she serviced johns in back. His father beat him regularly so severely, his sister covered her own head in the next room trying to muffle his cries. So Tonee could intuit need in a child's eyes, feel the hesitancy in uncertain features. He was, it seemed, searching for himself in every hurting kid he encountered ... as if the man he'd become could console the child he'd been.

Credit for his own survival, Tonee attributed to his Hayward High School counselor, Robert Berndt. Often truant, when Tonee did come to school, he was usually on something simply to ease the pain of being. Mr. Berndt would take him into the counseling office and let him sleep it off, then get him to whatever classes he could. He also gave Tonee his home phone number should he need help after hours. The first time Tonee called, it was another male teacher who answered. "I suddenly got it," Tonee told me. "My counselor and my art teacher were a couple," and he laughed. "It made such a difference for me." Tonee revered Robert Berndt as the father his own father could not ... or would not be ... and stayed in close touch till Robert died in 2009.

But he didn't talk about his growing up with my students. That past had roots deeper even than Vietnam. What he talked about on this occasion was his work with Food Not Bombs and the Needle Exchange programs he helped set up ... and my students were riveted ... alternately silent as they absorbed his experiences ... then competing with each other to ask questions before the bell.

Perched on a student desk, his levied knees angled comfortably up, sneakered feet on the seat, Tonee injected humor into the dialogue as he described salvaging and prepping veggies and fruits, just past expiration dates, gleaned from markets ready to toss them. He talked about the camaraderie among volunteers, many of them latter-day hippies, as they cooked nourishing vegan soups in cauldron-like pots, finally driving the food to an ocean-side park, at the same time each day, where they unfolded tables and served their hot meals and day-old bagels.

Two of the girls leaned toward each other whispering behind their hands, then waved them enthusiastically. "Can we do that, Mr. Schmidt?"

Tonee's handsome features broke into a grin as I said, "Of course. Maybe Tonee can connect us with a Food Not Bombs group."

"Absolutely," he said. "I have the number for the Santa Cruz group right here," he added, taking a slip of paper from his wallet and borrowing a pencil from a boy at the next desk. Chatter rippled through the classroom like an electric current.

But only four were willing to commit when they heard the hour they would need to be up on Saturday to drive with me to Santa Cruz to wash, peel, chop and stir the steaming vats of zesty vegan soup, then load them next to the containers of salad and day-old bagels in the volunteer's van for the drive to the park. But those four ninth graders dove into community activism with fervor that day. I watched their faces literally mature before my eyes as they served their clients, some rumpled and unwashed, others neatly dressed but down on their luck ... and there were kids from babies to adolescents my students' age. It was an experience that these four would carry with them as they encountered other homeless people in the course of their lives, an experience they were excited to share with their classmates the following Monday.

For a long time, Tonee had been driving his own van, which lately sported a bullet hole in the side, down into Mexico. Keenly aware of what his country had perpetrated in Vietnam ... and what he'd been sucked into through his service there, he became more and more caught up in the plight of the Mexican people, especially the indigenous tribes who live in dire poverty in the shadow of their wealthiest-in-the-world neighbor to the north. The growing harping of fundamentalists about the United States' Christian roots had no spill-over effect in generosity toward these people the Spanish had vanquished and Christianized. Lighter skinned Mexicans with traces of the conquistadores in their features were privy to advantage that the Mixe, the Zapoteca and other indigenous tribes did not enjoy and Tonee simmered over that difference ... "There are fifteen separate languages spoken just in the state of Oaxaca," Tonee once told me, "and many of these people cannot speak Spanish, much less English."

The president of Mexico, Felipe Calderón, cared little or not at all about improving the lot of these tribes or that of Mexicans in general. Similarly, in June of 2006, Governor Ulysses Ruiz Ortiz cracked down with brutal force against students and teachers striking for improved conditions in universities.

Tonee's decision to move to Oaxaca surprised none of his friends. He was sickened by U.S. policies such as NAFTA, Bill Clinton's North American Free Trade Agreement, which had a devastating effect on the poor of Latin America, and by American corporations such as Monsanto imposing the production and sale of American-grown corn on Mexicans. Mexico's indigenous tribes had, after all, originated the planting and harvesting of corn or maize. Free Trade is clearly not Fair Trade. American "corporate persons" sought only profit, not the well-being of the poor. Putting himself on the line among the oppressed became a way for Tonee to assuage his anguish for his country's crimes.

Tonee returned periodically to visit his son and other family and friends in California, staying with me in my Treehouse when he came to San Francisco ... and we would talk. More and more he was involving himself in the plight of indigenous Oaxacans and poverty-stricken youth with no future. In the process he'd attracted the attention of the Mexican authorities. In 2006, the year American journalist Brad Will was shot and killed while covering the violent response of the police against striking teachers, Tonee helped the university students to maintain their radio station as they broadcast information to remote villages about planned marches and protests at the governor's palace across from the zócalo in Oaxaca. In fact, Tonee had helped supply those villages with the radio transistors essential to that purpose. He told me that a police vehicle had started sitting outside his apartment at night. He gave me the name and phone numbers of the American consular agent in Oaxaca and said, "If you don't hear from me and can't reach me in a reasonable period of time, call this man." I tacked the numbers to the bookshelves on my desk, hoping against hope I would never have to make such a call.

In spite of all that, he kept essentials in sight ... and his sense of humor. In advance of his too-infrequent visits, he would ask me if I could tap into AIDS organizations in San Francisco and request free condoms to take back to Oaxaca for the youth who hung out in the zócalo and frequented gay bars as well as straight venues. Another Tony at the Stop AIDS Project in the Castro always came through with a couple of boxes. The last time it was three boxes with one thousand condoms each. When Tonee was returning to Oaxaca, he opened the cartons and spread the contents ... three thousand condoms ... through his luggage. He called when he got home. "Ron, you should have seen the expressions on the security guards' faces as they opened my luggage coming back into Oaxaca. They looked up at me wide-eyed as I patted my chest and said, 'For my personal use.' They respectfully zipped up my luggage and let me through." That was Tonee, Class Act...ivist with a sense of humor.

And then, he had me to instruct. Oftentimes, my exuberance over gay rights victories spills over into my day-to-day interactions. Tonee was visiting during the five-month window in 2008 when same-gender marriage had been declared legal in California and 18,000 gay and lesbian couples were legally married in this state. The Castro was charged with an energy that was hard not to savor. Domestic-partnered couples had, for several years, begun parenting as well. A wonderful documentary on the subject, Paternal Instinct, had just screened in the San Francisco International Lesbian and Gay Film Festival and Tonee, and I had attended at Herbst Theatre, one of the venues in the festival. Next morning as he and I were strolling past sidewalk tables of brunchers at Bagdad Café, we came upon a pair of gay fathers with twin daughters on their laps and, spontaneously, I burst into a broad smile and modest clap. The fathers glanced up. One smiled. The other did not.

As we walked on by, Tonee was clearly aghast. He looked at me, saying, "Ron, how could you do that?"

I looked at him as we reached the intersection and crossed to Café Flore. "What do you mean?" I said. "They're beautiful! They're just like the fathers and daughters in Paternal Instinct."

"But how do you expect those little girls to feel like they're part of a normal family if people applaud when they see them?" His expression smouldered.

I was embarrassed ... chastened ... I hadn't thought that one through.

For Tonee it was not just paternal instinct; it was a sense honed in the forge of his own abusive childhood ... innate and inherently classy. I was again reminded of that conversation with him in front of the fire at Saratoga Springs when, in the presence of that white light, he had detailed his efforts to effect change with small but significant steps. I had interrupted him at one point saying, "Tonee, you scare the shit out of me!"

He looked at me, startled. "Why?" he said.

"Because you're so far ahead of me, and you're where I need to be," I replied.

He shook his head, surprised. "Oh, no," he said. You're out as a gay teacher for all those kids. You're right where you ought to be."

I felt touched by his words but understood that he was, indeed always would be, ahead of me ... and so, my mentor.

Class Act defined everything Tonee turned his energy to. In the latter stages of their father's life, Tonee's estranged and abusive father reconnected with Tonee and his sister. He'd grown infirm and needed them. He was no longer able to handle day-to-day necessities. Characteristically, they responded, traveling to Oregon to get him set up in a care facility. But the senior Mello was so verbally abusive to rest-home staff that they refused to keep him. No stranger to risk, Tonee brought his father to Oaxaca, set him up in a home near his apartment and hired skilled and sensitive round-the-clock attendants to care for him. Tonee visited regularly, took his father on outings and was always as near as the phone. The elder Mello settled into a retirement he hadn't deserved, quite content for the remaining year of his life.

Two years ago, with what remained of his share of his father's estate, Tonee bought a modest home on a quarter acre of land on the outskirts of Oaxaca. His sister had urged him, "Put what you've got left in dirt, or you won't have a cent for yourself." She knew her brother only too well. He'd been generous with needy friends and ever-needy causes. Fixing up his casa, he was excited and happier than I've ever seen him. Casa Tlalixtac became his Eden. He flourished vibrant Mexican colors throughout the house, planted a splendid garden in which every flower bloomed lushly and every vegetable produced prolifically. "If I accidentally drop a seed, it grows!" he said and laughed appreciatively.

Tonee began to step back from his more overt activism to concentrate on his home, hosting friends, activists among them, and providing work for his indigenous neighbors as well. He had turned 62 and was experiencing the aches and pains that presage aging. He hired local artisans to help him build raised adobe planters to ease his sciatica as he scooped rich loam around newly planted vines and vegetables. He devoted extra attention to bracing and cleaning the well so its pure, cold water could cool the koi pond's glimmering shapes, nourish the garden and refresh him and his guests. He adopted three dogs, two cats ... and Mr. Lucky, a burro with a broken foreleg.

When I flew down to visit on Valentine's weekend of 2009, Tonee had overseen the building of a chicken coop, acquired seven exotically feathered hens and a strutting, arrogant rooster. Fresh eggs every day for his table and neighbors as well. He tossed great salads with home-grown kale, three kinds of lettuce, pungent garlic and plump, juicy Heirloom tomatoes. On the stereo, Leonard Cohen's husky baritone crooned "Suzanne," "Hallelujah" and "I'm Your Man" as we shared supper my last evening with him.

Tonee had never had an absence of beautiful young men in his life, and that was still true. But people of all ages were drawn to him. You knew you meant something when Tonee Mello engaged you in conversation and took an interest in what you were doing.

In his years of chugging across the continent in his beat-up VW van, Tonee had created an ever-growing network of friends, so one's own network expanded as well. His friend Stuart Loomis said it best: "Tonee was the hub of a very large wheel. Many of us knew each other only through Tonee's stories about us."

At Casa Tlalixtac, he further augmented connections through couchsurfers.net, hosting visitors from Denmark, Sweden, Italy, Australia, Thailand, Ghana ... Tonee's was a global consciousness, a universal sense of belonging ... with governments, corporations and organized religion corrupting that sense of belonging. He hated the violence he witnessed those entities perpetrate on the innocent, and he choked up talking about it.

But the violence Tonee had spent his life fighting so hard against, breached the gates of Casa Tlalixtac on April 11, 2011, when a pair of intruders who burgled his home and vehicles, shot and killed this beautiful man. He died, at least, where he'd found his greatest peace, his greatest happiness ... at Casa Tlalixtac ... Tonee Mello left a legacy of uncommon caring and compassion for others. He was my friend, my mentor. God, how I miss him.

CHAPTER 33

OBSCENITIES IV: WHERE WERE YOU?

My fourth-period ninth graders were quiet ... absorbed in Act 1 of Romeo and Juliet. Our own practiced reading scene by scene, act by act, I rewarded with the screening of Franco Zeffirelli's sensuously opulent rendering of Shakespeare's masterpiece of youthful passion with stars essentially my students' own age, the stunningly handsome Leonard Whiting and spontaneously beautiful Olivia Hussey. (Ironically, Miss Hussey was too young to attend the 1968 premier of the film rated R because of her nude love scene with Whiting.)

By Scene 4, Romeo and his Montague buddies had set out to crash the masked ball at the home of their sworn rivals, the Capulets. En route, Mercutio, Romeo's volatile best friend, launches into such a prolonged and raving soliloquy about Queen Mab that Romeo approaches, puts his hands on either side of Mercutio's head and drawing it against his own, says, "Peace, peace, Mercutio, peace! Thou talkst of nothing ..."

As the youthful foreheads touched, one of the callow youths in my own class blurted, "Faggot!"

Immediately, I stopped the video ... "Let's talk," I said. There had been a few chuckles at the slur and heads turning toward me. Some students were clearly sobered by the insult. One petite olive-skinned girl stared at me with timid, dark eyes, then down at her own hands, her black hair buckling on her jean jacket collar. Indeed, everyone knew I was gay. I didn't ask the culprit to own up ... asked, instead, "Why was that epithet inappropriate?"

"Not 'spost to talk during a movie," one boy said.

I nodded. "Okay, that's true, Duncan ... It disturbs other people's concentration. Anything else?"

Quiet ... Still more quiet ...

Then ... "Well, obviously, it was a put down ... and I don't know why we just can't live and let live," a girl volunteered. "Anyway just 'cause Romeo pulled that other guy's head against his doesn't mean they're gay. They're just good friends and that Mer ..." She looked up at me.

"Mercutio," I said.

"Yeah, Mercutio ... He's just goin' off about this Queen Mab. Romeo's tryin' to calm him down. Don't need to put him down for that."

"That's pretty insightful, Brenda," I said. I scanned the twenty-two visages struggling toward maturity and asked, "Is Shakespeare suggesting Romeo is gay ... or Mercutio?"

"That still don't make it okay to slur the dude," Duncan volunteered. "'Sides Romeo isn't. He's all hot for this Rosaline, and he's about to get blown away when he sees Juliet, so he's not gay."

Laughter ...

"But, Duncan, can we pursue what you just said about it not being okay to 'slur the dude' if he is gay? Why isn't it okay?"

A hand went up across the room ... "This play happens in Mantua, right? And Mantua's in Italy?"

I nodded. "Mantua is in Italy, Zaq, that's correct. And that's significant because ...?"

"Well, Michelangelo and Leonardo da Vinci were Italians, and look at them ..." Zaq said, his clean, handsome features sharpened with focus.

"What's that 'spost to mean?" Duncan pressed.

"Two of the world's greatest artists, dude .... both Italian and both gay," Zaq said. "Leonardo was a genius in science, too ... even designed plans for airplanes ... in the fifteenth century! You going to call them faggots?" he said turning to the boy who had used the slur. "You got something better going for you than they did?"

The offender shrugged uncomfortably, doodled on his notebook, face flushed.

"Maybe the point to be made here is that we're all of equal value regardless of what sexual orientation we are. Why should it matter which gender we love as long as we love and we're not hurting anyone else? All of us have gifts to bring to the world, and ..."

The bell rang, and the hustle to get to lunch interrupted. "Thanks for that insight, Zaq ..." I said, wishing I had one of him in every class.

"Hey," Zaq said, hefting his books against his slender hip as he rose. "I think we should all be hetero-flexible ..."

Laughter as students exited the room.

At the end of the lunch break, I checked my teacher's mailbox before the next class began. A note on binder paper, folded in quarters, was among the materials I retrieved. I glanced at the signature first as I unfolded the page. It was from Danae, the petite olive-skinned girl with dark eyes who had looked at her hands during the class discussion.

"Mr. Schmidt,

I just wanted you to know that I really appreciated what you said in class today about the slur and that we all have equal value. I've had things like that happen to me and it really hurts.

Thanks ...

Danae"

I thanked Danae for her note next day after class and said that if she ever wanted to talk, my door was always open. The occasion for that happened two years later when she called me one Sunday morning. She hadn't realized she was calling me at first. She'd found my number on a hotline list because of my work with the Bay Area Network of Gay & Lesbian Educators (BANGLE). She simply began by saying, "I go to high school in a conservative district, and it's really difficult ..."

Her voice began to break.

"I understand," I said, "I teach in a conservative district ..."

Suddenly there was a pause and then recognition.

"Mr. Schmidt?" she said.

"Danae?" I said, and we laughed. She explained how things had worsened after leaving the ninth grade ... that she felt so alone. I told her there was a youth group that met every Sunday afternoon at the Billy De Frank LGBT Center in San José and that if she would like to go, I would be glad to take her. Even as I spoke, I knew this meant altering my plans with my lover, Degnan, hoping ... knowing he would understand.

I met her at Martin Murphy Middle School, the northern boundary of Morgan Hill Unified School District, but in the city limits of San José, where she had been my student in ninth grade, and drove her to the De Frank Center in time for the 1:00 youth group meeting. I graded essays while I was waiting and was delighted to see her emerge an hour-and-a half later beaming, her expressive brown eyes alight with relief. I didn't need to drive her back; she would get a ride with one of her new-found friends.

Degnan was pleased when I got home and told him as well, but our plan for the day had been severely altered.

I had been lobbying my administrators to embrace awareness training on the needs of LGBT youth virtually since my first semester in the district when an eighth-grade student committed suicide, but met with huge resistance initially ... Danae was correct: it was a very conservative community.

In my continuing search to address the issue, I met an amazing woman, Ann Davidson, at a weekend workshop related to expanding perspectives conducted by another amazing woman, Jane Vennard. I spoke to Jane about my desire to introduce awareness training about LGBT youth in schools. The former wife of a gay man, Jane enthusiastically addressed the issue in the last session of the workshop, and Ann Davidson, mother of two sons, one straight and one gay, approached me about wanting to work together on the concept. Ann was a member of PFLAG, Parents, Family and Friends of Lesbians and Gays.

Together we created The Invisible Minority in Our Schools: Lesbian, Gay, Bisexual, Transgender Youth Workshop that we successfully lobbied every school district in Santa Clara County to schedule as part of their in-servicing ... but not without immense effort. Behind us were the other educator members of South Bay BANGLE ... in particular, Rob Birle, the inspiring young co-founder of BANGLE and the deeply dedicated and determined parents of PFLAG. We presented to administrators, counselors and staff in every district, bringing panels of parents from the districts we were in-servicing ... as well as LGBT students who were willing to risk revealing what their closet in the classroom and on campus had cost them in terms of their self-esteem and often suicidal tendencies.

When finally we were successful at convincing MHUSD administration to accept the Invisible Minority Workshop, I called Danae and invited her to tell her story on the youth panel. She was one of three students and four parents from the district who participated. The workshop was held in the MHUSD boardroom, the presenters seated on the dais in the board members' chairs. At least three-quarters of the expected district personnel attended ... although one counselor walked out during the youth presentations. Those who remained became quickly caught up as parents told of their sons' or daughters' struggle for acceptance and search for a receptive ear within the school district. They had been dismayed by the taunts directed at their children ... their visceral fear of going to school every day ... and the relentless determination of an ever-present percentage of students bent on exposing and harassing classmates with real or perceived difference ... especially sexual orientation. Even worse were the adults who pretended not to notice ... or dismissed the harassment by saying, "Teasing has always taken place. It's part of growing up. You can't stop it. It toughens kids up for the real world."

When Danae spoke, she leaned in close to the microphone on the desk and in her shy manner began detailing her experience in the middle school. Taunts were so routine, some teachers even allowed them to go unchallenged in the classroom. "I remember one class," she said, her olive fingers now clenching the stem of the microphone, her eyes burning as she spoke, "where the teacher set aside the lesson plan and let the students say whatever they wanted about gays the whole period and yell faggot and dyke and queer ... and ... and I was so afraid they were going to look at me and say, 'You're one of them, aren't you?'" She looked at the assembled educators and burst into tears, sobbing, "WHERE WERE YOU? ... WHERE WERE YOU?" Not a single person moved ... not another sound echoed in that chamber, only this young woman's wrenched sobs. I moved to the chair next to her, put my hand on her shoulder and handed her my clean handkerchief to stem the flood of tears. I have never washed that handkerchief. Indeed, I took it with me to every workshop I ever presented after that to remind me of my obligation there. This is what relics are about ...

An assistant principal from the high school approached Danae after the in-service to thank her for telling her story, expressing regret for what she'd had to endure.

The superintendent mandated that all teachers and staff be in-serviced in this training at the opening session of the next school year. There were discontented rumblings, of course, and there were die-hards who opposed such training on religious grounds. I had become a lightning rod around the issue, the only openly gay teacher who found a way to bring the topic into every district meeting. Indeed, the first time I said the G and L words in a district meeting, the oxygen evaporated from the room. In time it was just taken for granted that if I was there, so was the topic, and I had the backing of both CTA and CFT.

We recommended other well-respected presenters to do the district-wide in-servicing, and that seemed to meet with broader agreement. Our goal had never been that we had to do it; we just wanted it done by competent presenters. Besides, we had other districts to whom we were committed ... as well as CTA's Good Teaching Conference, NEA's Human Rights Conference, and California Self-Esteem Conference. Ann Davidson and I and another PFLAG couple, Pat and Pete Koopman, felt that we'd made significant progress at long last. We became almost complacent for the next year or so regarding MHUSD.

So it was a jolt when I received a phone call during the mid-semester work day in 1998 from Alana Flores, a young woman who had graduated from Live Oak High School the previous June, saying that she and five other students had been continuously harassed for their perceived sexual orientation for virtually the whole of their high school careers. I was stunned but made arrangements immediately to meet with Alana. She told me that when she'd gone to the assistant principal in tears with her complaint that she was being called a dyke, the assistant principal responded, "If you're not gay, why are you crying? Are you a lesbian?" This was the same woman who had gone up to Danae after her tearful account in our initial board room in-service to express regret for what she'd suffered.

Dismayed at Alana's account of what she and her classmates had endured, I said, "Alana, we've been to the Board, we've done all the talking, we've done the workshop ... even had the whole district in-serviced. If students are still suffering this treatment, the only thing the administration will listen to is a lawsuit. If you want me to, I will take you to an attorney and to the ACLU ..."

There was no hesitation. "Absolutely," she said ... and neither did I have any hesitation.

Immediately, I consulted Anne Rosenzweig, a labor rights attorney and Morgan Hill resident who was among the first to support the sensitivity training. On her recommendation, I took Alana and one of the other aggrieved students to meet with San José attorney Diane Ritchie and ACLU's Ann Brick. Pat Koopman from PFLAG joined us ... and the lawsuit was filed.

The district dragged its feet for six years, claiming ignorance of the harassment ... They settled finally in 2004 for $1.1 million, the largest amount ever awarded in such a case at that point in time, plus mandated awareness training annually for all staff and students. One would hope that other school districts would take note and make the necessary changes ... but sadly, the harassment continues in school districts around the country. Alana Flores served as the spokesperson for the other five students, an articulate, immensely brave young woman. Morgan Hill Unified should be proud to have her as an alumna.

I retired at the millennium, so assisting these students with filing the lawsuit was essentially my parting gift to my district. No student should ever again have to ask school personnel: "Where were you? Where were you?"

CHAPTER 34

LETTERS TO LOVED ONES

"Hi, Ron, this is your sister," said the voice on the recorder. "A problem's come up about dinner tomorrow, and I need to talk to you. Give me a call when you guys get in, okay?"

"What do you suppose that's about?" Degnan asked, the tree lights shimmering in the hall mirror behind him. Little Drummer Boy cadenced the quiet with Christmases past, and I sensed that we were about to lose our grip on another holiday. For the second year now, Degnan and I had absented ourselves from my family's table rather than endure the stone-eyed rebuke of my sons and one nephew.

"I don't know," I replied, shaking my head as I dialed, "and I'm not sure I want to find out." The likeness of two little boys caught in the arms of a dark-bearded me smiled in the glow of green-shaded desk lamp, a gilt-and-glass fondness come through old despairs. The boys' mother and I had just divorced when that photo was taken. I'd been prepared to run to Canada with them had I lost custody.

The ringing stopped. "Hello?" A chorus of "Joy to the World" swelled my sister's end of the line.

"Kathleen," I said, "Degnan and I just got in. What's up?"

"I don't know why we can't have normal holidays like oth..."

"Normal holidays are a Rockwell fiction, Kathleen. Just tell me."

"I know you told me at Thanksgiving that Tracy had a college friend with no place to go at Christmas and he wanted to know if he could bring ... What's his name? ... Geoff?"

I closed my eyes. "That's right. Geoff."

"I even checked with my kids at the time, and they both said, 'No problem.'"

"So what is the problem?"

"The problem is, my son has changed his mind. Darwin says he won't sit at the same table with a black."

I began to shake. Degnan moved behind my desk chair, put his hands on my shoulders.

"What are you telling me?" I said, incredulous.

"I'm telling you that I'm not going to put my own son out on Christmas so your son can bring a black friend."

"Oh, Christ!" I said into the mouthpiece.

"What is it?" Degnan asked, his hands working my shoulders.

"You've known for a month, and you expect me to tell Tracy on Christmas Eve that he can't bring his friend to Christmas dinner because Darwin won't eat with a black man? Christ, Kathleen, he won't eat with his faggot uncle, he won't eat with his cousin's black friend. Have you thought about letting Darwin spread his own table?"

"Jesus," Degnan murmured.

"I'm sorry," Kathleen said, "that's the way it is."

"Sorry doesn't cut it, lady. You call Tracy. You tell him how you're letting Darwin fuck up his Christmas!"

"I won't do that. Anyway, what about your own sons? They were coming here because they won't eat with you and Degnan either."

I slammed the receiver in its cradle. Degnan took me in his arms. My hands were fists, and I couldn't stop shaking. Soft, stereophonic "hah-hah-hah-hah-h-hs" piped goodwill to the world. "GOD-D-DAMNIT!" I shouted, leaning into my lover's shoulder. "It's their own fucking fault; it is. She's right about that."

Degnan listened, hugging.

"If Drake and Tracy weren't so adamant about you and me, they'd be coming here to our home where they wouldn't have to ask whether Geoff is welcome. Why can't they see that?"

Degnan's head nodded against my own. "I know," he said, "I know. And maybe now they will. Maybe this is what they needed to understand what they've been doing to us." His fingers coaxed the tension from my nape. "Let's not be too hard on your sister. She's been very accepting of us, very supportive. She's let her emotions about her son get in the way this time. I know that doesn't make it right, but it's a part of parenting you can identify with. It's hard to be objective when it comes to your kids. You, of all people, know that."

I nodded, silent.

He kissed my hair. "Do you feel up to calling Tracy?"

Insinuated tremor lingered the length of my spine like recalled trauma. "I'll be all right," I said. "I need to get hold of Drake too."

"Tell you what," Degnan said, "see if they'll bring Geoff here tomorrow. This could be our disguised blessing, worthy of a feast."

I looked at him. "Your folks are expecting us," I said, my voice filling up.

"They're having a crowd. They'll understand if we explain. Stores are still open. We can pick up a last-minute bird and enough trimmings to make it work ... Ask."

The dial blurred as I sat down to call. Tracy now lived with my former brother-in-law's family. I'd arranged for his move into Terrence's home three-and-a-half years earlier when it became necessary to distance him from the red-necked mentality of the Sierra town we'd lived in for seven years. I was newly sober, needing to come out and desperate to get a teaching position in the Bay Area where I hoped Tracy and I could move in with Degnan, although I suspected he would say no to that ... and did. Drake had started college and was on his own ... the emotional distance between us palpable. Growing up had happened too suddenly. Both sons understandably felt betrayed and fearful hearing the words, "I'm gay" from their father's lips ...

Despite months of adjustment, Tracy had seemed to thrive with his uncle, his Aunt Becky and two cousins, the younger of whom was Tracy's age. Last June, in fact, paired both cousins in mortar boards with high school diplomas in their hands.

The arrangement, I hoped, would provide Tracy needed space and distance to deal with his father's homosexuality. Together in the year following my coming out to them, we had made little headway toward healing. Their betrayed reaction to my revelation, coupled with my drying-out from alcohol, in fact, skewered the three of us to the same tenterhook the whole of Drake's senior year. He was growing into manhood and needing to stake claim to his own direction. At eighteen he decided to attend community college in San José and moved out. It was a wrenching parting, albeit mixed with relief. I dreaded the possibility of losing Tracy, too, and appealed to Colleen's brother. Clearly, he loved his sister's sons.

From the beginning, Terrence and Becky had tried to support my coming out. Their espoused goal in taking my son into their home was to return him to me. But three-and-a-half years later, I had still to search for signs of acceptance. My visits with Tracy went fine until I mentioned Degnan, and suddenly I was talking to myself. Whole areas of our lives did not intersect. In his new environment I was that curious real father who drove in and out of his life from a distance, and little in that pattern seemed given to change. Despite all I'd risked to come out, I was still cast in a role, and my frustration steeped in the telling of Darwin's holiday sabotage once Tracy came to the phone.

"My God," Tracy exclaimed incredulously, "how could he do such a thing?"

"You're asking what I'm asking," I said, grateful that at least my aversion to race hatred had rubbed off on my sons.

I listened to his youthful resonance break as he railed against his cousin's betrayal and his Aunt Kathleen's complicity. When his pitch dropped on the last, "God!" I suggested, "It's still possible for you to drive up north with your cousins and Terrence and Becky to her relatives tomorrow …"

"Dad, do you know how far away that is? I have to work the next day."

Degnan's proposal had just escalated to the reasonable alternative. To ask now was to risk the baldest sort of rejection. On the other hand, it could pierce the transom of hostile years like fresh web in the unstrung relationship. My throat went tight. "Look, Degnan and I would really like to have you and Drake bring Geoff here tomorrow. We're scheduled to go to his folks, but they're having a crowd and … Tracy, we'd love to have you guys here."

There was silence. Swallowing was difficult. I became conscious of a pulse on the periphery of the receiver and I thought, "That is my pulse in my temple," and I wondered if Tracy could hear it.

"Well, can I let you know?"

"Tracy, it's Christmas Eve. The stores will be closed in a couple of hours. If you're coming we have to shop … now. What's to decide?"

More silence. I glanced at my lover leaned against the door jamb, the soft pierce of lights etching his gentleness. His eyes said there was no point, but I could not let it go.

"Tell me," I said, "how this reaction to Degnan and me differs from Darwin's reaction to your black friend? Tell me that. Magnify the anger, the hurt of your cousin's rejection by four-and-a-half years, Tracy, and you'll get some sense of what Degnan and I feel. Isn't it time you came to terms with us?"

More silence.

"I guess I have your answer," I said, finally. "Have a Merry Christmas, Trace."

Drake, when I reached him, four-lettered his cousin so vehemently that I rechecked the number to see if I'd really dialed him at work. The alternative invitation he dismissed with, "Thanks anyway. I've gotta go, Dad."

My sons took Geoff to a restaurant for Christmas dinner.

For weeks I could not respond to calls from Tracy or his uncle. Despite what I owed Terrence and his family for kindnesses to my son, I needed much more. I needed delivery on their promise to return my son to me. Yet, so far as I could tell, that was the issue they had not really addressed. While I was a topic at their table, Degnan was not. He existed, it seemed, in that peripheral netherworld to which straight folk consign same-sex housemates of people they care about. When Terrence dismissed Degnan's and my spousal relationship with, "I would have trouble with any partner you have who is not my sister," I feared that the environment I had negotiated for my son would not nurture the understanding I so longed for. Phone messages from Terrence insisting that I communicate provoked me to write a bitter missive of blame for which I quickly apologized and, ultimately, a wrenchingly naked letter that would, in the end, be viewed by Terry's wife as my effort to rewrite history to satisfy some need in myself. What follows is a mix of those conflicting intents, of purposes crossed without trying, the measure of which the heart alone can read:

Dear Drake and Tracy,

Your uncle has characterized my silence as emotional withdrawal, but he is mistaken. It is simple self-defense as I cut you both free. At 18 and 21 you have reached legal benchmarks of manhood and in so many ways I am proud of how you demonstrate those levels of maturity. Maturity is a funny thing though. Just when you think you've got it, it moves a distance ahead. That's how it's been for me, at least, especially with both of you.

Years ago in my Washington classroom, I picked up a book entitled

Why Am I Afraid to Tell You Who I Am? and even before I opened the cover, I knew the answer. I was afraid that if I told you, you would not love me. I'm afraid, even now, I was right.

In one week I will be fifty years old. That is the age which Plato defined as the philosopher-king, the age of wisdom. What my last forty-nine years have taught me is how exquisitely remote I am from wisdom. If I have reason to celebrate my half-century mark, it is that I am, I think, a bit more mature ... not wise, just mature.

I've made so many mistakes ... most of them lies I've tried to live, some of them the zeal with which I've tried to correct those lies. The one thing I remain convinced was not a mistake was my decision to tell you who I am. The mistake was in not doing it when I first picked up that book.

Living with your uncle's family, Tracy, I hoped would prevent the deep scarring that marked Drake's and my relationship during his last year at home. I hoped, in fact, that closeness to them would somehow make both of you closer to me. And living there has been good for you, Tracy ... of benefit, indeed, to you both. And I am grateful to your uncle, to your Aunt Becky and to your cousins ... though they must think I have a piss-poor way of showing it. Everyone has different expectations about how gratitude should look and how often be expressed.

The graduation party last June spotlighted my gratitude and what remains of my closet. I had, in truth, not expected to speak. It was your aunt and uncle's party. I was there in my role as Uncle-Dad, as Tracy's something's-not-quite-right-about-him father, as your cousins' well-we-just-call-him-that uncle. When Terrence asked me, prior to the toast, would I like to say a few words, I looked at the relatives gathered from his and Becky's bloodlines, at the friends come from their society ... and I looked at my son who had in so many ways benefited from their largesse, and I said what was expected of me. I tried to be as lavish with my gratitude as your aunt and uncle and cousins had been in giving me cause for it. And I have smarted ever since; smarted with the denial that a role demands; smarted with the knowledge that while my gratitude warmed all those couples gathered about the cake that my spouse was timing his flight to miss the celebration that would not celebrate us; as I now smart with the rejection of a son outraged at the rejection of his black friend ... and I know as never before that you have not been returned to me, that

that end has scarcely been addressed.

I was gratified by your dismay at the ignorance that kept your cousin from gracing a table attended by your friend, but the incident sharpened focus on the two of you, Drake and Tracy, and the two of us, Degnan and me.

Degnan suggested that, if you would come, we would change our plans for Christmas with his family and fix dinner for you in our home where Geoff would be welcome. You declined, preferring each other's offended but very straight company among strangers whose orientation you knew nothing about. I have not forgiven that. I'm not sure that I ever can. The one hope for it is that I still love you. It was, however, as if after kicking us in the teeth for so long, you had dropped your aim to your real target. You could feel righteous about your anger at your cousin and still sanitized about your treatment of us.

Last Father's Day you both expressed your appreciation for my support of your separate endeavors and of your relationships, oblivious to your continuing denial of mine. That time is over. Understand that I love you both, but be clear that I love you not only as your father but as Degnan's lover and spouse. I will no longer court your prejudice in the hope that it might miraculously change. I have exhausted my sources of persuasion and you reject my relationship with my lover with a vigor equal to Darwin's rejection of your black friend.

Degnan did not seduce me into homosexuality; he seduced me away from an addiction that was killing me. It was Degnan who talked me down from tumblers of gin at my lips, in whose arms I accepted my value, in whose heart I can be myself. I would hope you could be grateful for that. The clear alternative was the grave.

I am grateful to Degnan but it is not gratitude that holds me at his side or in his bed. He alters the quality of my living with his gentleness, his thoughtfulness, yes, and his flesh. I love this man whose name causes you to fall silent, grow distant. I intend to spend the rest of my life enhancing his as he enhances mine.

I'm letting go so that you can learn to reach back. Does that mean that to have me, you must also have Degnan? It does. Should you remain steadfast in your rejection, that at least will be your choice. I will no longer exercise responsibility by holding on. I will have earned whatever you feel for me with my self-respect intact. André Gide once wrote, "It is better to be hated for what one is than to be loved for what one is not." I believe that passionately.

One day, not I hope till Degnan and I are very old, one of us will scatter the other's ashes in the white-capped bay. Between now and then I hope that both of you and whomever you choose to love will shore up with us tender, poignant memories made strong by the measure of our combined embrace. We can if you will. If you do not, then a piece of me will always mourn simply because I love you ... but it will be that piece that I long ago traded to others' expectations, a piece that in these pages I have labored to amend. My decision to detail who I am risks setting you more solidly against me and, while I desperately want that not to be so, I am committed to that risk for the option it offers us each as a person. I would not, for anything, go back. Risk has features too dear to rescind.

Your Aunt Becky suggests that I have rewritten history to serve some need in myself and, without intending it, she has summed up the effort of these thirty-four chapters. Anyone who exchanges a closet for life has a past to re-script. The habit of deception gives way to wholly different perspectives and that's often uncomfortable. You know me now not as the person you thought I was because of the person I pretended to be but as the person I am. That is a communication few ever achieve and if we own that then the interim pain has been worthwhile ... infinitely more so than the pain of unrelenting deception. One must move beyond ... at least in spite of ... fear. Ultimately, otherwise, we lie beneath a stranger's epitaph. So, yes, the rewriting serves some need in myself, as I trust it does in you, as I hope it will in others ... a need that goes all the way back to distances that defined me as once-removed and traces their transformation into my canticle ... my song.

Albert Camus wrote with particular eloquence about that need:

"The world in itself is not reasonable, that is all that can be said. But what is absurd is the confrontation of this irrational and the wild longing for clarity whose call echoes in the human heart."

I hope that in my wild longing you will make some sense of the world, savoring the fullness promised within you. It is the measure that above all guarantees my commitment to you.

Love,
Dad

EPILOGUE ...

Twenty-four years have passed since I penned that letter to my sons. On June 28, 2009 both Drake and Tracy marched with me in the PFLAG contingent of the San Francisco Gay Pride Parade ... It was Tracy's sixth time, Drake's first. Their girlfriends accompanied us ... as did my sister, who looped our mother's platinum wedding band on a chain around my neck. (Even her son, Darwin, has made progress.) It was affirmation beyond my wildest dreams ... confirmation that the bond of blood ... father-son ... is stronger than the societal fictions foisted on us from every conceivable side ...

We are close now ... very close ... and easily share confidences ... In 2005, the three of us revisited Tacoma, Washington ... the sites of their childhood and the onset of their mother's illness. There had been piercingly beautiful as well as wrenchingly painful moments in that Puget Sound remoteness. We sat on the beach at Harstine Island, where their mother and I had honeymooned and reflected, the slight lap of wavelets on the rocky shore. It was a cathartic interlude as I reminisced and apologized for the pain of my drinking in the growing absence of their mother ... and my initial fear that I had caused her illness. We had, of course, made it through ... the illness ... and my coming out. Drake said, "We never doubted that you loved us, Dad."

In another conversation, Tracy said, "Uncle Terry was really angry about the letter you sent, Dad. He *did* try to talk to me. In fact, he said to me once as I was walking through the living room, 'Tracy, you have got to come to terms with your father ...' but I wouldn't listen ... I wasn't ready ..."

More recently still, Tracy said, "I really regret the way we treated Degnan ..." and I was so moved ... as was Degnan when I told him ... But what might have been in that regard was affected by what had been ... by circumstances of which neither of my sons had control ... They were acted upon in a societal convention that seemed to offer comfort and safety ... and suddenly that was turned upside down. Not enough that they had grown up without their mother ... their father revealed to them as adolescents that he is gay ... a father steeped in recovery from alcohol and a convert to gay activism ... My response to my sons needs to be: "I really regret the way I treated you ... but like you, I did the best with what I had in me to work with at the time ... and we have come to this place of mutual understanding, respect ... and love."

Degnan and I separated in 1990 after attempting couple's therapy ... It was the yellow stickies that did it ... His innate need for serenity in his home was increasingly threatened by my activism ... He understood that my need to be an advocate on GLBT issues in schools was directly related to my sobriety and tried in every way to be supportive of me, but more and more my support for him was found wanting. Caught up as I was in prepping for classes, grading papers, teaching Invisible Minority in Our Schools workshops, BANGLE meetings and phone calls ... yellow stickies proliferated on the mirror of my medicine chest directly opposite his in the bathroom ... Even if I was out at a meeting, the reminders were there ... and, in particular, if I was out at a meeting, he had only the cats to keep him company in front of the fire ... or eat popcorn alone watching television. He had a lover ... but he didn't ...

The pain of parting was exacerbated by learning that he'd met someone else. At the San José Gay Pride celebration that June, I was one of several South Bay BANGLE members staffing the booth at the fairgrounds with PFLAG parents. I knew Degnan was bringing the new fellow to the event, but I was nonetheless ill prepared when Degnan brought him up to the booth briefly to introduce him. Watching them walk away, the other fellow's arm around Degnan's waist, choked me up, and I grieved the loss of that intimacy, but knew I'd earned that loss. I hadn't been good at balancing ... I wanted to be glad for him.

In time, I moved on to other lovers as well ... Ted, yet another gentle-spirited fellow I met at the Body Erotic workshop ... a derivative of the Body Electric ... where men were encouraged to delve into their sexual nature to get in touch with their inner needs in the company of twenty or so other men naked in the same pursuit. A quick friendship emerged between Ted and me, and we decided to move in together ... a Victorian flat on Noe Street in San Francisco, just two blocks from the ever-vibrant Café Flore. We had many interests in common ... including the desire that the relationship should be open ... Both of us had come out of monogamous relationships and agreed that, at that moment, we wanted more flexibility. The intimacy was good between us, but the reality was that, unlike Degnan with whom I'd fallen in love, I'd chosen to love Ted ... and I would come to understand that the difference is palpable.

That was dramatically demonstrated for me when, three years into my relationship with Ted, a stunning Swiss-Italian happened to me at Cala Foods on Eighteenth Street in the Castro. Thirty-six years younger, Gianni had come to San Francisco to explore his attraction to men ... older men, in particular. Given the open relationship Ted and I enjoyed, I had no hesitation in opening my arms to this breathtaking being. We made love with abandon that first afternoon. He burst into tears after climaxing, and my fate was sealed ... Taking him in my arms, I said, "I could fall very quickly and very deeply in love with you" ... and, indeed, it was already happening. His face nestled in the crook of my neck, his damp lashes against my shoulder.

Gianni's visa would expire in mid-April, so he had to return to Switzerland then. It was September 27, 1996 ... essentially six months to explore and assess what could be. But Ted, seeing how utterly captivated I was by Gianni, was immediately threatened by him. A few faltering efforts at ménage à trois did nothing to salve his discontent and eventually he said, "I can't handle having this other person in our lives ..." He gave me an ultimatum: I must choose. Torn, I reminded Ted that Gianni must return to Switzerland in April, that I didn't know whether I would ever see him again ... That didn't matter. I knew that it would not be fair to Gianni to end the deepening relationship with him, feeling as we did about each other. Neither would it be fair to Ted to sever my bond with Gianni and pretend it didn't matter. Clearly, it would not be fair to me ... "Then I will move out," I said ... and set about searching for a place for Gianni and me to move into together.

The separation from Ted has, unfortunately, remained one of strain ... best characterized, perhaps, by the last comment he made to me after much negotiating around the relationship ending: "You've gotta make yourself right ..." He smiled sardonically, and repeated, "You've gotta be right ..." It's an ever-present part of any memory I have of Ted ... an obvious sadness.

Thus began a trans-Atlantic relationship that would consume the next six years of my life. My heart belonged to Gianni ... My soul belonged to Gianni ... Others would sometimes ask, "What do you have to talk about with someone who is so much younger?" But that was never an issue between us ... I was the age he anticipated; he was the youth I never had ... Infidelity became the issue. Given the distance and lengthy periods apart, I understood his youthful need for sexual expression, but my own need, at least as intense, was an issue for him. "I'm so afraid I'll lose you," he said, bursting into tears on the phone when I told him I'd met a fellow his own age with whom I was intimate in his absence. He would then push for monogamy again, but he could never maintain that. For my part, I was totally mesmerized by Gianni and would gladly have borne the monogamy despite the distance if I knew he would. He could not, despite his good intent.

In those six years we traveled much of Europe ... Switzerland ...Italy ... Germany ... the Netherlands ... Belgium ... France ... and here, in addition to San Francisco ... Manhattan ... Santa Fe / Taos ... Puerto Vallarta and Oaxaca in Mexico ... Gianni was a sensitive artist and photographer with an eye for the erotic in nature. His inner beauty unquestionably matched his exterior beauty. I could not get enough of him and struggled to be content with what I could get.

Gianni and I planned two months together in Europe in the summer of 2000 when I retired after thirty-three years in the classroom. We had arranged to exchange apartments with a Parisian lesbian couple for three of the eight weeks. Sitting at my desk in our apartment with a view of Twin Peaks the afternoon of June 26, I was about to confirm my Air France reservations for July 17 when the phone rang. I answered to find Linda, the woman who had for the last few years cared for my former wife, calling to say that Colleen was dying. I was stunned. I'd kept in touch with Linda and the previous caregiver every three to four months just to check on how Colleen was. In the throes of her schizophrenia, Colleen had cut off all contact with our sons and me as well as with her own side of the family twenty-four years earlier. It was, I am convinced, simply too hard for her to have only occasional contact with our sons and then prolonged periods without them in her life. I'd always urged Colleen's caregivers to please let me know immediately if any dramatic changes in her health occurred between my calls. So I was startled by this news.

"She's dying?" I said. "What's happened?"

Colleen had been suffering with kidney cancer but had kept her discomfort to herself till remedy was no longer possible. It had progressed without staff realizing it. "Is death imminent?" I asked. "Do we need to come immediately? I have to call my sons and Colleen's brother, and they're all at work."

"Sorry I didn't call you sooner, but you're not the legal husband anymore," Linda said.

"Who else did you have to call?" I asked.

"We didn't have anyone. My husband said, 'Call the ex-husband.'"

Colleen's doctor expected she would probably live five or six months. Relieved, I made the three calls, all to message recorders, asking both sons and Colleen's brother Terrence to call me at once. Each of them sensed what it had to be about. Terrence met my sons and me the next morning at the care facility in Milpitas. We spoke with the director and Linda, Colleen's principal caregiver, who in yesterday's phone call had emphasized they needed information on the mortuary to be contacted when death occurred. I suggested to Terrence that he give them the name of the funeral director who had served the family in San Francisco for years, assuming that Colleen would be buried there.

As we talked, a middle-aged Asian-American woman entered ... Emily was Colleen's hospice worker ... A soft-spoken woman with the energy of miracles flowing through her, she asked, "Do you want to see Colleen?" The question was weighted with over two decades of separation.

I looked at her, at my sons, at my former brother-in law, then said, "I would love to see her, but ... I'm not convinced Colleen would want to see me ... or her brother. What is important is that she see our sons and that they see her."

Emily nodded. She suggested we go for lunch at Chili's two blocks away. Meanwhile she would talk with Colleen about seeing the boys. She would call us on Terrence's cell phone.

The mood at lunch was charged with the surreal ... We were on the verge of a life-changing experience ... certainly for Drake and Tracy. The woman most intimate to their existence, yet a virtual stranger to them now, was on the brink of re-entering their lives twenty-four years after she cut off all contact with us. Midway though our lunch Terrence's phone rang. Emily had talked with Colleen, raised the reality of the terminal cancer diagnosis and asked, "Colleen, is there anyone you'd like me to contact for you ... anyone you'd like to see?" Colleen's answer was immediate: "My sons," she said, "I'd like to see my sons."

We finished quickly and drove the few blocks back to the facility.

As we waited in the visitors' lounge, Emily went in to tell Colleen her sons had arrived. Tracy, in the immensity of the moment, burst into tears. I put my arms around him. Drake was fighting tears himself ... Emily came back in. "Colleen is ready," she said. I hugged both sons, and they followed Emily. Terrence and I sat quietly, aware of the murmur of voices audible through the wall ... the residue of old wounds very present between us.

I scarcely knew how to assess what I was feeling ... the scourge of schizophrenia had intruded and taken their beautiful mother from our sons ... They grew through childhood without her love ... without her tenderness ... her absence her only presence. Tracy had been three and Drake six when, in desperation, I filed for divorce. Terrence signed her out of Western State Hospital, returning her to her parents in San Francisco. Tracy had few memories of the woman he was now visiting ... albeit special glimpses ... such as helping him blow out candles on his birthday cake ... Drake remembered more ... most fondly her hands ... and the gold-colored robe she used to wear in the mornings.

The visit was brief, only about forty-five minutes ... but both sons came back into the lounge relieved and buoyant. Their mother had been sitting up in bed, smiling ... holding out one hand to each of them ... and calling them by name ... "I knew you at once," she told them, her effervescent smile setting them at ease. She wanted to know about them but avoided mention of me, her brother and family ... She was glad to know both sons had graduated from college; to learn that Drake now owned the Schmidt family home ... and that she had a granddaughter. Tiring soon from the unanticipated excitement, however, she asked could they come back next day ... which they did ... and every day for the rest of her life.

The four of us drove back to San José and sat on the large cool porch of the 1904 vintage Valley House that had been the family home for five generations ... now Drake's ... on South Fifth Street ... and talked ... debriefed about the remarkable event that had unraveled in the last twenty-four hours. Terrence mostly listened. His own disconnect with his sister seemed deeply rooted in her rejection of him and her side of the family during her protracted illness. I expressed my immense relief that Colleen had not died without us being able to reconnect. Always I feared that might happen. The boys felt grateful for that as well, and an unwarranted sense of guilt at not having sought her out before this.

They'd actually come close once several years earlier. I had taken them at their request to meet Betty, the woman who had been Colleen's previous caregiver for over ten years and let the three of them talk at length over lunch in Marie Callender's. It was Betty's suggestion that we just show up at the door one day and visit Colleen. None of us felt comfortable with that and I, in fact, refused. Ill though Colleen still was, she had stabilized at a functioning level in the context of managed care, making regular visits to her doctor, taking her meds, and basically maintaining a very private but seemingly comfortable existence for herself. If showing up to visit unannounced were to shock her out of that routine, there was nothing I could offer that was any better surely. I would not risk that. Drake and Tracy agreed.

After that the subject had lain dormant until this call. Now they were equally agreed that they would see their mother every day that remained to them. Terrence returned to San Rafael, and I drove Tracy to his girlfriend's in San José. On the way he asked, "What are you going to do about Europe, Dad?"

"Yeah, that was in my mind as you and Drake were with your mother," I said. "I think that with what's happened today, I've accomplished what I always intended by keeping in touch with the caregivers. You guys and your mother have been reunited ..." Tracy nodded. "The expectation now is that she may have six months, and that will be precious time for you and her. I'll be back in two months ... I think that I should go on to Paris as planned with Gianni."

Tracy nodded. "I agree, Dad ..."

As often as I could, I came down to help Drake with the yard ... There is always so much to do around an old house. It seemed particularly important then, given their visiting schedule as well. On one such afternoon, I'd finished mowing the lawns and was watering when both sons came down the front steps, ready to visit their mother. Pausing, they approached me, and Drake held out his hand closed protectively on some object.

"Dad, Mom asked us to show you this to prove she's the right woman," he said, then turned his closed fist and opened his hand to reveal the engagement ring I'd given her. It was not a huge diamond. It was small and brilliant ... and I'd had it set in a cluster of antique gold leaves. I caught my breath.

"My God!" I exclaimed ... "I gave that ring to her at our Sea Castle in Carmel."

"That's what she said," Tracy smiled, adding that she no longer had the wedding ring.

"I have the wedding ring," I said, "and when I come down next I'll bring it so you can prove to her that I'm the right man."

And I did.

Drake and Tracy brought my broad golden band that had matched Colleen's and presented it to her. She was pleased, but when Tracy said, "Look at the inscription inside, Mom," she said, "Oh, that's too small. I can't read it." Drake took the ring and read, "I am responsible for what I have tamed ..." and Colleen broke into laughter, clasping her hands together and exclaimed, "Oh, The Little Prince!"

The Little Prince by Antoine de Saint-Exupéry had figured importantly in our lives from early in our courtship ... the beautiful tale of the boy who lived on an asteroid and flew to earth tethered to a flock of wild birds. On earth he met a fox who invited him to come every day at the same time to visit ... each time sitting a bit closer ... and by so doing, the Little Prince would tame the fox ... But, the fox cautioned, once the Little Prince tamed the fox, he would become responsible for him ... That taming had remained the tenuous thread prompting my periodic calls to Colleen's caregivers over the years, I see as I look back now. Always, I shared with the boys what I learned about their mother's current condition.

With the ring exchange, Colleen had tentatively reached out to me. Next, she wanted to know had I remarried ... did I live alone ... They said "no" and "yes" respectively, and as I looked at them, Drake said, "Dad, we're not going to go there ..."

"No," I said, "nor would I expect you to ..." But, unspoken was the reality that my re-emergent homosexuality would, of course, have eventually ended the marriage had the schizophrenia not. My sons understood that.

Drake and Tracy made a habit of visiting their mother every day in the early evening. Her room had a view of the walkway up to the facility, and she could wave as they approached. Clearly, it was a taming process after the lapse of twenty-four years, and gradually they grew closer. It was amazing to watch. But before leaving for Paris on July 17, I cautioned them: "One disease took her from you, another is giving her back ... but just for a while. You must both keep that in mind. Savor the joy in this, but know there will be further pain ..."

"It is sunrise over Iceland," I wrote in my Journal at 12:34 A.M. aboard my Air France Flight 083 to Charles de Gaulle International Airport. "Amazing beauty. It is even more amazing that people live there. Remote. A region of the world that most people would not think of tolerating ... probably could not, in fact. It is, in a way, as if that's where Colleen has been these past twenty-four years and suddenly she is coming back. Betty (Colleen's previous caregiver) once said that she believes that in mid-life some schizophrenic people simply decide to get well. How much, if any, could such a theory account for Colleen?" Terrence seemed influenced by that idea as well, and therein, perhaps, lay a margin of his hurt.

I was surprised and deeply touched when Arlene, another hospice worker, said to me, "You have worked a miracle ..." by staying in touch all those years and making possible this reunion between mother and sons. That was humbling to hear.

Gianni strode toward me at 2:03 Paris time, embracing me for the first time in four-and-a-half months and hurried me, luggage and all, via the Metro to our swapped flat on Rue des Pyrénées and breath-taking lovemaking ... then supper on the terrace ... tortellini with funghi, asparagus and salad ... Italian soda ... "The sun is setting," I wrote in my Journal. "The breeze is light and cool on this garden terrace with chimneys rising Utrillo-esque above wrought-iron balconies ... It seems years since we sat down to share a meal he cooked. It's four-and-a-half months and too long, by far, at that. What a magical ambience. Paris with my beautiful lover."

Later, Gianni and I walked to a vista point overlooking the City to watch the Eiffel Tower light up like thousands of sparklers in celebration of the millennium. This would happen every night during 2000. His remarkably beautiful face smiled as he watched my expression. I hugged him fiercely. It was a wildly romantic dream I seemed to be living, and I had no desire to wake up.

The next two days: Notre Dame's stunning rose windows and brooding gargoyles; Ste. Chapelle, the jewel box of stained glass and gilded arches; cappuccinos and glaces at Café Med ... Gianni sketching and I journaling; Musée Luxembourg's exhibition of Renoir's Bust de la Femme, Brazille's two male nudes fishing a stream, El Greco's St. Dominic; shopping for fresh broccoli and risotto for supper on the terrace ... and intense lovemaking as Gianni threaded his way toward me, naked, between the jasmine trellis and luxuriant, densely scented roses ... coaxing me down on the Thermarest mattress we'd bought for camping in Firenze later in the trip. I had no desire to wake up.

But wake up, I did, next morning when the phone rang as Gianni and I were setting out for Musée d'Orsay. "Drake ...?" I said, surprised at hearing my son's voice ... then, "Oh, my God ..."

"Yeah, Dad ... Mom passed about an hour ago ..." Fatigue weighted his voice.

"I'm sorry ... I'm so very sorry, Drake."

Tracy had stayed with their mother till McAvoy O'Hara arrived, bringing her back to San Francisco for what would turn out to be her last time. Colleen had expressed a desire to be buried near my parents in Santa Clara Cemetery. That was problematic for Terrence, but it was her wish ... and the boys next morning asked that she be returned to Santa Clara. No one had thought, in the flush of reconnection, about changing McAvoy O'Hara's name on the critical-information list at the facility. We'd thought there would be six months. Terrence arranged for the transfer to happen.

"What are you going to do, Dad?"

I suggested that I felt I'd fulfilled my goal in reconnecting them ... that was what I'd wanted most ... "If she had asked to see me ..." I began ...

"Dad," Drake interrupted. "I think she was really close to that ... I think she'd have wanted you here ... You're our main link to Mom ... I would like you to be here."

Gianni had sat down next to me, hearing the drift of the conversation. He put his hand over mine. "Of course you must go," he said, and when I hung up, "I love you so much ..." an assurance I needed. We needed the whole two months for our relationship, but I must honor the relationship that had been as well. Time was when I loved Colleen "so much" ... Indeed, in some dormant dimension beneath the scars of her illness and my realization that no cure had rendered me straight, that had remained true ... I loved her.

Gianni made the Air France reservation while I packed.

The next four days were a whirlwind of intense emotions anchored by too little time to make the necessary arrangements for Colleen's funeral and too little sleep ... and yet it all came together. There in the dining room of the home that had housed five generations of our family, my sons and I created the plans for the funeral. Around the table that had gathered Finns and Schmidts for Sunday dinners and holiday feasts for nearly one hundred years ... we selected music from Colleen's favorite recording artists ... "Morning Has Broken" by Louis Armstrong; "Who Am I?" by Nina Simone; "Evening Prayer" from Humperdinck's Hansel and Gretel ... to be played in the funeral parlor the morning of the burial.

My sister had volunteered her home for the post-funeral gathering of immediate family. My brother and his wife would help with food. Selection of a casket for the woman whose sons had only begun to know her ... Drake and Tracy rose to the unanticipated role of seeing to their mother's end-of-life affairs with grace, dignity and sensitivity ... and I was immensely proud ... as I know Colleen had to have been as she got to know them in those final twenty-four days of her life.

Fatigued as we all were, we discussed what they knew of her wishes ... and extrapolated from those certainties to what else we assumed she would want, both sons keen to honor their mother's wishes ... In the warm July night, they had moved onto the wide porch, dark but for their separate laptops on which each typed out what he would say to the gathered few at the service.

I'd been assembling a collage of photos from the family albums I'd given each of them the last Christmas we were together in the Sierras and walked to the screen door to find their intent features leaned into the pale glow of their separate computers and, clearly, her features at work in theirs. Drake's daughter, Celine, prepared a reading from The Little Prince concluding with: "'Goodbye,' said the fox. 'And now here is my secret, a very simple secret: it is only with the heart that one can see rightly; what is essential is invisible to the eye.'"

Drake and Tracy, when we arrived at the funeral parlor, were first to view their mother, and there were tears ... Tracy asked did I want to see her, and my chest grew tight.

"I'm not sure she would want that," I said, but he and Drake were convinced that she would. I nodded. "Then I would like to see her alone first," I said.

"Oh, absolutely," they both agreed.

Tracy put his hand on my shoulder as Drake opened the chapel door for me. Nina Simone's "Who Am I?" had begun playing on the sound system. I walked toward the casket, Colleen's features coming into view as I neared, then stood revisiting the beauty beneath the two-and-a-half decades of difference ... It was wrenching after all those years to come finally to her side again ... like this ... this woman I had loved, this wife whose anguish tore open my heart, this mother who had blessed my existence not once but twice with sons to do any man proud. "Who Am I?" indeed ... I leaned to kiss her forehead, and my Tibetan locket with a wisp of Gianni's hair swung into the space between ... and my own tears came. I cried ... cried for what had been ... for what might have been ... and for what was ... I cried for the wasted years and the loss of loving; the dilemma of estrangement; the perceived abandonment; the self-imposed exile. She who had loved these two sons with such exquisite depth. How had it been possible to be thus engulfed by such a distortion of consciousness? ..."Who Am I?" Who among us ever knows?

I pushed open the door ... Drake, Tracy and I embraced ... The others had arrived. Terrence, with his wife and sons and their wives, shook hands, but said little. Nor did he approach the casket to see his sister one last time.

There was no mass ... A priest who had visited Colleen in hospice spoke sensitively about her reconciliation with our sons ... and with me ... about coming to terms with dying ... could she die in "holy grace" if she had really been schizophrenic ... Drake and Tracy had tried to reassure her in that regard ... and God being bigger than she gave Him credit for. Emily spoke ... that wonderful hospice worker who made the reconciliation happen between Colleen and our sons. Drake and Tracy shared heartfelt thoughts they'd typed on the darkened porch the night before about having lived virtually a quarter of a century without their mother ... and the sudden gift of her return for so short a time ... twenty-four days ... one day for every year she'd been out of our lives.

As we left the grave, the casket lowered, and awaiting the shovels full of earth, I asked Terrence to return with me to the graveside and let go the hurt. "I can't ..." he said. "I can't ... I'm not ready" ... and I remembered Tracy's comment when his uncle implored him to come to terms with me ... "I wouldn't listen ... I wasn't ready ..." So much of our lives are on hold waiting to be ready ... Colleen's mother had said during the depths of her daughter's illness, "This business is breaking her father's heart," and I reflected that no one who loved Colleen had merged with heart intact. That was surely true of her brother. It was Terrence who had introduced me to Colleen thirty-eight years earlier following dinner with me and a mutual ex-seminarian friend. "I've met the man for you," he'd told her. It was Terrence again who, when I came out to him and his wife on the deck of a Tahoe cabin several years after the divorce, said, "Give me your hands." The mountain air was chilling with the sun's descent as he clasped my hands in his own and said, "I loved you when you married my sister and nothing you have just told me changes that ... I love you still."

The reality is that my sons, especially Tracy who moved in with his uncle's family in high school, are the men they are today significantly because of that family's love and generosity ... and I ache for Terrence's unresolved pain.

At the gathering at my sister's there was a sense of relief ... and more words from Drake and Tracy ... With the other loved ones present, I listened ... humbled and moved by what they shared about their mother's prolonged absence and sudden, brief return.

"Colleen taught me the meaning of radiance," I said, and that was true. She had, in those early days of our courtship and marriage, defined radiance better than anyone I'd ever known. It was that quality that her illness would alter and I would eventually describe as the landscape of that molten soul.

Both sons drove me to San Francisco International next morning for my return flight to Paris and Gianni. As I walked through the gate, Tracy called, "Have a great trip, Dad! You deserve it!" They both waved. I waved back, the immensity of my relief ... my gratitude ... and my love for these two wonderful young men overwhelming me.

RESOURCES FOR LGBT YOUTH

Parents, Families, and Friends of Lesbians and Gays (PFLAG):
San Francisco (415) 921-8850
San José (408) 292-0720
Check on-line for national/international contacts. www.pflag.org.

Trevor Project for LGBT/AT RISK YOUTH:
(866) 4-U-TREVOR/866-488-7386
www.thetrevorproject.org

IT GETS BETTER PROJECT
www.itgetsbetter.org

Gay-Straight Alliance Network (GSA Network):
(318) 795-4282
www.gsanetwork.org

Gay, Lesbian and Straight Education Network (GLSEN)
www.glsen.org
(BANGLE evolved into GLSEN)

www.ingramcontent.com/pod-product-compliance
Lightning Source LLC
LaVergne TN
LVHW041607070426
835507LV00008B/168